Managerial Thought for Public Finance Officers

A Practitioner's Perspective

Edward Anthony Lehan

Also By The Author

The Practice of Municipal Budgeting - A Self-Istruction Text
Bureau of Governmental Research, University of Rhode Island, 1975

Simplified Governmental Budgeting
Municipal Finance Officers Association, 1981

Budgetary Thought for School Officials
Cantabrigia, 1982

Budgetmaking: A Workbook of Public Budgeting and Practice
St. Martin's Press, 1984

Budgetary Thought for Budget Officers: A Practitioner's Perspective
Amazon, 2016

Noteworthy Monographs:

- The Future of the Finance Directorate. (Municipal Finance Officers Association) 1977

- Rebuilding a City: Modest Adventures in Hartford. "Public Management" (International City Managers Association) 1967. Louis Brownlow Award, 1968

- Budget Appraisal: The Next Step in Budget Betterment. 'Public Budgeting & Finance" 1996 Jesse Burkhead Award, 1997

- Organization of the Finance Function. **Local Government Finance** (Government Finance Officers Association) 1991

- Public Budgeting (Institute of Public Service. University of Connecticut) 1967

- Determinants of Local Government Capability (Institute of Public Service,. University of Connecticut) 1978

- Articles on various public finance topics in "Governmental Finance "
  (Government Finance Officer Association) 1976 & 1979

© 2016 Edward Anthony Lehan

All rights reserved. Except for brief quotations, no part of this publication may be reproduced, stored in any retrieval system, or transmitted in any form or by any means, electronic, mechanical, photocopying, recording or otherwise, without the prior permission of this copyright owner. Contact data follows: :

ISBN: 1535363932
ISBN 13: 9781535363938
Library of Congress Control Number: 2016912433
CreateSpace Independent Publishing Platform
North Charleston, South Carolina

Edward Anthony Lehan
89 Rumford Street
West Hartford, CT 06107
(860) 521-7097
ealehan@att.net

Managerial Thought for Public Finance Officers

CONTENTS

Acknowledgements xi

To The Reader xiii

    I. Core Agenda 1
    II. Instrumentalities 7
    III. Authority 43
    IV. Rationale: Aims of Attainment 53
    V. Organization: Means of Attainment 81
    VI. Management: Pursuit of Attainment 121
    VII. Concluding Notes 247

ACKNOWLEDGEMENTS

First, I must acknowledge the debt I owe to three educators, all of fond memory, who influenced the course of my life: Bernice Owen, my English teacher at Hall High School, West Hartford, Connecticut; Dean Pascal Poe, Hillyer College, Hartford, Connecticut; and Professor Karl Bosworth., Department of Government, University of Connecticut. Each not only contributed to my intellectual development, but, equally important, provided wise counsel.

Moreover, I was blessed to work with competent civil servants who provided me with essential practical experience and guidance in the craft of public administration, public finance and public budgeting: Robert Duffy, several times a Finance Director; Bernard A. Batycki, a quintessential public executive; and Elisha C. Freedman, city manager, par excellence

Further, it may be taken as axiomatic that only authors really know what they owe to their reviewers. This is to attest to the depth of my debt to my reviewer, Joseph T. Kelley. Through his effort, I not only garnered encouragement, but gained valuable insights affecting the form and substance of this work. The manuscript was significantly improved by his wise counsel. Experienced as a finance director and international consultant, Mr. Kelley also earned credits as a lecturer and author. .

Therefore, it is fitting that I dedicate this book to Joseph T. Kelley, with my thanks for being a never-ending source of encouragement and intellectual stimulation.

TO THE READER

If you continue beyond this opening line, you will enter into a one-sided conversation with me about applying management thinking to public finance work. Considering this intellectual focus, the subjectivity of my thought on the topic, and my wish to speak directly, I have written a rather extensive essay. Although I hesitate to classify it as a contribution of the "how-to-do-it" literature, I certainly hope (as all authors do) that this "what-to-think-about-it" essay will affect practice—otherwise, why bother?

Clearly, the advance of computer technology has reduced the need for traditional "how-to-do-it" finance literature. Software, when well designed, now embeds much of the "how" of finance work in automatic sequences and linkages. The computerization of finance work is an altogether happy development because it permits public finance officials to devote more of their time and energy to process controls and less to process — to shift from concerns about finance facts to consideration of their meaning.

My interest in the mental dispositions of public administrators, in general, and public finance and budget officers, in particular, dates from a study of L D. White's 1926 classic, *Public Administration,* which I first read when I was a graduate student. Commenting on the establishment of integrated finance directorates in American state and local governments, Professor White expressed his concern about the mentality of the leaders of these powerful centralized units. He worried that they could, and perhaps, would, assert the primacy of finance values at the expense of the programmatic purposes of democratic government. Although subsequent experience with integrated finance directorates did not justify Professor White's particular worry, his general concern about the mental disposition of public administrators was not misplaced.

Many supervisory officials take the trappings of their office very seriously. One's office can easily become the measure of all things. Indulging their conceit, and masking their fear, they strive to defend and extend the power of their office, to the detriment of programmatic purposes. Even though they may be technically qualified by education and experience, supervisory officials need models of appropriate management thinking and behavior to condition their conduct. This concern causes professional societies to adopt ethical codes to define and recommend best practices. In seeking the same end, governments adopt "conflict of interest" regulations governing official conduct, with the intent to influence mental dispositions.

Our subject is the *management* of public finance, not public finance, per se. The term refers to persons (and practices) responsible for the coordination of the factors of production. Personalizing the point, *managers* are supposed to think (and act) strategically, that is:

> *Ever striving to attain desired objectives, "managers" deploy resources in time and space, giving due weight to resistance and opportunities.*

Accordingly, throughout this essay, readers will note that I have assumed that public finance officials entrusted with supervisory responsibilities consider themselves "managers," and accept the intellectual and behavioral implications of that identification. On my part, such an assumption is necessary, for otherwise, my commentary would lack focus. However, I freely acknowledge that this assumption is not universally valid, for I know public finance officials who rather define themselves as professionals or technicians who happen to be burdened with supervisory responsibilities. They express little or no enthusiasm for the "management" aspects of their jobs, at least in the manner described in

TO THE READER

this essay. Naturally, as an author, I harbor the hope that even those who feel thusly will find this essay illuminating, if not energizing.

Looking Inward. Finance cuts across all public programs—an important strategic fact in the design and operation of every government. By its very nature, public finance, and its management, is intrusive. The arithmetic of finance touches every government activity. Thus, procedures related to finance provide a system of order, supplying government leaders with a prime vehicle for regulating the formulation and execution of public policies. If properly organized and well-led, a finance establishment can provide 1) finance-related information and controls, useful in the execution of policies, projects and programs, 2) a means of representing and attaining the values of effectiveness, efficiency and economy, (the efficacy triad) throughout the government, and 3) a source of reasoned advice on the financial implications of issues, problems and opportunities facing the government.

The saying, "on tap, not on top" aptly describes the proper instrumental role of finance and finance establishments. Except to misers, money has no intrinsic value. Government financial requirements, and the management thereof, derive their essential value from programmatic activities. The cost of financial management, including capital costs, is, therefore, universally considered as an overhead burden, to be justified by a positive relationship to the programmatic activities of government.

Typically, public finance establishments carry on specific activities, principally, budgeting, accounting, revenue collection, procurement, administration of accounts receivable and payable, and the management of cash. These activities embrace procedural details. Applying the methods of management analysis to these procedures, accountable officials should strive for operational effectiveness, efficiency and economy. These three values comprise an efficacy triad for all who supervise other people's work. In addition to supervising finance-related operations, finance establishment leaders must apply intellectual resources to the issues, problems and opportunities associated with the ***availability,*** *cost, productivity and recovery* of public capital. This essay directs the reader's attention to the application of managerial thought to these four prime concerns.

Looking Outward. The exercise of fiscal power regulates the relationship between government and the financial and economic marketplace, touching and influencing the arithmetic of the community. This relationship is most precisely formulated at budget time, when, in addition to appropriation decisions funding a service agenda, government leaders make collateral decisions on taxes, fees, service charges and loans.

Leading finance officials are expected to participate in financial policy formulation, contributing, at the highest level of finance thinking, recommendations concerning the fiscal policy of their jurisdiction, that is, the relationship of governmental finance (the arithmetic of the organization) to the local economy (the arithmetic of the community). Consequently, one also manages public finance by active involvement in resolving issues and solving problems facing the jurisdiction. This requirement places finance work within the broad perspectives of socio-economic thought. Officials struggling with the formulation of fiscal policy require and use information developed during the conduct of finance activities. The relevance, integrity and timeliness of this information are important managerial considerations.

Public Finance Ideals. It is regrettable that public finance work can never have the focused clarity that the "bottom line" confers on finance work in profit-seeking enterprises. Finance officials associated with enterprise organizations are unambiguously applauded for their efforts to optimize the use of capital. Further, representatives of the global investment community appropriately assess the financial *soundness* of profit-seeking enterprises by applying standard yardsticks - and the world listens respectfully. Certainly, we can fully subscribe to the proposition that, like their private sector counterparts, public finance officials

TO THE READER

should strive to optimize the use of capital, but we must hasten to add the qualifying caveat, "politics permitting." One must also take care when applying the concept of soundness to assess the financial condition of governments. When this term is applied to the finances of governments of general jurisdiction, the speaker is, more than likely, merely noting the fact that current revenues exceed current disbursements, including ample coverage of that crucial obligation so dear to the hearts of creditors: debt service. Obviously, the standard tests of financial soundness are fairly applied to public enterprises. But, even in those cases, we note that public enterprises are notorious for flunking the liquidity test—and not only is this trespass frequently forgiven by the leaders of the responsible government, they are likely to be rewarded with capital replenishment when they go "in the hole."

Yet, despite these necessary qualifications, abstractions like *optimize* and *sound* caress our ears, and serve to put our thoughts about public finance management on the right path. Although we cannot simply borrow and apply conceptions drawn from the commercial world, we can certainly test the limits of application, noting when and how they might be used.

Throughout this essay, the reader will note that I have sought to maintain a governmental perspective. As observed above, public finance management is counted as an overhead activity whose costs (direct and indirect) must be justified by reference to the programmatic thrusts they support. Therefore, to be useful, the criteria applied to the management of public finance must be suited to government—and the politics which drive it.

One last important point concerns my assumptions, which may affect the reader's expectations and the utility of this essay. As indicated by its subtitle, this essay presents a practitioner's perspective, in this case, the point of view and experience of a chief financial officer working within a comprehensive finance establishment, including a budget unit responsible for an executive-style budget. I have endeavored to take the reader into my confidence by discussing the considerations that caused me, over my career, to ponder and adopt the recommended prescriptions of preferred practice.

In closing, I sincerely hope that the reader finds my considerations and prescriptions useful in addressing the perennial issues, problems and opportunities of public finance work

Edward Anthony Lehan
West Hartford, Connecticut
July, 2016

I. CORE AGENDA

... explores the application of managerial thought to public finance work by addressing key questions: When public finance officials seek to "manage" public finance, what should they think about? Then do?

By all accounts, the practice of public finance varies from place to place. Sometimes, it seems that there are as many ways to practice public finance as there are governments. From one government to another, the variations in organization, procedure, technology and the competence of personnel can be striking. Even within a government, one often finds a series of relatively independent offices engaged in finance-related work, each doing business in its own way. Even more telling, on a world scale, despite years of effort by standard-setting professional groups, governmental accounting practice differs from place to place. And mark this, even when they are knowledgeable about differences from place to place, accountable public finance officials from place to place are prone to defend their particular organization, procedures and technology as efficacious, even exemplary, and, consequently, resist (and resent) criticism and suggested changes.

Variations notwithstanding, I think that we need not permit differences in organization and practice to obscure the underlying foundations of efficacious public finance work. At this point, consult Exhibit 1.1, *Foundations of Efficacious Public Finance Management.* In addition to providing this essay with its topical organization, this

Exhibit functions as a checklist, cutting through the thicket of operating variations to identify universal characteristics of efficacious public finance work. Drawn from many sources, including my experience, Exhibit 1.1 provides a list of preferred practices. In effect, this checklist represents an attempt on my part to identify institutional instruments which, when proficiently applied, contribute to the attainment of those grand, but elusive, ideals of public finance management:

- "Sound" public finance
- "Optimum" deployment of public capital.

Of course, these ideals are abstractions. Lacking specification, the terms "sound" and "optimum" deserve to be qualified by quotation marks. However, like all ideals, these statements are meant to inspire and embolden. Even more than that, they can, and do, act like gravity, exerting a constant influence on the minds and conduct of public finance officers. Thus, the concepts of preferred practice, outlined by Exhibit 1.1, serve to incline the thinking of public finance officers and concerned political officials along productive lines of inquiry and action, that is, behavior conditioned by reference to the above cited ideals of public finance management. Each practice has a natural foundation in public finance work and each may have an ideal development. Taken together, and applied, I believe that the concepts listed on the checklist provide us with the elements of a general model of exemplary public finance practice. This list also provides accountable public finance officials with an evaluation framework. In cases where practice falls short of ideals, the model points the way to improvement.

I. CORE AGENDA

EXHIBIT 1.1 Foundations of Efficacious Public Finance Management

A	AUTHORITY	PREFERRED PRACTICE
1	Financial Power	Jurisdiction limited to funding and financing programs and projects that cannot be provided privately.
2	Resource Acquisition	Jurisdiction raises substantially all its revenue from its own sources and unconditional subventions.
3	Borrowing Money	Jurisdiction borrows only for capital investments.
4	Rate Regulation	Jurisdiction sets budget-related tax and cost-covering fees and service charges.
5	Resource Utilization	Jurisdiction's organization and management practices enable and encourage solution-centered, results-oriented budgeting.
B	**PRIME CONCERNS**	
1	Availability of Money	Pay obligations when due.
2	Cost of Money	Minimize finance management costs, Including interest charges.
3	Productivity of Money	Maximize socio-economic returns on investments in services and facilities.
4	Recovery of Money	Minimize subsidies related to regulation, services and enterprises.
C	**ORGANIZATION**	
1	Structure	Designed to promote efficacious finance management.
2	Leadership	Unified and accountable.
3	Staff	Qualified by education and experience.
4	Staff Deployment	Flexibly assigned tasks related to issues, problems and opportunities.
5	Technology	"State-of-the-art" capitalization of production, supported by depreciation.
D	**MANAGEMENT**	
1	Preliminary Work	Fiscal and budgetary perspectives.
2	Resource Acquisition	Revenue mobilization methodology.
3	Resource Utilization	Solution-centered, results-oriented budgeting.
4	Controls	Dynamic monitoring.
5	Management Motivation	The will-to-achieve.

With regard to financial authority, I regretfully acknowledge the situation facing finance officials who work under laws that do not facilitate efficacious finance management. I have reserved comment on the difficulties of this situation for Part 3, where I comment on the subject of public finance authority. Suffice it to say, at this point, that public finance officers have a responsibility to promote the adoption of laws encouraging efficacious financial practice. This imperative deserves a prominent place on the "to do" list of public finance officers, especially finance establishment leaders.

Managerial Thought for Public Finance Officers

In my introductory note, *To the Reader*, I observed that the usual perspective applied to public finance work is procedural. In the work-a-day world, public finance management is commonly identified with the conduct of finance-related activities, variously identified as budgeting, accounting, revenue collection, procurement, accounts receivable and payable, and cash management. (One also notes that finance establishments are often assigned responsibility for sundry centralized process agencies that have no direct connection to finance work) These finance-related activities provide a basis for the distribution of authority within finance establishments, resulting in the maintenance of organizational units, variously identified as divisions, sections, etc. Unquestionably, the finance-related activities form a domain for the exercise of organizational arithmetic.

In the domain of organizational arithmetic, finances qualify as "managed" when accountable officials attain production goals on time and at relatively low cost.

Working within the mental framework of organizational arithmetic, accountable officials can appropriately apply management efficacy criteria (effectiveness, efficiency and economy) to production procedures. Significantly, taking governmental jurisdictions as a whole, I noted that finance-related procedures reach into every nook and cranny. Universally, governments exploit this intrusive feature by using finance-related procedures to secure and maintain a modicum of administrative order. Finance officers are well-positioned to provide government leaders with

1) information and controls, useful in the execution of policies, projects and programs; and

2) a means of representing and attaining the values of effectiveness, efficiency and economy (the efficacy triad) throughout the government.

I. CORE AGENDA

I further observed that, looking outward, the exercise of government financial power regulates the relationship between government and the financial and economic marketplace, touching and influencing the arithmetic of the community. Finance officials help their jurisdictions resolve issues, solve problems and seize opportunities. If properly organized, and well-led, finance officials can provide government leaders with wise counsel on the perplexities of the day, including, of course, advice on financial policy. Considerations concerning the relationship of government finances to "community arithmetic" represent the highest form of public finance thinking.

Consequently, in addition to applying management criteria to the conduct of finance-related activities, accountable officials also "manage" public finance by assisting government leaders address socio-economic issues, problems and opportunities.

At this point, again consult Exhibit 1.1. Section B lists the prime concerns of public finance officers. Defined succinctly, these concerns are:

Availability of money. Refers to the acquisition and possession of cash to pay obligations, when due.

Cost of money. Refers to 1) interest on borrowed funds, and 2) the cost of conducting finance-related activities.

Productivity of money. Refers to the benefits conferred by allocating public funds and finance to programs and projects.

Recovery of money. Refers to the application of the beneficiary payment principle.

Managerial Thought for Public Finance Officers

At any given time, in any given finance establishment, specific objectives derived from these concerns form an agenda of public finance work. Working on an agenda linked to these transcendent concerns provides accountable public finance officials with consequential opportunities to apply managerial thought to their work. The reader will find a detailed discussion of these prime concerns in Part 4, *Rationale: Aims of Attainment*.

Although some public finance workers, notably cashiers, actually handle currency, most work with figures representing money. In this symbolic environment, chief financial officers conduct bond sales, controllers keep books of account and authorize payments, treasurers issue checks and reconcile bank statements with check registers, and accountants make ledger entries and test their appropriateness with trial balances. In the largest sense, attaining these desired effects requires "management," defined as the active coordination of the means of production, principally, in this case, personal services. For those public finance officers who supervise the work of others, "management" means attaining work objectives through the coordinated services of subordinates and colleagues. Considered as "managers," they must possess and demonstrate the ability to think and act "strategically," that is, attain desired goals by efficaciously deploying resources in space and time, giving due weight to resistance and opportunities. As will be explored in detail in Part 2, *Instrumentalities*, the habit of strategic thinking, and resulting action, can be facilitated by the adopting recommended concepts and associated practices.

II. INSTRUMENTALITIES

... identifies selected instruments which require and foster the application of managerial thought.

Instruments of management thinking serve to incline the minds of public finance officers along lines of inquiry, reflection and practice which help them formulate valid judgments about the efficacy of their work. These instruments include metadata, integrated data, accounting, and performance measurement. This discussion of instrumentalities will conclude with the significance of credit ratings and financial and administrative process controls.

Metadata

The term "metadata" refers to pertinent facts about particular facts. Metadata provides a basis for principled, efficacious management action, that is, action justified by reference to the values of effectiveness, efficiency and economy—the efficacy triad. Metadata provides essential raw material for managerial thinking applied to finance work.

Finance facts, such as those typically found in financial statements, are numbers representing money. Without past, present and prospective references, such facts are essentially meaningless. As in every sphere of mental life, *relationships provide meaning.* A finance fact acquires management significance by its association with other pertinent facts. For example, a particular denominated receivable is a finance fact, pure and simple. Minimally, accountable officials should also know the age of that receivable, and the time, effort and cost related to its collection. Indeed, with regard to overdue receivables, efficacious action depends on the assembly of information concerning particular debtors. As attested by experienced revenue collectors, the collection of overdue receivables is a fairly complex activity, requiring a judicious mix of information, and management vigor, rigor and discretion.

Similarly, the estimated prices assigned to purchase requisitions resting in a procurement office queue are also finance facts, which, in some governments, might be duly recognized by accountants as "bookable" contingent liabilities. We can (and should) track the number of such queued requisitions, noting the time, work hours and cost required to transform them into purchase orders. Procurement processing time is a critical variable to dependent programmatic agencies awaiting supplies and services. Like all centralized process agencies, procurement units are queue-driven. In general, ill-managed queues are very damaging and costly to the programmatic agencies compelled to use the services of centralized process agencies. Although difficult to specify, queue-related damages and costs incurred by user agencies deserve consideration in assembling metadata concerning the efficacy of centralized process agencies. Metadata is also indispensable in responsibly managing queues affecting parties depending on finance agency action, especially vendors awaiting payment, and taxpayers awaiting refunds.

Profit-oriented enterprises tend to attack the productivity problems of centralized process agencies by establishing their "accountability" to "users" within the enterprise. For example, production units might pay for their share of the cost of centralized procurement or payroll processes, adding the cost of these centralized services to the costs of production. This apparently works best when the users are granted the option of access to a competitive market environment, representing an economic, rather than administrative approach to productivity. After analysis of, let us say, the cost of processing purchase orders by a centralized procurement unit, a service charge might be assessed which provides a reasonable return on funds invested in the

II. INSTRUMENTALITIES

service by the jurisdiction. Users of the service then pay at this rate for a specified period. Because the revenue flow to the central process agency is thus determined by the volume of its output, the managers of centralized process agencies have strong incentives to manage prudently, invest in technology, and avoid fixed costs which do not vary directly with production.

The management utility of any given data array depends on its organization. Managers express their intent through format selection and the procedures specified for data assembly and verification. Relevant data usually rests in disparate records. Consequently, it is necessary for accountable officials to visualize insight-provoking data relationships, then devise and implement data assembly formats. Ensuring the availability of metadata is, in itself, a fundamental act of managers, a condition precedent for subsequent managerial thinking and action. The assembly and use of organized metadata is a defining characteristic of competent public finance managers.

Because we use pertinent data about finance facts to execute policy and practice, metadata deserves as much care as prime finance facts appearing in finance reports. Consequently, criteria of relevance, integrity, accuracy and timeliness must be rigorously applied to the recording and reporting of metadata.

Information is the raw material of finance management. If not properly focused, information and advice distract and confuse, wasting the time and energy of policy-makers and administrators. As information and advice illuminate issues, spotlight options and stimulate thought, the organization and presentation of information and advice must not be left to chance, or to caprice. Even before computers increased the availability of information, reporting was never a trivial point of organizational theory because reporting requirements, such as budget formats and the layout of finance reports, were known to have significant affects on managerial attention and action.

Recognizing its value, public finance officers should embrace and relentlessly implement this controlling, energizing management instrumentality. Acting continuously upon systematic data about finance facts most certainly enhances the ability of accountable public finance officers to attain desired results. When considering how to organize and furnish the minds of public finance officers, I give this instrumental concept high place in my lexicon of most desirable mental dispositions. Its importance in organizing managerial thought applied to public finance work cannot be overstated.

Integrated Data

Although finance practice differs from place to place, differences in procedure cannot obscure the following two axioms: 1) the underlying similarity of all data handling processes, and, 2) the often repetitive use of the same information. Considering the first axiom, regardless of their assignment (budgeting, accounting, treasury, etc.) finance workers act on a stream of facts and documents in typical ways:

- sorting and routing
- numbering and coding
- processing, according to rules
- summarizing
- recording and filing
- transcribing and reporting

Considering the second axiom, finance workers frequently record, re-record, file and re-file, report and re-report the same data (purchase order numbers, addresses, invoice numbers, payroll data, etc.) And, mark this, even in computerized offices, finance workers frequently transcribe existing information, in effect, creating new records. While some data redundancy is useful for proving and checking, most transcription work is sheer waste, representing a failure to think through the recording and reporting problem. Although computer technology provides document

II. INSTRUMENTALITIES

processing facilities and multiple points of access to stored data, reducing the amount of redundant effort and documentation, finance workers will still be acting upon relevant data in the characteristic ways listed above.

Finance-related activities embrace many routines. By all means, finance managers should analyze separate routines for effectiveness, efficiency and economy, but should reference the dominating concept of Integrated Data Management (IDM). This perspective promotes the elimination of superfluous routines to produce a continuous assembly of outputs—a master key to efficacious operations.

Obviously, any routine can be studied in relative isolation. By applying techniques of management analysis, methods of attaining work goals can be rationalized, reducing, avoiding or displacing effort and costs. Paradoxically, however, isolated attempts to bring each routine to a peak of efficiency through management analysis may produce a relatively inefficient overall operation, if finance units still process and re-process the same information. In tackling the productivity problems of financial management, then, it is the beginning of wisdom to recognize that efficiency of the parts may not necessarily produce an efficient whole.

The two axioms noted above, provide a solid foundation for systemic thinking about public finance work. In addition to utilizing methodic approaches, public finance officials should apply systemic thinking to their work since data, useful to others, can be captured or created once, then stored and transmitted in a "common" medium, such as, paper, film, electronic files, etc., making this data repeatedly useful with minimum, or no, further processing.

At this point, examine the following IDM checklist. It provides a set of statements defining the key operational characteristics of the IDM concept. As a checklist, this set of statements can, and should, be used to test particular procedures and records for compliance with IDM principles. In cases where practice does not contribute to the realization of the IDM ideal, reference to the checklist can certainly point the way to improvement.

1) Store and transmit data recorded in one finance operation, also used in another, in media making re-recording unnecessary.

2) To ensure that later users can absolutely rely on its accuracy, use "proving" procedures to verify data at the time of recording.

3) Thoroughly review recorded abstractions of primary information (summaries, batch totals, compilations, reports, etc.) for accuracy and utility.

4) Regardless of recording media, regularly purge records according to a records management plan.

Some may say, this list is very good, but many governments are too small to afford the equipment and services which seem needed for integrated data management. It is true, of course, that equipment is best justified by volume, giving larger jurisdictions an advantage in technological applications. However, this advantage is more apparent, than real, because the concept of integrated data management can be applied in any administrative environment—even in offices which have no technology at all. Indeed one can visualize an office efficiently organized by multi-part forms, well-planned coding and recording practices, etc., provided that work sequences minimize or eliminate the repetitive re-recording of data in the various stages of processing. (For example, assigning the same number to both requisition and purchase order(s) facilitates processing, recording and filing related to procurement transactions.) Without doubt, a systemic approach to finance work, based on the commonality of data and administrative tasks can be tried and successfully implemented in every government, large or small.

In the larger jurisdictions, the volume of work clearly justifies greater use of technology. Even in such units, however, it is not so much the use of technology, but the way technology is used which creates an

II. INSTRUMENTALITIES

efficient operation. Moral of the story: Equipment is good, but a plan for integrated data management is better! For additional observations about "technology in the countinghouse," turn to Part 5, *Organization: Means of Attainment.*

Jurisdictions lacking plans for integrated data management (the situation of most governments of general jurisdiction) can not get such plans without investing in a formal records management program. Based on research and analysis, such programs probe the reasons for record creation and retention. If vigorously implemented, the resulting plan will minimize the volume of records by rationalizing their creation and retention. In putting a plan together, finance officials are advised, in colloquial terms, to "start from scratch, "work from the bottom up," and "cover the waterfront." It is necessary to map pertinent data from point of origin, through all stages of processing to final disposition. Every routine must be examined, placed in its operational context, and documented by means of flow charts, volume counts, work hour tabulations, etc. All recommended changes must be justified by favorable cost comparisons or speed, accuracy and quality considerations. It is painstaking work. Keeping a plan up-to-date, in the face of changing technology, and demands for new information, also requires a commitment to research and analysis.

Data management processes are inseparable from reporting procedures and requirements. Presumably, reported data is affective, that is, influential. If reports do not affect policy and management behavior, data aggregation activities represent a waste of organizational energies and resources. Qualified observers have noted that between those preparing and those receiving reports, persons preparing reports learn the most, and tend to react to the information entered therein most vigorously and appropriately. Reports come in all shapes and sizes. Obviously, "before-the-fact" reports are far more valuable to report recipients than those submitted "after-the-fact." This observation prompts a conclusion that reports that do not cause or help the report preparer to act are a waste of time and energy. From the recipient's point of view, performance reports should reference standards and targets with performance tendencies noted, especially impending failure to attain expected goals. It is safe to say that much time, energy and material are wasted on ineffectual reporting by subordinates to superiors. Unless periodically reviewed for decision-related utility, administrative and financial controls, and the reporting thereon, tend to expand over time because policy and operating problems and issues continuously crop up, requiring management responses. Where possible, reporting should be skewed toward prevention rather than cure.

Accounting (Chart of Accounts and Cost Centers)

It can be truly said that accounting is not just an instrument of business, but is an expression of its essence: Assets less liabilities equals owner's equity, which business officials work to protect and increase. The role of accounting in governments, excepting in their public enterprises, is fundamentally different, but no less important. The accounting equation applicable to governments (lacking ownership) results in fund balances, rather than ownership equities. These fund balances include amounts of "free cash" that is available for future expenditure. Thus, government accounting is not a fundamental expression of its essence, but is an indispensable managerial instrument.

Program managers and finance officials striving to improve the efficacy of government operations require access to an elaborate and flexible accounting system, a system which can provide supervisors at every hierarchical level with desired data on costs, efforts and performance. Accordingly, accounting formats classify and code data which can be related to measures of results, permitting the calculation of performance ratios, such as unit costs and unit times. Denoted by programmatic titles, "cost centers" aggregate the evidence of applied resources (money and work time) which can be related to "results" produced by their application. Exhibit 2.1, *A Sample Chart of Accounts: Finance Director's Office,* provides a classification and coding scheme applied to the leadership of a public finance establishment.

II. INSTRUMENTALITIES

EXHIBIT 2.1 A Sample Chart of Accounts: Finance Director's Office

EXPENDITURE LEDGER

Classification and Codes								Significance
1	2	3	4	5	6	7	8	Significance
01								Fund
	General Fund							
	1							Function
		General Government						
		03						1st Level of Oganization
			Finance Department					
			1					2nd Level of Organization
				Finance Director's Office				
				0				3rd Level of Organization
					No Third Level In This Unit			
					1			Subsidiary Ledger
						Activity (Work Plan)		
						1		Cost Concept *
							Variable	
							001	Expenditure Object
							Salaries	

REVENUE LEDGER

Classification and Codes								Significance
1	2	3	4	5	6	7	8	Significance
01								Fund
	General Fund							
	1							Function
		General Government						
		03						1st Level of Oganization
			Finance Department					
			1					2nd Level of Organization
				Finance Director's Office				
				0				3rd Level of Organization
					No Third Level In This Unit			
					1			Subsidiary Ledger
						Activity (Work Plan)		
						03		Type of Revenue
							Service Charge	
							051	Source of Revenue
							Copies	

PERFORMANCE LEDGER

Classification and Codes								Significance
1	2	3	4	5	6	7	8	Significance
01								Fund
	General Fund							
	1							Function
		General Government						
		03						1st Level of Oganization
			Finance Department					
			1					2nd Level of Organization
				Finance Director's Office				
				0				3rd Level of Organization
					No Third Level In This Unit			
					1			Subsidiary Ledger
						Activity (Work Plan)		
						01		Activity Indicator
							Fiscal Policy	
							025	Production Indicator
							Report	

* This sample chart of accounts uses variable (code 1) or fixed (code 2) to characterize costs for management purposes. Such costs may also be identified as direct or indirect.

Every well-ordered accounting unit maintains an updated chart of accounts listing the titles and code numbers to be used in identifying, recording and reporting budgetary decisions and transactions. The chart of accounts should list appropriately entitled *cost centers* for the aggregation of receipts and disbursements, satisfying the criteria listed in Exhibit 2.2, *Cost Center Criteria*. Cost, itself, must be precisely defined, as the concept is open to different formulations and interpretations, depending on the accounting convention applied.

In Exhibit 2.1, the coding scheme embraces eight code levels, using a total of twelve digits. Note also that expenditure object classifications are logged the lowest level. Programmatic classifications, Code Levels 3 thru 6, located in the middle of the code scheme, provide a zone where cost centers are most likely to be correlated with measures of results. Code level 6 refers to subsidiary ledgers which list activities/tasks recorded in associated work plans. In appropriate cases, costs can be refined by identifying them as fixed or variable, employing code level 7. The coding scheme's complexity may be greater or less than illustrated, depending on management's need for information and/or control. In accordance with the "lump-sum" allocation concept of solution-centered, results-oriented budgeting, code level 4, the finance director's office, might be the allotment limit beyond which no further expenditures would be processed for payment. Setting control points this high in the code scheme cuts paperwork and significantly enhances official accountability.

Given the possibility that jurisdictions using the fund concept to organize their accounting system will have more than nine funds, the sample classification and coding array shown in Exhibit 2.1 provides Code Level 1 with two digits (1 to 99 possibilities), providing for the identification of 99 separate funds. As shown in the sample, Fund 1 is usually designated as a general, or consolidated fund, recording transactions related to a jurisdiction's array of service programs. Transactions related to capital projects are usually lodged in a separate Capital Projects Fund. Of course, if a jurisdiction has more than 99 funds, three or more digits will be required, depending on the number of funds. This qualification applies to all the codes listed in the sample classification and code scheme. In general, a proper philosophy of coding stresses economy in their use, specifying that no more digits be provided than are needed, reducing coding effort and the possibility of coding error.

II. INSTRUMENTALITIES

Using the same set of codes, levels 1 through 6, for the classification of expenditures, revenues and performance data facilitates the coordination of program information when linked to work plans, considered as subsidiary ledgers. Worl plans can log and report data related to effort, such as, workloads, work targets, staff paid hours, staff work hours, energy usage, equipment utilization and performance information drawn from reports and invoices submitted by contractors, etc. Obviously, a resulting consolidated cost center record can have great managerial value as it can stimulate analysis and facilitate presentations. Moreover, assigning the same code sequences to program expenditures and program-related revenues focuses managerial attention on net financial results (plus or minus) of program activity. As managers are customarily preoccupied with spending, a consolidated program report showing net program-related financial results serves to engage them in resource acquisition. Using cost center formats and procedures to facilitate program manager participation in revenue production is an important point which will be discussed again later on.

EXHIBIT 2.2 Cost Center Criteria

CRITERION	
SIGNIFICANCE	Center aggregates costs devoted to an important purpose.
PRODUCTIVITY	Center linked to specific, measurable performance results.
ACCOUNTABILITY	Center assigned to a manager accountable for resource applications and performance.
REPORTABILITY	Center supported by procedures for recording, relating and reporting financial and performance data.
ACCEPTANCE	Center understood and endorsed by affected staff and interested parties.

Governments seriously committed to performance establish and maintain appropriately identified cost centers for the aggregation of costs, related revenues and results. Ideally, all cost centers should be associated with output/outcome/impact indicators. Best defined, cost centers are aggregations of disbursement, expenditure or expense which can be related to results. As prime organizing concepts, cost centers should be closely associated with supervisory accountability. As the building blocks of budget structure, each cost center should be tested for its contribution to efficacy by applying the criteria listed in Exhibit 2.2, *Cost Center Criteria*. A brief commentary on cost center criteria follows:

1. **Significance**. As organizing concepts, cost centers should focus attention on important activities, purposes, and goals. Testing a proposed aggregation for significance helps to discourage the proliferation of cost centers identifying instrumental tasks and processes, such as processing applications, issuing permits, etc., which are more appropriately incorporated in work plans. Although subjective evaluations inevitably determine "importance," specifying decision criteria can help to mitigate their influence in the establishment of cost centers.

2. **Productivity**. Every cost center should relate to output/outcome/impact indicators, preferably specified mathematically. The designation of expected results requires management attention and, often times, a willingness to accept less-than-perfect indicators. This criterion also applies to inclusive, high level summaries, requiring, in most cases, an index of indicators of results. The productivity criterion must be applied to all cost aggregations, and foregone only where conceptual difficulties prove insurmountable. As displayed in Exhibit 2.3, *Indicators of Performance*, seven concepts are variously applied to define and measure the productivity of government agencies.

II. INSTRUMENTALITIES

EXHIBIT 2.3 Indicators of Performance

OUTPUT (Volume)	Production quantities, stated in units of service or products. .
OUTPUT (Quality)	Production qualities, defined by specifications (Service waiting time, accounting error rates, in-hospital infection rates, etc.).
OUTCOME	Social, economic and physical consequences of program activity. Outcomes require interpretation and evaluation.
IMPACT	Specifies changes caused by program activity. Impacts require interpretation and evaluation..
EFFECTIVENESS	The degree of attainment of an ideal, a goal or an intention, calculated as a percentage, with results serving as the numerator and the ideal, goal or intention, numerically stated, as the denominator. Interpretation requires comparative reference, time series, standards, etc,.
EFFICIENCY	The relationship (ratio) between a result and the resources used to produce it, calculated by dividing results by input or the reverse. Interpretation of the ratio requires comparative reference (Time series, standard cost, market price, etc.).
ECONOMY	A relative evaluation that finds that a certain means of production is less expensive than alternative methodologies. Evaluation rests on comparative references.

3. **Accountability.** To establish accountability, every cost center should be formally assigned to a manager who is accountable for the behavior of both allocated resources and expected results. In order to provide needed flexibility, cost center managers should be granted "lump-sum" allotments validated by reference to work plans and performance reports. Further, to truly qualify as an accountable cost center, its manager should be entrusted with the following duties: 1) cost center budget and work plan formulation; 2) cost center budget reallocation, when

necessary; 3) maintenance of measurement records regarding results; 4) performance monitoring and reporting; 5) supervision of staff and contractors funded by the cost center; 6) discipline of staff funded by the cost center; 7) work time and/or payroll certification; 8) authorization of requisitions and/or purchase orders; and 9) certification of receipt of purchases and vendor payments. In complex governmental organizations, the distribution of hierarchical and functional authority will modulate assignment of these duties.

4. **Responsibility**. In order to avoid excessive accounting and reporting, each cost center should be assessed for recording ease, accuracy and relevance. Complex cost allocations and extensive splitting of work time will be necessary in some cases, but, as a rule, should be avoided. In general, the standards for recording costs are governed by established accounting conventions, supported by auditing procedures. As budget reports should reference results, standards governing the collection and reporting of performance data are as important as the standards for controlling and reporting payrolls and other disbursements, and should also be regularly audited.

5. **Acceptance**. Simply stated, those doing the work, especially accountable cost center managers, should understand the cost center concept and its productivity implications. Securing a sufficient degree of acceptance cannot be left to chance as accountable officials may be expected to vary in their willingness to resolve issues of cost center definition and specification of expected results. Attaining the required degree of acceptance throughout a jurisdiction requires leadership attention, and unambiguous commitment to the cost center concept.

II. INSTRUMENTALITIES

As a general rule, each criterion should be given equal weight in measuring the merit of any particular cost center. Therefore, the failure to satisfy any one criterion renders the cost center substandard. However, with reference to the productivity criterion, in those cases where a mathematical linkage between input and output/outcome cannot be specified, the cost center may still be qualified as satisfactory if it is supported with documentation providing factual information defining rationale, goals, clientele, service standards, etc.

As prime organizing concepts, cost centers should be closely associated with supervisory responsibility. In addition to providing building blocks for budget arrays, cost centers provide a basis for work plans and subsequent performance reviews. In Exhibit 2.1, *A Sample Chart of Accounts: Finance Director's Office,* expenditures supporting the office of a chief financial officer are identified as a cost center, requiring the formulation and execution of a work plan. Typically, work plans list activities and tasks. A work plan example is provided in Part 6, Exhibit 6.11, *Work Plan: Finance Director's Office.* It lists the key activities/tasks of a chief finance officer as 1) fiscal policy formation, 2) systems development, 3) general administration, 4) miscellaneous tasks and 5) performance reviews.

Also note the reference to subsidiary ledgers documenting work plans. Formulated and implemented by cost center managers (officials who supervise the work of others), work plans register anticipated activities/tasks, work hours assigned to each, performance targets, performance ratios, and expected completion dates. As noted above, work plans can record other productions-related facts, such as, energy usage, equipment utilization and performance information drawn from reports and invoices submitted by contractors, etc. Nevertheless, planning and control of work time, rather than cost, is the primary purpose of work plans, re-enforced by periodic performance reviews. Although it is possible to classify and code the detailed activities and tasks displayed in work plans in a Chart of Accounts, work plan detail is usually too extensive to be so listed. Consequently, cost center managers must organize and maintain their work plans as subsidiary ledgers, regularly reconciled to the reports produced by the accounting system of their jurisdiction.

EXHIBIT 2.4 Cost Center Array Related to Performance Data

COST CENTER	COST	OUTPUT	UNIT COST	TREND
BUDGETING				
Budget Preparation	83,992	Submitted Budget	83,992.00	Up
Projections	9,773	4 Reports	2,444.50	Up
Status Reporting	9,773	11 Reports	888.92	Down
Quarterly Adjustments	3,942	4 Close-outs	985.50	Up
PURCHASING				
Processing	16,394	10,000 Orders	1.64	Down
Formal Bidding	38,425	370 Awards	103.55	Up
ACCOUNTS PAYABLE				
Vendor Payments	63,490	33,600 Payments	1.89	Down
Pay Checks	63,490	81,620 Payments	.78	Up
REVENUE COLLECTION				
Taxes	74,303	37,000 Accounts	2.01	Up
Utility Charges	20,082	225,000 Payments	.08	Down
Delinquent Accounts	72,294	17,800 Accounts	4.06	Down
ACCOUNTING				
Reporting	21,263	144 Reports	146.97	Down
CASH MANAGEMENT				
Depositing	1,205	2,000 Deposits	.60	Down
Reconciliation	8,312	50 Accounts	166.24	Down
Investing	21,163	370 Investments	57.20	Up

* Trend tendency derived by comparison to prior period results, not displayed.

Exhibit 2.4, *Cost Center Array Related to Performance Data,* provides a sample application of the cost center concept applied to finance work. Incorporating an array of finance management variable/direct cost estimates divided by output measurements, the Exhibit displays resulting unit costs of production. The right-hand column in this array serves to draw management attention to those cost centers with rising unit costs. As the desired tendency is "down," the reasons for rising unit costs bear investigation, and, if feasible, timely corrective action.

II. INSTRUMENTALITIES

It is important to note that, in complex organizations, the attainment of any given objective frequently requires effort by more than one organizational unit. For example, in a jurisdiction with centralized procurement of goods and services, the process will involve: 1) programmatic units requisitioning goods and services, then certifying receipt and vendor invoices; 2) a central procurement unit soliciting bids and issuing purchase orders; 3) a central mailing unit distributing paperwork and posting; 4) an accounts payable unit authorizing vendor payments, 5) a central accounting unit (controller) certifying availability of funds and recording transactions; and 6) the treasury issuing checks and reconciling accounts. Obviously, attempts to rationalize the cost and performance of centralized process agencies require the identification of associated efforts and costs throughout the jurisdiction. Further, subsidiary ledgers and/or temporary accounting procedures may be needed to split or allocate costs, or previously recorded disbursements. Personal service budgets provide a case in point. As they usually involve both specific allocations, organizational unit by unit, and "lumpsum" (also called global) allocations for employee benefits, personal service costs present a problem in maintaining the integrity of a cost center scheme. To ensure that total personal service costs are properly distributed, jurisdictions may use temporary accounting procedures which permit pay checks to be issued when due. These "direct costs" are subsequently "loaded" with the "indirect costs" of employee benefits before charging them to appropriate performance cost centers.

Every well-run government maintains a well-thumbed Chart of Accounts prescribing how certain facts related to financial transactions are to be identified and recorded in its accounting system. As custodians of the system, accounting personnel tend to prize Chart of Accounts stability. To avoid confusion and reduce error, and to maintain period-to-period reporting comparability, many finance officials resist the concept of a flexible approach to classification and coding.

Discounting the management imperative, they favor a stable chart of accounts, standardized and extended, unchanged, over many fiscal periods. However, management-minded finance and programmatic officials see the overriding advantages of a flexible approach to the structure of accounts. Given sufficient flexibility in its application, the Chart of Accounts becomes the primary instrument for establishing and tracking relationships between costs, efforts and results. Using the accounts structure for managerial purposes requires that a Chart of Accounts be easy to amend. Although period-to-period comparability is valuable, from a policy and managerial point of view, it is much more important to be able to relate costs and efforts to programmatic issues, problems and opportunities, as they arise and are addressed by accountable officials throughout the government. Regrettably, conservative accounting staff attitudes and system rigidities impede management-minded officials who wish to provide program officials with a flexible scheme of cost/effort centers. Although we can overstate the influence of form on decision-making, people do tend to think about what appears before them. The classifications listed by an organization's Chart of Accounts influence thinking and discussion, thus shape action agendas.

Charts of Account are typically issued by central finance authorities, granting program officials of central governments and subordinate governments little or no discretion in establishing revenue and expenditure classifications. Management-minded finance officials trapped in this situation must consider maintaining subsidiary ledgers incorporating an alternative Chart of Accounts, even though this policy entails redundant accounting.

When all is said and done, cost centers provide an indispensable tool for the organization and interpretation of data about finance facts. Despite acknowledged problems, it is difficult to exaggerate the importance of an adequate scheme of cost centers for managing investments in public policies, programs and projects. The important topic of accounting support will be further considered in Part 5, *Organization: Means of Attainment*.

II. INSTRUMENTALITIES

Performance Measurement

If accounting is the heart of financial management, performance measurements are surely its soul. Although it concentrates on finance activities, the general concepts of performance measurement are applicable throughout government jurisdictions. Certainly, applications of efficacy triad measurements are critical factors in establishing the *intrinsic* merit of budget allocations. Performance ratios, such as unit cost and output per work hour, are useful because they automatically relate measures of investment and measures of effort to results. Input-output relationships help to reveal relative efficacy, provided that, in a given period, inputs and results can be measured, and then united by ratio calculations which facilitate comparisons. Unit measures are formed by dividing numbers representing effort by numbers representing results, and the reverse. Exhibit 2.5, *Unit Measure Concepts*, displays commonly used unit measures.

EXHIBIT 2.5. Unit Measure Concepts

CALCULATION*		UNIT MEASURE	DESIRED TENDENCY
Cost/Results	=	Unit Cost	Down
Results/Cost	=	Units Per Cost	Up
Work Time/Results	=	Work Time Per Results Indicator	Down
Results/Work Time	=	Results Indicator Per Work Time	Up

* Results can be identified as output (measure of production), outcome (measure of effectiveness) or impact (measure of transformed conditions or situations).

Evaluation implies comparison. Provided that the measurement in question can be compared to a measure rooted in similar circumstances, the magnitude and direction of its variance can be noted and evaluated. Measures can be compared to:

- Targets
- Similar measures arrayed in a time series

- Similar measures produced by alternative production methodologies
- Similar measures produced in similar production situations

Data about annual cost, effort and production displayed in Exhibit 2.4 indicates that processing vendor payments cost $63,490, required 12,360 work hours and produced 33,600 vendor payments. As shown below, this raw data can be converted into a series of ratios useful in making performance comparisons:

$$\$63{,}490/33{,}600 \text{ Vouchers} = \$1.89 \text{ Per Voucher}$$
$$33{,}600 \text{ Vouchers}/\$63{,}490 = 0.53 \text{ Vouchers Per Dollar}$$
$$12{,}360 \text{ Work Hours}/33{,}600 \text{ Vouchers} = 0.37 \text{ Work Hours Per Voucher}$$
$$33{,}600 \text{ Vouchers}/12{,}360 \text{ Work Hours} = 2.70 \text{ Vouchers per Work Hour}$$

In passing, it should be noted that the cost of $63,490 is an aggregation of variable (direct) expenditures, such as salaries, supplies, etc. Deriving the total cost of processing vendor checks would require adding fixed (indirect) costs, such as space costs, fringe benefits, depreciation charges on equipment, etc. It is usually instructive to calculate and compare performance ratios in the following situations:

- Ratio produced during a given period compared to a set target ratio.

- Ratio produced in a given period compared to similar ratio(s) for other periods.
  (Time series comparisons)

II. INSTRUMENTALITIES

- Ratio produced with a specific production methodology compared to ratio(s) produced by alternative methodologies.

- Ratio produced in a particular production situation compared to ratio(s) produced in a similar situation elsewhere.

As shown in Exhibit 2.5, each type of measure has a desired comparative tendency, as follows:

- Cost per unit of output should go down.
- Units of output per cost should go up.
- Work hours per unit of output should go down.
- Units of output per work hour should go up.

Variances between similar unit measures may be traceable to:

- Changes in prices.
- Changes in production volume and type of resources applied.
- Changes in performance of assets employed.
- Environmental contingencies, that is, uncontrollable changes in the production situation which invalidate original production assumptions.

As pointed out above, performance ratios acquire meaning when compared to one or more ratios based on similar output indicators, and the same input considerations. For example, unit costs can be compared in a time series, to standard (or expected) unit costs set up during the budget process, and to market prices, if suppliers are available. Time series unit cost comparisons are frequently displayed in performance-style budgets. Time series unit measure variations focus attention on the relationship between fixed and variable costs and a fluctuating workload. By using unit costs, cost center managers can be held accountable for those costs which can be made to vary with output: salaries, overtime payments, supplies, contractual services, etc.

As a rule, over the short run, fixed or indirect costs do not fluctuate with output. But, through policy and/or management action, fixed costs can be made variable, reduced or eliminated. It has been truly said that, "there are no fixed costs." So, over time, the amount of space, equipment, depreciation charges, and other fixed costs which are assigned to specific procedures can be made to vary in desired ways. In short, the introduction and maintenance of a comprehensive scheme of unit measures helps to ensure that investments, fixed and variable, in finance procedures are related to workloads and results..

Obviously, performance ratios are dynamic, changing from period to period, due to changes in cost factors and production variables. Consider this: For any given cost center, costs may go up, stay the same, or go down. During the same period, production may go up, stay the same, or go down. The interaction of these variables results in nine possible unit costs. Three combinations of these variables will definitely produce the favored tendency, that is, down. Three will not. In two of these combinations, the direction of change will be indeterminate. It must be determined by calculation. The remaining combination produces no change. Be warned, if quality considerations are also related to cost and production variables, the range of possibilities rises from nine to 27.

Most important, a comprehensive scheme of unit measures makes it difficult for cost center managers to shun responsibility for productivity improvements. The unit costs and unit times of a procedure, such as payroll processing, often can be resolved into a set of subsidiary unit measures, each worthy of study. The administration of payroll deductions might be one such subsidiary cost center. Suppose it is found that the cost of administering payroll deductions is so much per check. This figure can then be referenced to market prices for the service, and this activity assigned to a contract supplier, if the market price is favorable. Or, cost reducing changes in the production procedure can be effected

In general, it is unwise to maintain unit measures at high levels of aggregation, as this may hide opportunities for a series of perhaps minor changes in procedure which can add up to an impressive productivity improvement. To successfully implement a scheme of unit measures, one must identify units of production, and then assemble data about production volumes and the related work time and costs. The identification and establishment of cost centers is, therefore, dependent on management's expectation that the results will merit the effort.

EXHIBIT 2.6 Quality Criteria Applied to Finance Functions

COST CENTER	QUALITY STANDARDS
BUDGETING	
Budget Document Submissions	On time %
Projections (Estimates)	% accurate to set standard
Status Reporting	On time %
Budget Adjustments	% accurate to set standard
PURCHASING	
No-Bid Requisition Processing	Elapsed time to issue purchase order
Formal Bid Processing	Processing time
ACCOUNTS PAYABLE	
Vendor Settlements	% paid within given time
ACCOUNTS RECEIVABLE	
Taxes	% paid while current
Utility Charge Payments	Time lapses between receipt, deposit and recording
Delinquent Accounts	% change in accounts outstanding 30 days or more
ACCOUNTING	
All Transactions	Entry error rate
Reporting	Time to report after closing
CASH MANAGEMENT	
Depositing	Time lapses between receipt, deposit and recording
Reconciliation	Time lapse reporting & correcting statement errors
Investing	Interest earnings comparisons

We should not conclude this general discussion of performance measures without reference to quality considerations. Up to this point, I have concentrated on the cost center, unit cost and accountability approaches to productivity. These approaches rivet attention on the volume of production, rather than on its quality. Yet, the quality question intrudes deeply into every production situation. For example, finance officials should be concerned about the time lapse between receipt of a vendor's invoice and the date of settlement check issuance. Long delays in this sensitive matter not only produce time-consuming inquires from vendors, but damage the reputation of a jurisdiction, and, may reduce the number of enterprises competing for a jurisdiction's business. Exhibit 2.6, *Quality Criteria Applied to Finance Functions*, lists a variety of performance concepts and quality of performance indicators.

The reader will recall that I noted that the integrity, relevance and timeliness of finance information should be an important concern of finance officers responsible for the formulation of fiscal policy. Obviously, data integrity, accuracy, relevance and timeliness are quality considerations. Just as obviously, the best way to attain operating qualities is to design them into procedures, rather than try to attain them through after-the-fact inspections or close supervision. And, even then, the attainment of desired qualities may cost money, increasing unit costs. This dilemma is illustrated by the following examples:

- A centralized purchasing unit may show a significant reduction in the number of purchase orders by concentrating the energy of its staff on bid scheduling, resulting in fewer low-volume orders. As a consequence, *ceteris paribus,* the unit cost of producing purchase orders will rise. To be sure, this increase in unit cost might be offset by cost reductions throughout the accounts payable cost center structure: fewer requisitions, invoices, payment checks, less recording, etc. But, even if the increase in the unit cost of purchase orders is not completely offset, a purchasing unit which can accomplish its work with fewer orders is doing a higher quality job. In this case, "less" means "more" in the qualitative sense.

II. INSTRUMENTALITIES

- In a certain treasury, the unit cost of investing idle funds was perceived as comparatively low, a sign of apparent productivity. Upon investigation, however, it was found that this unit cost (derived by dividing administrative costs by the number of notes issued) reflected a large volume of short-term investments. The subsequent introduction of better cash forecasting and new controls on the issuance of vendor payments resulted in fewer investments for longer terms at higher rates of interest. Because administrative costs did not decline appreciatively with the introduction of the new procedures, (a common occurrence), the reduction in the number of investments drove up the unit costs.

In many financial management activities, a single-minded drive for low unit costs can be damaging. In property assessment work, for example, the accuracy of appraisals should be the dominant productivity criterion. Luckily, in this activity, finance officials can compare the unit costs of property assessment work to market rates for appraisals and to a well-accepted quality criterion: the coefficient of dispersion (a measure of the difference between assessed values and market values. Indeed, in most financial management activities, it seems entirely possible to associate unit costs with a credible scheme of quality criteria acceptable to the staff involved, superiors and the public. Error rates, time lags and service frequencies are frequently used to specify quality criteria for financial management activities.

A note of caution: Periods of price inflation reduce the comparative value of year-to-year unit cost measures. One way to combat this involves the application of price deflators to the data. Of course, this procedure, while excellent, increases the burden of calculation.

Maintaining productivity records which relate work hours to output measures is another way to avoid the distorting influence of currency inflation. Furthermore, work hour output calculations stimulate thinking about capital/labor ratios as they point up productivity trends in labor-intensive financial management activities.

EXHIBIT 2.7 Selected Performance Measurement Concepts

	MEASUREMENT FOCUS	METHODOLOGY
1	Accounting Accuracy	% Original Entries/Total Entries
2	Timely Vendor Payments	% Invoices Paid Within 30 Days
3	Competitive Procurement	% Competitive Purchases
4	Revenue Collection	Collection %
5	Investment Earnings	% Cash Balances Invested
6	Timely Finance Reports	% Scheduled Reports Duly Submitted
7	Budgetary Accuracy	Actual Minus Adopted/Adopted Times 100%.

Exhibit 2.7 offers a set of selected finance management measurement concepts. The following notes amplify the methodology applied to each of the seven performance concepts:

1. Accounting Accuracy. Total entries minus correction entries divided by total entries, times 100%.

$$\frac{\text{Total Entries less Correction Entries}}{\text{Total Entries}} \times 100\% = \text{Ratio}$$

As a general rule, the accounting accuracy ratio should approach 100%. Patently, original entries in files of record should be correct. But, even those finance establishments which maintain strong controls on the data entry process experience erroneous entries. Reliance on reconciliation of records to one another is the main technique for after-the-fact discovery of erroneous entries. Finding and correcting entries is expensive, however, and very frustrating, especially when reporting deadlines are approaching, or already past.

2. Timely vendor payments. Checks issued within 30 days of receipt of vendor's invoice divided by total vendor checks issued, times 100%. Selecting 30 days as the invoice-processing standard, a timely vendor payments ratio for any reporting period can be derived by the following calculation:

$$\frac{\text{No. of Payments Within 30 Days of Invoice Receipt}}{\text{Total No. of Invoice Payments}} \times 100\% = \text{Ratio}$$

Commercial standards require the payment of invoices within 30 days of submission. Governments should select a processing period that falls within this commercial standard. As a general rule, given the selected invoice-processing standard, the timely payments ratio should equal or exceed 95%. Invariably, governments make payroll payments on a strict, periodic schedule. In contrast, although many governments try to regulate the vendor payment process (paying invoices received before the 10th and 25th of each month on the 15th and 30th of that month, respectively), a strict scheduling standard is less frequently applied. Indeed, delays in vendor invoice payments are often not the fault of the finance establishment, but are traceable to lax receiving report and invoice processing by program officials. Strict government adherence to an established vendor payment schedule enhances its repute among suppliers. For governments which do not accrue liabilities, the strict scheduling of vendor payments also assists them in preparing periodic reports which better reflect their current financial position. Additionally, a policy of timely settlement of vendor invoices promotes efficient finance-related processing in all units, as well as in the accounts payable units. Finally, the strict scheduling of vendor payments provides a firm foundation for the management of cash.

3. Competitive procurement. Vendor checks associated with purchase orders issued subsequent to competitive price quotation divided by total vendor checks issued, times 100%.

$$\frac{\text{Purchase Order-related Checks Issued}}{\text{Total Vendor Checks Issued}} \times 100\% = \text{Ratio}$$

Although circumstances (namely sole sources or emergencies) may require non-competitive procurement, procurement efficacy depends on comprehensive competitive tendering processes. Additionally, competitive procurement processes reduce opportunities for favoritism and corruption, ever-present risks in every jurisdiction. Consequently, the higher the proportion of vendor checks associated with competitively awarded purchase orders, the better. Additionally, one may assess the benefit of competitive procurement by aggregating the difference between award-winning prices and the next best price, providing a proxy for savings ascribed to the competitive bidding process. To derive a benefit/cost relationship for any given period, this total of presumed "savings" may then be divided by the cost of the procurement process, yielding a ratio.

4. Revenue collection. For specified periods, amount collected divided by the revenue estimate, times 100%.

$$\frac{\text{Revenue Collected}}{\text{Estimated Revenue Collection}} \times 100\% = \text{Ratio}$$

This calculation can be applied to any given period, provided the amount outstanding at the end of the previous period and the amount expected during the period are known. As a general rule, tax collection ratios should equal or exceed 95%.

II. INSTRUMENTALITIES

Calculating coverage ratios provides another way to measure effectiveness. A case in point, potential revenue is lost when subjects avoid and evade sales and use taxes by making purchases in districts with lower tax rates and prices. Calculating coverage ratios not only helps to identify and collect additional revenue, but also helps to provide revenue equity by establishing the revenue liability of all appropriate subjects and objects. The coverage ratio is derived, as follows:

$$\frac{\text{Registered Subjects, Objects or Revenue Amount}}{\text{Potential Subjects, Objects or Revenue Amount}} \times 100\% = \text{Ratio}$$

Using survey methods or by securing access to records and files maintained by relevant agencies, accountable officials deliberately seek information on the potential subjects, objects and/or possible sources of revenue. The concept of coverage also includes "leakage." Leakage refers to amounts collected by agents of the government, such as business operators, but not remitted to the government. Consequently, attaining a revenue coverage ratio close to 100% implies little or no "leakage," if the estimate of potential revenue is accurate.

As it costs money to collect money, governments should be interested in the relative cost of collection. This measure requires the determination of the cost of collection for each tax and regulatory revenue. With regard to taxes, governments should strive to reduce collection costs, increasing the net sum available for funding desired programs and projects. With regard to fees for licenses and permits, revenue should equal or exceed costs. Also, with regard to charging beneficiaries for service, payments should equal or exceed collection costs and costs for service provision. Costs should include "direct" costs (salaries, supplies, etc.) and "indirect" cost allocations, (supervision, space costs, equipment depreciation, etc.) Recognizing the critical importance of collection and service delivery costs in the revenue collection process, finance officers should establish accounts and procedures to record and report expenditures related to collection and service. This step will facilitate the annual calculation of cost of collection and revenue/cost of service ratios. For more on this topic, see the commentary on resource acquisition in Part 6.

5. Investment earnings. Average daily investments divided by the total amount of cash and equivalents, times 100%. In general, the proportion invested should be close to 100%.

$$\frac{\text{Average Daily Invested Amounts}}{\text{Average Daily Balance of Available Assets}} \times 100\% = \text{Ratio}$$

Measuring the earnings efficacy of an investment program presents a more challenging problem as it requires the establishment of interest rate yardsticks. Data on market rate quotations must be assembled to provide a basis for comparisons with the rates actually obtained.

6. Timely financial status reports: As a general rule, the timely report ratio should not be less than 100%, calculated as follows:

$$\frac{\text{Number of Timely Reports (Including Projections)}}{\text{Total Number of Scheduled Reports}} \times 100\% = \text{Ratio}$$

The value of financial reports, especially interim reports (monthly and quarterly), depends on their accuracy and timeliness. Timely interim reports, accompanied by projections of end-of-period financial condition (revenue, expenditure and balances), are particularly useful in monitoring and revising projects and programs during implementation. Monthly reports lacking a projection through the remaining months to the end of the fiscal year are sub-standard, thus do not qualify as timely

II. INSTRUMENTALITIES

reports. Consequently, year-to-date monthly reports (including a projection of year-end financial condition) should be submitted to the chief executive and legislature no later than 10 days following the end of each month.

7. Budgetary accuracy: Calculate the difference between original estimates (adopted budget) and final audited figures for all, or a representative sample, of cost center classifications. Divide this difference (without regard to sign) by the original estimate, times 100% to derive a percentage of variation. Then, average the percentages of variation.

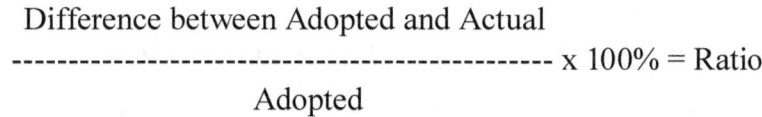

$$\frac{\text{Difference between Adopted and Actual}}{\text{Adopted}} \times 100\% = \text{Ratio}$$

Ideally, the budgeting accuracy ratio, measured by the average percentage of variation should be 5% or less. Experience indicates that this objective is attainable at high levels of aggregation, say at the jurisdiction as a whole, or at departmental levels where pluses and minuses throughout the aggregation cancel one another out in summaries. Experience also indicates that variances are largest at the lowest level of classification and coding, that is, the least inclusive level.

Budgets are usually constructed by aggregating a large number of detailed estimates. In almost every case, the actual revenues and expenditures recorded against these estimates will differ from these estimates, plus or minus. The better budgeting establishments strive to minimize the amount of variation by promoting procedures which produce accurate original estimates. Striving to minimize variation between original budget estimates and budget results enhances the credibility of program officials, and the accountability of the political leadership. Reasonably accurate budget estimates also provide a firm foundation for the formulation of cash flow projections. Additionally, striving for accurate budget estimates stimulates the establishments of cost centers and associated work plans and periodic performance reviews. Consequently, the accuracy of original budget estimates provides an important clue to the quality of a government's finance system.

A final note concerning performance measures: As shown by Exhibit 2.8, *An Indicative Performance Ratio Index,* performance data may be presented in an index format. Indexing permits multiple measures to be prioritized (weighted) and then combined into a single abstract performance indicator.

EXHIBIT 2.8 An Indicative Performance Ratio Index

MEASURE	RATIO		WEIGHT		INDEX
Accounting Accuracy	95%	x	10%	=	9.5%
Timely Vendor Payments	65	x	15	=	9.8
Competitive Procurement	85	x	20	=	17.0
Timely Revenue Collection	97	x	25	=	24.3
Investment Earnings	99	x	30	=	29.7
			100		90.3

Exhibit 2.8 displays an index assembling ratios for five measures of financial management performance. The assigned weights reveal the relative value placed on operating effectiveness. (A ratio of 100% represents perfection) The ratio displayed for Accounting Accuracy means that during the reporting period in question, 95 % of original entries were accepted as accurate. The assigned weights signify that the accountable officials think that Investment Earnings (30%) are three times more valuable than Accounting Accuracy (10%) and twice the value of Timely Vendor Payments (15%). Obviously, cost/benefit assessments underlie the assignments of weights.

II. INSTRUMENTALITIES

Credit Ratings

The most serious questions about quality of management thinking do not arise in connection with "bread and butter" service activities, such as, accounting, purchasing or treasury operations. They arise only when the finance officials try to apply the logic of productivity to the highest function of public financial management: the formulation and execution of fiscal policy. Credit ratings are an important measure of the overall quality of a jurisdiction's financial management. Provided to the investing public by private rating services, credit ratings reflect appraisals of the relative riskiness of public debt instruments. Because these ratings tend to influence interest rates, and thus the cost of acquiring debt capital, government agencies are well advised to pursue fiscal policies which enhance their reputation with the rating services. Since the rating services base their appraisals on a review of the information displayed in documents produced by each jurisdiction, principally, budget documents, financial reports and official statements accompanying an offering to sell bonds, the quality of these documents and any associated evidence of the jurisdiction's financial status and planning, become an important index of the quality of its financial management. Consequently, governments should strive to improve the quality of these documents, and the supporting planning and analytical capability.

Ultimately, the quality of fiscal policy depends on the quality of analytical and planning work, and the support given the results of this work by the political leaders of the jurisdiction. It has been my experience that the reliance of the credit agencies on the content of public documents as criteria of the quality of fiscal policy has a thoroughly beneficial impact on the financial policy and procedures of subject jurisdictions. In other words, the very requirement of periodic composition, publication and submission of critical documents tends to guarantee that the supporting analytical and planning work will be done with precision and proficiency, and that the supporting data bases will be maintained. A fair assumption!

On the whole, the subject of government reporting has not received the attention it deserves from those seeking to improve the productivity of government. The concept of *reporting discipline* is an important (but neglected) technique of productivity. Reporting requirements can stimulate and sustain analytical and planning work by finance and program officials. Therefore, government leaders, and especially the citizenry, are well advised to encourage the formatting of a jurisdiction's basic documents to display integrated programmatic and financial information

Process Controls

In everyday language, "control," has a restrictive, negative connotation. In management practice, however, the term takes on an additional, altogether positive meaning. In addition to specific financial controls providing defenses against wrong-doing, a scheme of administrative controls is required to provide timely, valid knowledge concerning productive processes. This cybernetic effect is popularly called "feedback." Of the three criteria of efficacious management (effectiveness, efficiency and economy), goal attainment, or effectiveness, is the most important. Process controls have to do with getting things done economically, efficiently and on time. Obviously, process controls are important instruments of efficacious management throughout entire governments, not just within the finance establishment. .

Unquestionably, administrative and financial controls add costs, measured in work-time and other expenses. It is also certain that the enforcement of *financial* controls produce benefits (albeit impossible to measure) by discouraging misappropriation of public assets and procurement corruption. The benefits of *administrative* process controls are also impossible to quantify, but lax organizations undoubtedly experience a significant loss in efficacy. If systematically embedded in operating standards and progress reports, administrative process controls provide managers with timely information about the status of production. After all, goal attainment failure is a great source of waste in government, greater, by far, than losses by misappropriation and procurement corruption. Only by the vigorous use of administrative process controls can accountable officials learn of impending production shortfalls in time to effect corrective action to ensure goal attainment.

I offer further observations regarding the management significance of financial and administrative process controls in Part 6, *Management: Pursuit of Attainment.*

III. AUTHORITY

> *... identifies preferred practices conditioning the exercise of public finance management, with specific reference to 1) financial power and its limitation, 2) acquiring resources, 3) borrowing money, 4) regulating rates, and 5) using resources.*

Obviously, the day-to-day exercise of finance management must have an authoritative base, embracing injunctions and prohibitions defined by law. It is equally obvious that, in every jurisdiction, the specifications of public financial authority have a critical bearing on the practice of finance management. However, as noted below, specifications vary by jurisdiction in their impact on the ability of the subject finance officers to perform *efficaciously*, that is, to execute their tasks with steady reference to the values of effectiveness, efficiency and economy. To get to the heart of the matter, one needs to apply a philosophy of public finance. This I have done in constructing Exhibit 1.1, a list of preferred practices enabling efficacious public finance management. For the reader's convenience, Exhibit 3.1 reproduces Section A, of Exhibit 1.1, specifically outlining preferred practices concerning grants of financial authority. Further, I concluded this discussion of authority by citing a philosophy of public finance that reflects my experience as a public official in the USA and as finance and budget consultant in many countries.

EXHIBIT 3.1 Foundations of Efficacious Public Finance Management

A	AUTHORITY	PREFERRED PRACTICE
1	Financial Power	Jurisdiction limited to funding and financing programs and projects that cannot be provided privately.
2	Resource Acquisition	Jurisdiction raises substantially all its revenue from its own sources and unconditional subventions.
3	Borrowing Money	Jurisdiction borrows only for capital investments.
4	Rate Regulation	Jurisdiction sets budget-related tax and cost-covering fees and service charges.
5	Resource Utilization	Jurisdiction's organization and management practices enable and encourage solution-centered, results-oriented budgeting.

Although all governments worthy of the name raise revenue; borrow money; set tax, fee and services charge rates, and allocate and use resources; they do so in diverse ways. Across the world, the authoritative basis of government finance varies significantly from place to place. Further, from country to country, and within countries, finance laws and regulations tend to be prescriptive. Restriction of official discretion seems to be the rule. This is especially true of countries trying to "have their cake and eat it too" by devolving power to sub-national governments, while maintaining central controls. A recent example can be found in Indonesia where, in 1999, the central government delegated substantial fiscal powers to provincial and local governments, subject, however, to certain central government approvals. Among the many jurisdictions in the United States, and in many other countries, sub-state autonomy is compromised by subventions which provide potential and actual sources of superior government control of the behavior of "independent" units. Operating internationally, public and private donor agencies provide many governments with finance and funds. Almost

III. AUTHORITY

always, however, these loans and grants are "earmarked" for particular programmatic purposes, presenting recipient governments with a "take it or leave it" situation. It is undeniable that restrictions on the allocation rights of donee governments tend to strengthen programmatic interests at the expense of centralized financial management capabilities. Hence, the favorable references in Exhibits 3.1 and 3.2 to unconditional subventions as a preferred revenue situation.

Although the prime responsibility for efficacious financial management rests with the accountable officials in all jurisdictions, provisions of financial authority, together with organizational and procedural arrangements for its exercise, represent fundamental conditioning factors. When implemented together, the preferred practices listed in Exhibit 1.1 provide a strong foundation for the exercise of efficacious management thought. A brief commentary on preferred practices with regard to financial authority follows:

1) Financial Power. Obviously, governments require financial power, notably the right to tax, borrow and spend. However, the lessons of history strongly suggest that limitations are critically important. First and foremost, the exercise of financial power should be limited to funding and financing programs and projects that cannot be provided privately. Next, the intertwined history of depreciated paper money and government debt (especially current 21st Century experience) attests to the manifest hazards of excessive government borrowing. The verdict of history is clear: limits on government use of credit are absolutely necessary, especially the practice of borrowing to fund service programs. Effectively, governments should borrow only to finance capital projects. Finally, budgets funding public service programs should be equated (balanced) with conservative estimates of revenue receipts.

2) Acquiring Resources. Preferred practice requires that government jurisdictions raise revenue, primarily from their own sources, and secondarily, from unconditional subventions. Both conditions support independent government, which tends to foster self-confident leadership interested in efficacious resource allocation. Who will disagree with the axiom that people tend to be more careful in keeping and spending their own, rather than other people's money? Excessive reliance on conditional subventions from other governments and "earmarked" donor grants similarly undermine the accountability of the leaders of recipient governments. Such "earmarked gifts" do not foster development of strong finance management procedures. Suffice it to say, efficacious finance management and autonomous government work hand-in-hand.

3) Borrowing Money. Preferred practice restricts borrowing to physical acquisitions which can be deemed depreciable assets by applying accounting logic. Also, according to best practice, such loan receipts are project-specific, and are made subject to special rather than general accounting arrangements. By limiting borrowing to asset acquisition, this practice prohibits borrowing to finance service programs usually recorded and controlled in a "general" or "consolidated" fund. This prohibition effectively assumes that programmatic, so-called operating budgets, be "balanced," that is, estimated revenues should equal or exceed projected expenditures when budgets are adopted, and are kept in balance during implementation by executive action. The balanced budget concept is controversial, as it strikes at the heart of the popular theory that government fiscal policies (in this case deliberate deficit spending) should be used to balance the economy rather than the government budget (shore up consumption when demand falls short of production). The exercise of government borrowing power is a prime concern of public finance officials. In Part 4, Rationale: *Aims of Attainment*, I suggest some unconventional approaches to the management of government debt.

4) Regulating Rates. Preferred practice requires that jurisdictions be free to set budget-related taxes and cost-covering fee and service charge rates. Obviously this preferred practice supports the concept of autonomous government, as discussed above. In theory, the pure purpose of

III. AUTHORITY

taxation, cost-covering fees and service charges is the funding of public services. However, in practice, revenue raising measures are shaped by the influence of politically potent formations seeking socio-economic aims. Progressive income taxes, a myriad of tax exemptions and import tariffs are examples where the revenue raising power is used for purposes other than the funding of public services.

Superior governments frequently set revenue raising conditions for subordinate units. Within jurisdictions, legislatures tend to do the same, denying administrators and finance officials any discretion over rate setting. With reference to programmatic activities requiring cost-covering fees and service charges, this arrangement is seriously deficient. The characteristic reluctance of legislators to raise rates results in revenue from fees and service charges lagging behind costs, when these are rising.. Recognizing this typical situation, finance officials should press for enactment of laws requiring them to periodically adjust fees and service charges to cover costs, provided that these administrative actions are promptly reported to the legislature, supported by pertinent calculations.

In my commentary on resource acquisition, Section 2 of Part 6: *Management: Pursuit of Attainment,* the readers will find further observations on this important topic, including model legislation designed to protect the purchasing power of government revenues against the erosive impact of inflation. This nodel incorporates procedures requiring the timely adjustment of fee schedules and service charges by the jurisdiction's chief executive, setting standards for executive action, public notice and reporting. The recommended procedure is deemed a reasonable delegation of rate-setting power. It has the additional benefit of requiring periodic cost determinations, a practice definitely promoting efficacious finance management.

5) Using Resources. Legal provisions regarding resource allocation and program and project implementation should include a) fiscal planning, b) solution-centered, results-oriented budgeting, and c) a dynamic approach to implementation. This latter procedure is briefly outlined below. Recommendations regarding these procedures are explored in detail in Part 6, *Management: Pursuit of Attainment.*

Even if their efforts are fragmented and inconsequential, accountable financial and program officials engage in some form of forward thinking in anticipation of the upcoming fiscal period. As recommended in Part 6, this anticipatory process should be organized to produce a series of consequential documents. The first two, covering Resource Mobilization and Financial Capability are summarized by publication of a Fiscal and Budgetary Perspective, and subsequent issuance of the chief executive's Budget Call.

The determinants of successful implementation include: 1) effective articulation and use of performance data; 2) an elaborate, flexible classification and coding scheme; 3) accounting procedures which facilitate the aggregation of non-monetary performance data, formally correlated with measures of effort and monetary data; and 4) continuous management utilization of four inter-related instruments of budget implementation. These instruments embrace a) work plans, b) allotments, c) dynamic monitoring via periodic formal performance reviews and d) timely corrective action to ensure goal attainment. Effective implementation (attainment of performance objectives) is best assured by using an institutional framework integrating these determinants, with accounting procedures providing the glue. These determinants are mutually reinforcing. The absence or limp implementation of any of these determinants reduces the effectiveness of the others. As noted above, Part 6, *Management: Pursuit of Attainment*, provides a detailed discussion of recommended "before-the-fact," dynamic monitoring procedures.

A Philosophy of Public Finance and Budgeting

What advice can be extended to finance officials in those cases where the legal provisions governing the exercise of financial power do not facilitate preferred practices? As an outstanding example,

III. AUTHORITY

jurisdictions experiencing cash flow problems may be permitted to borrow to finance current expenditure — not herein designated as a preferred practice. Obviously, accountable finance officials who believe that such borrowing is unsound financial policy should 1) clearly state their opposition to deficit spending and 2) work vigorously to help their jurisdiction avoid incurring cash flow shortfalls and operating deficits.

In sovereign states, if constitutionally prescribed, financial powers and key processes are not subject to the discretion of finance officials, or, for that matter, legislators. Where rules governing the exercise of financial power are legislatively set, finance officials may muster enough influence to attain desired changes, but, reflecting experience, success in such endeavors tends to be problematical. In sub-state jurisdictions, where superior governments set basic rules for subordinate units, securing desired changes favoring efficacious finance management may be difficult, even impossible. In these situations, finance officials are reduced to advocacy—or silence. However, if they subscribe to the philosophy of finance leadership espoused by this essay, they should never cease championing the laws and practices of efficacious public finance, regardless of active and passive resistance.

Most assuredly, the errors of the past are repeated by those who ignore the lessons of universal experience, or who indulge their conceit in thinking they are exempt from the consequences of practices proven many times over to be ill-advised. Time and time again, we note that governments, wanting in sound financial policy and management, impose economic hardship on their constituents, degrade public services, default on debt and debase their coin. Does universal experience provide us with instructions? What rules of exemplary public policy and practice might we distill from the book of ages? And, what of the lessons of contemporary events in the first years of the 21st Century? As indicated by Exhibit 3.2, I have drawn on my experience to fashion a general model of public finance and budgeting.

EXHIBIT 3.2 A Philosophy of Public Finance and Budgeting

- Match desired services to financial resources. Borrow only for capital investments.

- Fund or finance only those services and projects which cannot be provided privately.

- Require beneficiary payment for services, when technically possible.

- Minimize subventions. Strive for self-sufficiency at all levels of government.

- Strive for effectiveness, efficiency and economy by using the following instruments:

    ➢ Solution-centered, results-oriented budgets.
    ➢ Work plans.
    ➢ Periodic work plan-based allotments.
    ➢ Dynamic monitoring, featuring "before-the-fact," periodic formal performance reviews.
    ➢ Timely corrective action.

In my considered opinion, public finance officials will do well to frame a copy of this model of public finance and budgeting, posting it prominently on their office wall. Even where and when practice falls short of the suggested ideal, the model points the way to desirable improvements.

As previously noted, organizational arrangements and management practices for the execution of financial power vary significantly among government jurisdictions of the world, sovereign and sub-state. Key organizational concepts and associated preferred practices listed in Section C of Exhibit 1.1 are explored in Part 5, *Organization: Means of*

III. AUTHORITY

Attainment. See Part 6, *Management: Pursuit of Attainment,* for a discussion of preferred practices associated with resource acquisition, rate regulation and resource utilization

IV. RATIONALE: Aims of Attainment

...provides specific reference points for the work of public finance officers. Formal organizations are justified by goal attainment. Providing benchmarks for the assessment of performance, goals represent an indispensable, irreducible ingredient of managerial thought. Goals infuse work, and work plans, with meaning and direction. Because managers are justified by aims sought and attained, goal statements merit the most careful consideration.

This commentary dwells on the practical concerns of public finance work. It represents an attempt on my part to identify institutional instruments which, when proficiently applied, can contribute to the attainment of those grand, but elusive, ideals identified at the beginning of this essay, that is "sound" public finance and the "optimum" deployment of public capital.

Since the end of World War II, countless officials have tried various solution-centered, results-oriented alternatives to the traditional line-item form of budgeting. Their efforts to employ budgeting procedures incorporating targets have met with varying degrees of acceptance, enthusiasm and success in a variety of jurisdictions throughout the United States, including its Federal Government, and, increasingly, the world. In assessing this experience, one must admire the tenacity of officials, who, despite manifest difficulties and disappointments, keep trying to bring the benefits of solution-centered, results-oriented budgeting to their jurisdictions. As evidence of this tenacity, pursuant to the adoption of the Government Performance and Results Act, 1993, officials of the United States Government have been making yet another attempt to install the prototypical form of results-oriented budgeting, namely Performance Budgeting

The uneven experience with budget reform is instructive. It warns us that results-oriented behavior does not naturally or easily effervesce in government organizations. This experience also warns us that successful expression of results-oriented official behavior requires supporting institutions, including elaborate and flexible accounting, work planning at every level of supervision, and dynamic monitoring via formal, periodic performance reviews.

We must acknowledge that governments, as not-for-profit organizations, do not enjoy the stimulus and the objective clarity that the "bottom line" confers on profit-seeking organizations. This fundamental circumstance conditions the expression of goal-seeking behavior in governmental organizations. The political environment of government does not exclude the formulation and implementation of goals, but it certainly works to inhibit their use as managerial instruments. First, private interests seeking favorable legislation and/or access to the public treasury infest the political environment, supporting and encircling governmental organizations. "All sugar and no medicine" is the common watchword of interests seeking benefits from government action. Rarely do we see benefiting interests demanding the application of rational efficacy calculations to favored programs and projects. Further, accountable program administrators are not known to be especially fond of means-ends calculations either. Typically, administrators do not like to work to precisely formulated goals, that is, numerically denominated targets, deemed attainable within a given time (goal statement criteria). Many public employees happily confound process with goals, believing that their daily activity provides sufficient justification for their employment. Characteristically, they can be counted on to resist intrusions of management mathematics.

IV. RATIONALE: Aims of Attainment

However, the foregoing remarks are not meant to devalue the process-oriented duty that is the daily lot of finance officers. After all, process is the true reality of work. Goals are abstractions, designed to endow processes with programmatic consequences. Because goals are abstract, their formulation requires an intellectual commitment by accountable managers to a management ideal. And because goals are abstract, their definition and attainment depends on the actions of principled leadership. In Part 6, I will elaborate on the critical role of managerial motivation, briefly mentioned here.

No less than managers in every field of endeavor, finance managers attain goals by coordinating the work of assigned subordinates and colleagues. Although particular governments strive to achieve objectives unique to them, and their situation, in general, finance managers can not go too far astray in deriving their scheme of finance goals from the prime concerns outlined in the presentation of a core agenda in Section B of Exhibit 1.1, *Foundations of Efficacious Public Finance Management*, reproduced below for the reader's convenience:

EXHIBIT 4.1 Foundations of Efficacious Public Finance Management

B	PRIME CONCERNS	PREFERRED PRACTICE
1	Availability of Money	Pay obligations when due.
2	Cost of Money	Minimize finance management costs, Including interest charges.
3	Productivity of Money	Maximize socio-economic returns on investments in services and facilities.
4	Recovery of Money	Minimize subsidies related to regulation, Services and enterprises.

Four Prime Concerns

The following discussion amplifies our thinking about these important preoccupations by identifying each with relevant procedural variables and analytical approaches. With reference to each concern, attaining specific goals depends on effective performance across a range of contributing activities. These conditioning factors are identified as key variables. Each is thought to be responsive to management attention and action.

1. Availability of Money: Paying Obligations When Due

The **Availability of Money** refers to a jurisdiction's "liquidity," that is, its ability to meet its obligations, when due. With this goal in view, the following key performance variables and tools and techniques merit management consideration and action:

- **Key Performance Variables**:
    Cash Balances/Reservations
    Tax and Service Charge Coverage/Rates (see cost recovery concern)
    Receivables (depositing practices/billing/delinquency procedures)
    Payables (payment cycles)
    Loans, if needed

- **Tools and Techniques:**:
    Revenue Mobilization Methodology
    Cash Flow Projections

Thinking about a jurisdiction's cash position centers attention on a spectrum of policy and management variables, including revenue policies and practices, credit repute, reserves, billing cycles, payment procedures, past due receivables, and the temporary investment of loan proceeds and cash balances. Liquidity is properly regarded the "sine qua non" of finance work, public and private. Acquiring capital, and having it ready to pay wages and other due bills is the prime duty of every finance establishment. In precise terms, during any given period,

IV. RATIONALE: Aims of Attainment

the flow of revenues and loan receipts, plus available cash reserves, must equal or exceed the payment of disbursements due.

Achieving goals related to liquidity and cash management requires coordinated actions involving every sector of a government. In governments of general jurisdiction, cash flows toward the treasury from a complex of sources, including an ever-changing mix of taxes, regulatory fees, service charges, loans and grants. All these sources require unremitting management attention to ensure timely receipt, deposit and temporary investment. To ensure maximum investment earnings, every government should formalize its cash management process, frequently reviewing performance, especially the collection of outstanding receivables. To help register and evaluate such forecasts, cash managers are strongly advised to formulate work plans incorporating a cash flow projection, revising it regularly, based on accumulating experience. Benchmarked against recent history, cash flow projections provide treasurers with a basis for testing forecasts and assumptions about the flow of receipts and disbursements. In general form, for any given future period, cash flow projections include the following elements, an opening balance, plus expected revenues and receipts, minus expected disbursements, and the resulting ending balance.

Credit rating agencies show great interest in government liquidity, rightly seeing it as the tell-tale indicator of fiscal probity and, perforce, creditor security. Because they are fundamentally concerned with a jurisdiction's ability to pay its creditors in the future, the rating agencies place the liquidity issue in a context of socio-economic trends, assessing the long- term ability of a government to draw capital from its environment to finance essential services and debt payments. In this connection, governments which maintain multi-year plans, particularly for their capital investments, and actively support community development and tax-enhancing projects, generally enjoy better credit ratings.

Obviously, attaining and sustaining liquidity ultimately depends on a jurisdiction's success in drawing resources from its economic environment. In addition to cash management, the vital subject of resource acquisition is considered at length in Part 6, *Management: Pursuit of Attainment.* There the reader will find an extensive commentary recommending the formulation of a Resource Mobilization Methodology as an essential element of fiscal and budgetary planning.

2. Cost of Money: Minimizing Finance Management Costs

The **Cost of Money** refers to 1) interest charges on borrowed funds, and 2) the financial burden of administering the finance function. With the minimizing goal in view, the following key performance variables and tools and techniques merit management consideration and action:

- **Key Performance Variables**:
  Finance Establishment Organization and Methods
  Borrowing: Terms of Indebtedness/Credit Rating

- **Tools and Techniques**:
  Efficacy Studies

As pure "overhead, every government should strive to reduce net interest costs and the cost of finance management, not only in the finance establishment, proper, but also costs in all service programs. Needless to say, efficacious finance management cannot be achieved without strong centralized leadership and unremitting attention to the details of daily work.

It costs money to manage money! In the perspective provided by this self-evident truth, one defines "sound" financial management in terms of relatively low costs to get, store, reckon, and spend a given sum in a given time. Accordingly, finance officers should approach financial management as a series of production problems. As noted, financial management embraces a number of activities. The techniques of management analysis should be rather continuously applied to these activities. These techniques include work flow documentation, work

IV. RATIONALE: Aims of Attainment

measurement, work simplification, the rationalization of forms and procedures, and the matching of procedural costs against workloads and work standards. If reasonably accurate cost figures are available, for example, the annual investment made in, let us say, tax collection, or the payment of bills, can be related to workloads, and the resulting unit costs reduced by deliberate management effort.

Of course, this assumes that government personnel are sufficiently motivated to strive for productivity goals.. Reflecting my own experience, and that reported by qualified observers, the working atmosphere of many governments tends to be "low key," to use a colloquial expression. I have found that many officials find it convenient to dwell on the pessimistic side of the motivational issue, stressing productivity inhibitions and barriers, pointing to missing ingredients, making excuses for low productivity — thus, shun responsibility for productivity improvements. Counterbalancing such tendencies requires aggressive finance leaders who insist on pursuing procedural studies across functional lines – a "systemic" approach. It is highly unlikely that governments with fragmented finance leadership can muster the power and persistence to pursue and implement such studies.

As stressed in the discussion of integrated data in Part 2, *Instrumentalities*, isolated attempts to bring each finance procedure to a peak of efficacy may not produce an efficacious overall pattern of procedures, if finance units are permitted to process and reprocess the same information. Consequently, all procedural studies should be dominated by the concept of integrated data management, a perspective requiring the elimination of redundant data and superfluous routines in favor of continuous assembly of outputs. As the only sure road to efficacious finance work, the systemic approach both implies and produces an integrated finance organization. This conception of integrated finance work is not limited to centralized finance functions; it also applies to "line" agency "business affairs."

Characteristically, public service programs are assigned to "line" units, variously named ministries, departments, offices, agencies, etc.

These fiscally dependent line units must assign staff to manage their business affairs, which commonly embrace the forms and procedures related to payrolls, requisitions, purchase orders, receiving reports, vendor payments and expenditure controls. In governments of general jurisdiction, these scattered assignments are a significant cost, and a source of much redundant data handling and storage. The relationship between line agency business affairs officers and central finance units is rarely harmonious or efficient. Even in those jurisdictions where the chief financial officer exercises a good deal of functional supervision over line agency business affairs personnel, the relationship tends to be the locus of tension, confusion and error. The spread of computers and their linkage has provided an opportunity to cast this relationship in terms of the integrated data management ideal.

Despite the claims of computer manufacturers, there are few technological shortcuts to lower operating costs. Simple grafting of computer technology onto existing forms and procedures is quite common. Indeed, the advent of inexpensive desktop and hand-held computers sharply increases the potential for idiomatic, repetitive recording of data—the practice already identified as the source of inefficacious finance work, computerized or not. Reliance on a single, centralized computer facility promoted various degrees of data integration. The usage of decentralized computer resources provides no such incentive. Obviously, when a government provides its finance staff, and line agency business affairs officers with decentralized computer resources, the integrated data management ideal will be more difficult to attain. In the years ahead, the availability of small, powerful computers will produce an irresistible demand for such decentralization. Only strong, continuous planning for integrated data management, via coordinated files and coding protocols, can offset the inherent waste and duplication which will accompany a planless distribution of these fabulous resources.

The tendency to think about finance procedures in planless, segmented ways is nowhere better illustrated than in the haphazard introduction of micrographic technology. One frequently hears of microphotography

IV. RATIONALE: Aims of Attainment

applied to inactive records. Far less frequently does one hear of a government applying micrographic technology in daily operations. Rarer still is the jurisdiction which has developed a comprehensive plan which carefully balances and integrates the use of "hardcopy," micrographic and computerized records.

3. Productivity of Money: Maximizing Socio-Economic Returns on Investments in Services/Facilities

The third concern, the **Productivity of Money**, refers to the net benefit conferred by the allocation of funds to the various purposes of the government. With the maximizing goal in view, the following key performance variables and tools and techniques merit management consideration and action:

- **Key Performance Variables**:
    Program and Project Cost/Benefit Calculations

- **Tools and Techniques**:
    Solution-Centered, Results-Oriented Budgeting
    Community Analysis (studies of socio-economic patterns).
    Systems Analysis (assessments of effectiveness).
    Management Analysis (studies of efficiency and economy)

As indicated at the beginning of this essay, the task of assessing the comparative worth of project and programmatic investments is the highest form of finance management thinking—and, I must add, the most perplexing. Because finance intersects with all endeavors, chief financial officers are well-positioned to provide government leaders with information, and judgments, about the productivity of funds invested in the various programs and projects of their jurisdictions. The following discussion explores the concept that quality public finance work focuses on efficacious use of public capital. Citing the productivity of money as a prime finance management concern assumes that governments are productive enterprises, if not "making money," per se, investing in services and facilities which maintain and increase the wealth and well-being of their citizens. According to this perspective, "sound" public finance management should result in socio-economic "returns on investment" which equal or exceed the amount of investment. Successful application of decision-related allocation criteria in governments, then, depends on the ability of officials to estimate the value of the assumed benefits. Is there a more central, more difficult, yet more urgent task facing government leaders today, and in the future?

If the jurisdiction's finance establishment includes supervision of the budget function, its chief financial officer can turn to budget officers for reasoned advice about the wisdom of proposed deployments off public capital. However, in the jurisdictions that do not vest the budget function in its finance establishment, the capability of their chief financial officers to contribute to considerations about the relative worth of public investments is rather circumscribed. (The organizational position of the budget function is a serious issue, given the consideration it deserves in Part 5, *Organization: Means of Attainment.*).

Consciously or not, government leaders, no less than business officials, strain toward an "optimum" distribution of capital throughout the jurisdiction, measured in terms of relative returns on investments. Success in this endeavor hinges on the ability to match accurate program costs with credible estimates of program benefits. Based on observation and report, government officials rely on an array of subjective and objective criteria to weigh the merits of various spending proposals. To assist them in this inherently difficult task, finance and budget officers should strive to enlarge the role of formal, objective allocation criteria in their decisions by including benefit estimation data in budget documents and finance reports. At this point, consult Exhibit 4.2, *Allocation Criteria,* for lists of pragmatic and formal allocation criteria.

IV. RATIONALE: Aims of Attainment

EXHIBIT 4.2 Allocation Criteria

PRAGMATIC CONSIDRATIONS	FORMAL CONSIERATIONS

INERTIA
(Organizational and programmatic continuities)
 	
COMPLEMENTARITIES
(Services supporting other services)
 	
DISEQUILIBRIA
(Correcting imbalances; redressing grievances; restoring conditions)
	SERVICE STANDARDS
	Market Equity
	Equal Allocation of Resources
	Equal Results
	
	PERFORMANCE RATIOS
	<u>Efficiency</u>
	  Cost/Results
	  Results/Cost
	  Work Time/Results
	  Results/Work Time
	<u>Effectiveness</u>
	  Goal Attainment Percentage
	<u>Programmatic</u>
	  Unique Production Ratios
	
	MODELING
	Correlation
	
	INVESTMENT RETURNS
	Marginal Productivity
	Investment Yield
	
	WEIGHTING AND SCORING
	Ordinal Ranking
	Multi-dimensional Scoring

Characteristically, a high proportion of typical public budgets reflect "pragmatic" responses to circumstances by appropriation authorities. The left side of Exhibit 4.2 identifies three compelling considerations that account for the ready acceptance of proposed allocations on subjective grounds. The right side of Exhibit 4.2 identifies a range of "formal" considerations that, when *applied on principle,* justify adoption of proposed allocations on "objective" grounds. A brief discussion of the contents of Exhibit 4.2 follows:

Pragmatic Considerations: As frequently observed, governments tend to perpetuate expenditure patterns from year to year. Once established, government programs gather something akin to the physicist's concept of *"inertia."* The fact that governments exist to assist and stabilize society certainly favors service continuity, and supporting allocations. It is also a fact that program officials, who have a natural interest in program continuity, tend to define budget requests as "inescapable recurrent expenditure" even though, in many cases, program rationale may be weak, or weakening as times change. Moreover, budgets frequently include ***complementarities***, that is, they include appropriations required to support decisions previously made, such as operating and maintenance programs for public facilities, and continued funding for centralized process agencies serving diverse programmatic units. Finally, everywhere in the world, governments respond to social, economic and political ***disequilibria.*** Appropriation decisions satisfying this criterion for public expenditure are often made during emergencies, under duress, without serious debate. Less objectively critical, but found to be no less compelling, are decisions to appropriate funds to protect rights and right wrongs.

Formal Considerations: Redirecting budget allocations from ineffective and/or inefficient programs to new programmatic initiatives is a necessary strategy for government leaders who wish to address new socio-economic problems without undue recourse to financing new or expanded programs with additional taxes or loans. By requiring program officials to justify their allocation requests by reference to formal rather than pragmatic criteria, finance and budget officers help government leaders rationalize existing and future allocation patterns.

IV. RATIONALE: Aims of Attainment

Recognizing that a significant proportion of budgets are justified by pragmatic criteria, chief finance officers, and supporting budget officers, are honor-bound to strive to counter-balance this tendency by enlarging the role of formal allocation criteria in the formulation, adoption and execution of budgets. The application of efficacy considerations, principally performance ratios, help determine the intrinsic merit of programs and projects.

Comparisons of investment returns shed light on their relative merit. The relative worth of publicly financed programs and projects can be assessed by comparing rates of return, expressed as net benefits, (benefits minus costs) or as percentages of investment. Benefits can be ascribed and monetized for a certain number of public programs and projects. In those cases where benefits can not be ascribed and monetized, making the preferred benefit/cost approach impossible, yet results can be numerically, or physically specified, one can apply the concept of marginal productivity. If these approaches are deemed impractical, comparative values can be established by using weighting and scoring procedures.

Estimating the value of the benefits produced by any given program or project requires 1) the development and maintenance of a suitable database, and, 2) analytical capability. The relative worth of a publicly financed program or project can be assessed by comparing its "rate of return," expressed as a net benefit figure (gross benefits minus costs) or as a percentage of investment, to all other programs for which benefits can be monetized. For example, proposed Program X is estimated to return an estimated net benefit of $25,000, or 20%. (gross benefit of $150,000 minus costs of $125,000). In comparison, let us say, Programs Y and Z return 13.6% and 5.3% respectively. Having such comparisons available, the jurisdiction's budget authorities could set a minimum rate of return for program acceptance. If, referring to the example, the minimum rate of return is set at 10%, the funding of program Z would be jeopardized, unless redesigned to improve its projected return. This practice provides an objective basis for selecting programs and projects which can produce the highest overall return for a given level of total expenditure

Estimated benefits can be described and monetized, provided the appropriation authorities accept the benefit calculation methodology, such as, surveying potential beneficiaries to assess their *willingness-to-pay* for a proposed program or project. (This approach avoids the issues arising when *ability-to-pay* concerns are involved in budget considerations.) Of course, any form of prioritization, objective or subjective, implies the application of criteria. In the absence of objective criteria, accountable officials can adopt subjective allocation criteria to structure a weighting and scoring process. Because they serve to clarify and "objectify" values, weighting and scoring procedures help participants in the budget process to organize and test, but not eliminate, subjective judgments.

The simplest and most popular technique produces a priority list by requiring officials to rank proposals by assigning numbers (1, 2, 3, etc.), or letters (A, B, C, etc.). These numbers or letters frequently represent the application of defined prioritization concepts, such as, urgent, essential, required, necessary, desirable, etc. Proposals may also be sorted into broad priority categories, such as, High, Medium, and Low. Additionally, comparative values can also be established by using weighting and scoring procedures. Weights may be assigned by individuals, or groups, applying agreed-upon criteria and decision rules. Scoring procedures are required when proposals are assigned two or more priority designations.

IV. RATIONALE: Aims of Attainment

EXHIBIT 4.3 A Weighting and Scoring Model

	Priority	Legally Prescribed	Increase Tax Base	Reduce Unit Cost	Standard Service	Expand Service
		0	1	2	3	4
Safety	1	0	1	2	3	4
Health	2	0	2	4	6	8
Education	3	0	3	6	9	12
Civic/Cultural	4	0	4	8	12	16
Convenience	5	0	5	10	15	20

Exhibit 4.3, A *Weighting And Scoring Model,* provides an example of a two dimensional weighting and scoring matrix. Please note that in this example, zero is assigned to legally prescribed proposals, putting them at the top of the list, regardless of other considerations. Also note that the rankings drawn from each list are multiplied together to produce a combined ranking. Using the matrix, a proposal to expand a public health program, drawing a "2" from a list thought to express public priorities and "4" from the list of allocation criteria thought important by government leaders, receives a final combined priority score of "8." Proposal costs are accumulated down the scale of priority scores until the total reaches the margin of funds (or finance) deemed available. Priorities assigned to proposals on the list at or near the limit of available resources will undoubtedly receive further review.

This brief reconnaissance cannot do justice to the many technical refinements and qualifications which must enter into the application of formal allocation criteria to government programs, such as, the effect of time and interest rates in determining investment yield, and the procedures needed to apply the concepts marginal productivity and mathematical modeling. It remains appropriate to close this discussion by re-emphasizing the key role of finance officers in assessing, and enhancing, the productivity of the public's money. .

4. Recovery of Money: Minimizing Subsidies Related to Regulation, Services and Enterprises

The fourth concern, the **Recovery of Money**, refers to the proportion of program or project costs to be paid by those who directly benefit, or more to the point of concern, the degree to which those benefiting are to be subsidized by others. With the minimizing goal in view, the following key performance variables and tools and techniques merit management consideration and action:

- **Key Performance Variables**:
  Service, Regulatory and "Enterprise" Program-Related Revenue/Cost Ratios

- **Tools and Techniques:**
  Cost Accounting
  Cost Finding
  Efficacy Studies

Fees can be levied on regulatory services, tied to the issuance of licenses and permits. Service charges can be levied on a variety of services, on a services-rendered basis. Many, many governments own and operate enterprises funded in whole or in part by service charges. At minimum, the amounts collected should at least equal the cost of collection. Beyond that point, the amount of cost recovered will reflect the subsidy philosophy of the government concerned. Usually fueled by ability-to-pay considerations, equity issues always bubble up whenever governments seek revenues by applying the concept of "beneficiary payment," or "cost recovery" to their program and project activity. In total, governments of general jurisdiction spend relatively huge sums on services, and invest equally significant amounts on projects to remedy outstanding infrastructure deficits and to facilitate future social and economic activity. At one pole of policy, they provide services and

IV. RATIONALE: Aims of Attainment

infrastructure "free" to all and sundry. The relationship between benefactor (payer) and beneficiary (user) is indirect and formless. At the opposite pole, they provide services and infrastructure on the beneficiary payment principle, that is, regardless of the funding or financing method (appropriations and/or loans) the user pays part or all costs in proportion to use.

As the cost of service tends to reflect the impact of changes in the general price level, usually currency degradation, a policy systematically relating service charge revenues to service costs will help to protect the purchasing power of service charge revenues. Thus, an explicit legislative cost recovery policy (defined as a proportion of costs, e.g., 50%, 110%, etc.) provides a timely, fair and effective method of preventing the erosion of purchasing power by inflation. Of course, the adoption of this approach is dependent on an accurate calculation of costs, in itself, a problem in many jurisdictions.

Obviously, the issues of cost recovery can be completely avoided by "privatizing" the provision of infrastructure and service. On economic grounds, "privatization" often offers an attractive alternative to the investment of scarce public capital and subsequent expenditure for operation and maintenance by public forces. At the time of this writing, by all reports, governments across the world are actively pursuing the privatization option, especially those governments previously committed to the political philosophy of state capitalism.

Realistically, however, the scope of true privatization (no public subsidies or service contracts) is limited by policy and/or technical considerations, and the fact that there is simply no profit in supplying many services provided by governments. In truth, governments provide many services less by willfulness than default. Consequently, across a broad spectrum of programs and projects, the government's problem lays less in shedding responsibility for service and infrastructure investments than in determining an appropriate degree of cost recovery. Given this definition of reality, governments are well-advised to establish and maintain a resource mobilization process that can satisfy the demand for public capital by consistently probing the limits of cost recovery. Responsible finance officials can not evade this issue, mandated, as they should be, to provide recommendations for improvements in the equity and sufficiency of revenues related to infrastructure emplacement and service programs.

Policies depend on institutions for effect. Governments wishing to explore, let alone deeply embed cost recovery mechanisms within its system of public finance, must strengthen the institutions most likely to make them work effectively and equitably. To the extent that they are endowed with requisite authority, a cadre of competent officials, and an accounting system that records and reports costs, governments can, and should, try to enlarge the role of the beneficiary payments in funding appropriate infrastructure emplacements and services. Essentially, an experimental approach is recommended. In so doing governments acquire valuable decision-related data about service efficiency, effectiveness and the elasticity of demand which should be used to regulate its cost recovery policies.

The principal beneficiary payment mechanisms include property taxes, service charges, special assessments and development fees. As these are proven by practice in diverse parts of the world, no technical reason can be advanced to deny the feasibility of application in any particular jurisdiction. The chief barriers to enlarging the role of those beneficiary payment mechanisms are clearly political, not technical. In no case are the required procedures unduly complicated. In every case, requisite skills can be taught. Suffice it to conclude that the key finance officials must understand these mechanisms and, most crucially, grasp the essential conditions required for effective exercise. Part 6, *Management: Pursuit of Attainment*, provides further commentary on the merits of cost recovery, including an example of model legislation that facilitates the timely adoption of service fees.

IV. RATIONALE: Aims of Attainment

How should the accountable finance officials go about framing specific goals related to these prime concerns? A discussion of goal-setting methodology has been provided in Part 4, M*anagement: Pursuit of Attainment.*

Balance Sheet Objectives

In addition to the four key concerns, public finance officials are the guardians of their jurisdiction's financial position, popularly known as its "Balance Sheet." To effectively express this abiding concern, every government should strive to establish and maintain policies related to its financial position. Such policies should include:

- A minimum end-of-period cash balance.

- An annual program of investment in public facilities which equals or exceeds the amount of depreciation.

- An annual program of investment which attains and maintains capital/labor ratios required for efficient and effective work.

- Reserves for the orderly replacement of depreciated assets, and/or the timely acquisition of state-of-the-art technology.

Supplementing periodic year-to-date statements, projections of end-of-year conditions provide vehicles for the expression and control of "Balance Sheet" policies. If prepared and used prudently, such "pro forma" statements can become important reference documents for government leaders, encouraging them to set and attain objectives related to the policies outlined above. By preparing and updating pro forma statements, finance officers provide a perspective concerning the prospective financial position of the jurisdiction. Effectively, pro forma statements should be introduced at the very beginning of the budget formulation and adoption process, and updated continuously to register the impact of proposed budget decisions on key balance sheet amounts. Following budget adoption, the accountable finance officials should calculate the estimated effect of the newly adopted budget on balance sheet entries, projecting the jurisdiction's ending financial position, updating this statement periodically as the budget is executed.

Minimizing the Cost of Indebtedness

In addition to measures to reduce the administrative costs of finance management, discussed above, attention should be directed to the ways and means of reducing the cost of borrowed capital. Obviously, it is best to do no borrowing at all, thereby eliminating financing costs. Indeed, using this pay-as-you-go approach, the funds appropriated to pay for projects can be temporarily invested, earning interest. With sufficient lead time to build up reserves, even large projects can be financed without incurring debt. Next best, borrow for short periods, as the short-term market usually offers the lowest interest rates. If a jurisdiction issues long-term bonds, the most costly financing alternative, terms should be as short as possible to limit interest costs. Generally the credit rating agencies look with favor on governments that limit the life of their bond issues. Regardless of the reason for incurring debt, the ways and means of borrowing merit serious consideration by public finance officials.

In the United States, public infrastructure has been mainly financed by term-denominated debt, entailing significant issuance and interest costs. Moreover, infrastructure requires timely maintenance,

IV. RATIONALE: Aims of Attainment

which may, and frequently is, deferred. As indicated by the following list, a variety of financing techniques can be applied to the problems of financing cost and deferred maintenance:

- Use reservations to "monetize" the widely used multi-year Capital Improvement Program (CIP) concept – a step toward implementing a pay-as-you-go funding policy.

- Issue "perpetual" bonds – a paradoxical step toward the eventual elimination of borrowing for capital projects.

- Issue bonds directly to the public, eliminating underwriting costs.

- Use funded depreciation to a) foster timely capital replacements, and b) promote accurate costing of services, useful in setting service charges.

- Use deferred maintenance liability accounts to foster needed infrastructure maintenance.

A brief commentary on each of these approaches follows:

"Monetizing" Capital Improvement Programs. In thousands of jurisdictions throughout the United States, and elsewhere, proposed capital projects begin their journey though adoption and implementation by an initial inclusion in a multi-year Capital Improvement Program. This inclusion signifies that the proposed project has garnered significant endorsement. For about a century, the CIP concept has been employed as a prime vehicle fostering the orderly attainment of government infrastructure objectives. Its employment also reflects the common-sense understanding that coordination of capital deployments pays durable premiums. However, the CIP process, as practiced, has shortcomings, briefly described as deficient "linkage," casual treatment of project prioritization criteria, poor cost estimates and schedule instability. The failure of CIP-listed projects to support stated policies, plans and objectives (master plans, growth limits, etc) is a shortcoming noted by many knowledgeable observers. Although a serious criticism, addressing this deficiency is beyond the scope of this commentary. The other three shortcomings are traceable to the propensity of accountable officials to give CIP time commitments little weight during the press of capital budget adoption politics. Too often, a multi-year CIP is viewed as a malleable instrument - a sort of clerk's document requiring no official commitment to support its internal logic of timely movement of projects toward the year of formal adoption and implementation.

Frequently, the parties who are interested in proposed projects are potent enough to cause accountable officials to ignore the application of stated criteria and standard procedure, achieving the insertion of favored projects in the upcoming year's capital budget. If working within given financial constraints, the net result of such arbitrary action is to displace projects scheduled to move up into the year of adoption and implementation, and to disturb the orderly progression of other projects as well. This practice undermines the objective application of priorities and produces schedule instability.

Despite these shortcomings, an annually updated CIP has been a valuable instrument for organizing and conducting a capital deployment process – a process that is severely bounded by inevitable physical, financial and time constraints. Excepting the serious problem of "linkage," it is suggested that these CIP shortcomings, cited above, may be overcome or mitigated by adopting the pay-as-you-go philosophy of public finance, supported by the use of the accounting concept of reservation. This procedure effectively "monetizes" the CIP. Typically, governments formulating annual multi-year CIPs adopt its first year list of

IV. RATIONALE: Aims of Attainment

projects as their Capital Budget. Under the monetizing concept, herein advanced, listing a project in *any* year of the CIP requires an appropriation equal to a designated portion of the estimated project cost. This procedure would transform the CIP from a malleable schedule to a relatively firm instrument of capital programming and budgeting.

Except for appropriations for first year CIP projects (the capital budget), the amounts associated with projects listed in the subsequent years of a CIP are to be, by rule, proportionately appropriated and the sum reserved. (To ease into this procedure, jurisdictions may need to secure relatively inexpensive short-term loans.) It may be expected that this suggested approach, monetizing each year of the CIP, will have decisive affects on the behavior of the accountable officials, and, consequently, on project prioritization, project estimates, and schedule stability. Additionally, accumulated reserves can be increased by investing them at interest.

As an example, assume that a project is first listed in the fifth year of an annually submitted five-year CIP. It would draw a budget allocation of one fifth of its estimated project cost, which would be duly reserved, and invested at interest. The same amount would be appropriated and reserved in each of the next three annual CIPs as the project is moved along in yearly steps until finally lodged in the capital budget, At that point, the amount reserved must be made to equal the updated estimated project cost. This may require recalculation of the annual allocation as the reserves may have been tapped to fund engineering work finalizing project plans and the updating of cost estimates. This dynamic use of reserves is a key aspect of the monetized CIP concept. Assuming that reserves will be used for those purposes, it would be necessary to appropriate an amount for a project listed for action in the capital budget that would bring the total project reserve into agreement with an updated estimated project cost.

Most assuredly, the adoption of a pay-as-you-go approach, gradually implemented through annual allocations for CIP projects, duly reserved, will eventually pay significant dividends in reduced borrowing costs and more efficacious procedures. Across the country, the costs of bond issuance, principally, underwriting and legal services, eat up millions in taxes annually, money better spent on projects and programs. The savings in interest cost, and interest earned, produced by adopting a pay-as-you-go policy are so significant that, for any given level of capital spending, the recommended approach permits more project undertakings, in colloquial speech: "more bang for the buck."

The Case for Perpetual Bonds. As a rule, throughout the United States, public capital projects are financed by borrowing project-by-project, rather than funded by cash appropriations. To be sure, borrowed money requires interest payments, but payments for the services associated with bond issuance can be substantially reduced, and eventually eliminated, by issuing *perpetual* bonds. What can be said for bonds that pay interest periodically, but require no periodic amortization, or principal repayment at a date certain? Obviously, the current practice of issuing time-bound debt is deeply imbedded, and is supported by politically potent interests. Moreover, reliance on the periodic amortization concept reflects historical experience with the failure of government jurisdictions to honor their obligations. The deferrals and defaults which undermined the use of the theoretically sound sinking fund concept for debt retirement is instructive in this regard, as are the current revelations concerning government deferrals and defaults on contributions to government employee pension funds. However, perpetual bonds have been long-used successfully by Great Britain.

The important point: Although no American jurisdictions have issued what may be called "permanent" debt, ironically, thousands of jurisdictions are actually *permanently in debt*, as portions of their existing debt are periodically amortized and retired, and new serial bonds issued to finance new projects, running up underwriting costs again and again. The essential irrationality of this practice is obvious. In many cases, total debt remains relatively stable year after year. So, one can visualize

IV. RATIONALE: Aims of Attainment

swapping this ever-renewed mass of debt instruments for a perpetual debt of equivalent size. Consequently, that portion of a jurisdiction's annual debt service appropriation, which was here-to-fore applied to debt amortization, would now be available for pay-as-you- go project funding. Obviously, fiscal discipline is required. Prudently, jurisdictions with outstanding perpetual debt should appropriate, and reserve, annual amounts equal to, let us say, the amortization required to retire a 15-year serial bond of equivalent value. The reserve thus built up, invested at interest, can be deployed to fund projects at lower total cost, and/or redeem callable perpetual bonds. A jurisdiction pursuing this strategy cannot lose money, and most certainly will gain.

Of course, there are ramifications to consider. The concept must be tested to determine whether investors will buy bonds with no set redemption date, thus, be dependent on the open market for liquidation. Considering the volatility of capital markets, investors may demand and use "put" options, requiring issuing jurisdictions to establish redemption reserves (probably via lines of credit). Also considering the volatility of capital markets, issuing jurisdictions may wish to control their debt, and be able to eventually retire it on their own terms, if desired, by imbedding "call" options in every issue (which might increase interest costs).

To re-emphasize the point made above, making the use of perpetual bonds work, once reaching debt limits, the issuing authorities must be prepared to fund desired projects as they come along, adopting a pay-as-you-go approach. (To ease into this practice, the use of relatively inexpensive short-term loans will likely prove useful.) One thing is beyond doubt: if the concept of perpetual bonds were to take hold, associated with pay-as-you-go funding practices, the aggregate savings in bond issuance costs across the nation, over time, would total billions. Needless to say, the legal foundation for responsible issuance of perpetual bonds must be clear and strong, in terms of capital expenditure planning and execution, budgetary and accounting practice, and in the language of bond covenants.

Managerial Thought for Public Finance Officers

The Case for Directly-Marketed Bonds. What can be said for the concept of debt instruments sold by jurisdictions directly to the public? It is another way to secure project finance without incurring the customary underwriting costs. Surfacing in the Township of New Brunswick, NJ in 1978, this interesting idea was subsequently successfully tested by several municipalities and the State of Massachusetts. Those experimenting with marketing small denomination bonds directly to constituents noted what can rightly be called a "Hamiltonian" effect, as this process provides citizens with a convenient, profitable opportunity to invest directly in their community, as well as pay taxes. (The phrase refers to the policy of Alexander Hamilton to have the new Federal Government assume the Revolutionary War debts of the States as a strategy to build up loyalty to the new government.) Facts and observations about the experience with direct marketing, and its socio-economic aspects, can be found in my article, "The Case for Directly Marketed Small Denomination Bonds," Municipal Finance Officers Association: Government Finance, September, 1980. The concept subsequently came under sharp attack form parties involved in the traditional practices of the bond market, and regrettably faded from the scene. In seeking efficacious ways to manage the deployment of public capital, interested jurisdictions will find direct issuance of its debt instruments a rewarding procedure.

Capturing the Benefits of Depreciation. From an accountant's perspective, disbursements to provide public services deplete a jurisdiction's treasury, requiring bookkeeping entries to record the reduction of liquid assets. In contrast, cash spent to provide public infrastructure also depletes a jurisdiction's treasury, but gains a new accounting existence as a fixed asset. From liquid to concrete, so to speak. The purpose of the disbursement determines its accounting fate. Further, in the logic of conventional accounting practice, applied to enterprises, it is assumed that the new-born fixed asset immediately begins to lose value and is "depreciated" to zero value over an arbitrarily specified time. (Of

IV. RATIONALE: Aims of Attainment

course, aside from useful life assumptions, the accounting logic of depreciation is grounded in the fact that all things fabricated by the hand of man deteriorate over time, requiring maintenance to remain useful.) However, few officials serving governments of general jurisdiction in the United States support the application of the concept of depreciation, fearing its financial and budgetary implications. To what purpose, they say? After all, depreciation charges against income prevent the diminution of the equity of owners, the so-called "bottom line" of the commercial world. As governments have no owners, equity accounting conventions need not apply. It is also said that funded depreciation makes the taxpayer pay over again for an acquired asset.

This line of thinking seriously devalues the benefits conferred by the concept of depreciation. First, depreciation allowances, if funded, would help governments mitigate the damage caused by capricious capital budgeting, especially regarding facilities and equipment replacement. Government facilities are typically littered with abandoned, obsolete and inefficient equipment. In contrast to business leaders, government officials are not known for their concern about capital/ labor ratios. No less than in business, efficacious work is fostered by providing employees with state-of-the–art equipment. Funded depreciation can free the equipment replacement process from the vicissitudes of capital budgeting, as reserves can be deployed on rational, timely schedules. Moreover, depreciation entries, as an instrument of cost recovery, provide information useful in determining the true cost of services, placing service charges on a sound basis.

Mitigating the Damage of Deferred Maintenance. This brief reconnaissance into the limiting conditions surrounding the practice of capital programming, financing and maintenance would not be complete without a discussion of ways and means of mitigating the damage of deferred maintenance. It is frequently observed that many accountable officials tend to ignore or defer funding of public infrastructure maintenance. Who can argue that indulging this propensity is a prudent policy?

Maintenance deferred may not only reduce the safe use and serviceability of assets, but increases eventual costs, as the expense of repair tends to increase as time passes. The case for timely preventive maintenance is obvious, but, apparently not sufficiently persuasive for accountable officials in many jurisdictions. Given the damage caused by evasion of responsibility, can institutional conditions be devised that encourage, or compel, accountable officials to support timely investments in infrastructure upkeep?

Here again, accounting practice can help to attain a desired result. This is not uncharted territory. For some time, estimates of deferred maintenance have been reported on federal agency financial statements as liabilities. Expanding the reach of this idea, all jurisdictions owning capital assets should be required by law to establish general ledger liability accounts to record the value of "deferred maintenance" at the closing of reporting periods. This value should be determined by competent appraisers using standard survey methods, and be subject to audit. This procedure will disclose the financial implications of maintenance problems, and, the resulting estimates, posted as liabilities, will serve to reserve a portion of the jurisdiction's fund balance accordingly. This approach is calculated to promote more timely maintenance expenditure because the funds so sequestered can be made readily available to accountable authorities.

In summary, this brief exploration of possible solutions for outstanding infrastructure-related problems of financing cost and deferred maintenance directed attention to 1) integral use of accounting concepts in infrastructure programming, budgeting and maintenance, and 2) alternative ways of funding and financing the deployment and upkeep of public capital. If implemented, the recommended procedures can produce substantial benefits. With the exception of perpetual bonds, which have not been tested in the United States, the recommended procedures are not deemed radical. As presented, they can be given a natural foundation in government practice, and, with good faith implementation, enjoy an ideal development.

V. ORGANIZATION: Means of Attainment

.....explores the institutional conditions encouraging and enabling public finance officials to apply management thought to their work. By delegating authority, governments provide a structure of responsibility and accountability. A caution is in order: Delegations of authority do not guarantee management performance. Management behavior is not a natural human attribute. It must be learned, and once learned, steadfastly practiced, lest it atrophy or, worse, pass into an instrument of personal caprice or opportunism.

Although accountability for efficacious financial management obviously rests with the leading officials in every jurisdiction, financial authority, together with arrangements for its exercise, are fundamental conditioning factors. The management implications of laws governing the exercise of financial power cannot be overstated. As will shortly be noted, for several reasons, laws pertaining to public finance should not prescribe the internal organization of finance establishments. Despite the risk that improper motivations will influence the behavior of finance officials, it important that finance officers have flexibility to attain work goals efficaciously. Rather, constitutional provisions and legislation should be focused on enabling, encouraging, and in some cases, requiring desirable finance management thinking and action, that is, thinking and action illuminated by continuous interest in the efficacious use of public funds. Such incentives and injunctions are needed to counter-balance the ever-present tendency of political officials to favor expedient rather than principled action. For the reader's convenience, the key organizational concepts and associated preferred practices set forth by Section C, Exhibit 1.1, are reproduced by Exhibit 5.1, *Foundations of Efficacious Public Finance Management*.

EXHIBIT 5.1 Foundations of Efficacious Public Finance Management

C	ORGANIZATION	PREFERRED PRACTICE
1	Structure	Designed to promote efficacious finance management.
2	Leadership	Unified and accountable.
3	Staff	Qualified by education and experience.
4	Staff Deployment	Flexibly assigned tasks related to issues, problems and opportunities.
5	Technology	"State-of-the-art" capitalization of production, supported by depreciation..

1. Structure: Designed to Promote Efficacious Finance Management

As noted at the conclusion of the discussion of Part 3, the organizational and procedural arrangements for the execution of financial authority vary significantly among the government jurisdictions of the world, sovereign and sub-state. Given this variety, it is well to identify fundamental organizational conceptions which can support, encourage and require public finance officials to steadfastly pursue the ideals of "sound" public finance and the "optimum" employment of public capital.

Flexible Structure Desired

Drawn from a city charter in the United States, the following provision is illustrative: "There shall be a department of finance which shall be composed of the divisions of accounting and control, tax collection, and purchases and insurance." Significantly, this charter also granted departmental status to a property assessment unit and the city

V. ORGANIZATION: Means of Attainment

treasury, with the treasurer an elected official. With two finance department heads reporting to the chief executive, and one elected, this charter failed to establish a comprehensive finance department with unified leadership — a serious deficiency as it opens the way for finance units to work at cross purposes. (For example, in two cases known to the author, elected treasurers held up vendor payments to 1) embarrass a despised controller and 2) gain personal and political benefits.) Further, by establishing three supervised units as "divisions,' this charter can also be faulted for failing to grant the chief financial officer a desirable measure of discretion in determining the internal structure of the finance department, This level of organizational prescription is a serious defect.

Reflecting my experience, to promote efficacious management, responsibility for the internal organization of a comprehensive finance establishment is best left to its leader. Mandates concerning the internal organization of finance establishments tend to inhibit teamwork and fluid staff deployments to cope with the peak and valleys in work volume typical of finance activities, budgeting, accounting, payables, revenue collection, etc. Staffing these units to cope with peak workloads is not efficacious practice. Nor is meeting peak loads with extraordinary efforts from limited staffs, often requiring a wage premium. Important aspects of finance staffing are addressed in more detail later on. Organizational rigidities also encourage the creation and maintenance of redundant records, unit by unit, a topic treated in detail in the discussion of instrumentalities, Part 2. Moreover, mandated supervisory structures certainly afford possible points of resistance to technological change and other desirable operating adjustments.

Procedural Mandates Preferred

In contrast, whereas the case for organizational prescriptions is weak, the justification for procedural mandates is strong. After all, efficacious finance management depends entirely on timely administrative deeds expressing the values of the efficacy triad:

effectiveness, efficiency and economy. To ensure timely performance of key procedures, mandated administrative action is required. To be sure, authoritative procedural mandates do not guarantee faithful compliance, but they provide an expectation of performance continuity and certainty. Non-compliance with procedural mandates and administrative orders is a staple of bureaucratic life, evidenced by the use of multiple "feedback" mechanisms, including performance reporting, personal inspection, formal investigation, encouragement and protection of "whistle-blowers" compliant registers and reviews, suits invoking the concepts of *mandamus* and *ultra vires*, etc. The establishment of Inspector Generals throughout the United States Government is also testimony to the extent of the problem of official non-compliance (and neglect of duty) with procedural mandates and administrative orders.

Obviously, procedural mandates should clearly specify what is to be done, and when. The key procedures of efficacious finance work in governments of general jurisdiction are listed below. (They are also applicable in governments of special jurisdiction, which number in the thousands in the USA alone, depending on size programmatic complexity.) These procedures are explored in more detail in Part 6, *Management: Pursuit of Attainment:*

1) Prior to the issuance of the call for budget estimates, the jurisdiction's chief executive shall require the formulation of 1) a Revenue Mobilization Methodology, 2) a Fiscal Capability Statement, and 3) a multi-year Fiscal and Budgetary Perspective.

2) Prior to the beginning of the fiscal year, the jurisdiction's chief executive shall require the formulation of a solution-centered, results-oriented budget demonstrating effective management articulation

V. ORGANIZATION: Means of Attainment

and use of performance data, justified by program documentation, cost center by cost center, addressing the following topics:

- Rationale: Definition of Issues, Problems and Opportunities
- Goal(s)
- Collaborators And Affected Parties
- Conditions Of Performance
- Work Plan(s)
- Budget
- Alternatives

4) The chief financial officer shall establish and maintain accounting procedures which support a flexible array of cost centers and facilitate the aggregation of non-monetary performance data, formally correlated with measures of effort and monetary data

5) The chief financial officer shall require continuous utilization of inter-related implementation instruments These inter-related implementation instrumentalities form a Process Control Quartet:

- Work Plans
- Allotments
- Dynamic monitoring via periodic formal performance reviews
- Timely corrective action.

Mutually reinforcing, the absence or limp implementation of any of these four procedures reduces the effectiveness of the others. The thought conveyed by the last sentence deserves emphasis because it also applies to the entire set of the six procedural mandates listed above. This set of inter-laced recommendations can (and should) be seen as representing an integrated philosophy of public finance management. (Previously I alerted the reader to my perspective in Part 3, *Authority*, codified as Exhibit 3.2, *A Philosophy of Public Finance and Budgeting.*) Additionally, these six inter-locking injunctions comprise the essential argument of this essay. It is my considered opinion that the leaders of government finance establishments will not go far wrong in espousing and implementing procedures similar to those here recommended, mandated by law or not.

Accounting — Core Instrumentality

The remainder of this discussion about structure amplifies Point 4 above, concerning accounting arrangements. In every jurisdiction, accounting capabilities and performance condition the use of the appropriation process as an instrument of public policy and management. In short, budgets and budgeting depend on accounting for organizational lodgment. This axiom is widely appreciated, even where, in the eyes of budget officers, accounting support for budgeting practice falls far short of its potential. Accounting support for the appropriation process not only varies significantly among governments across the world, but, tends to be limited to bare essentials. In recent decades, financial accounting and reporting has attracted critical attention, with significant results. As governments with sub-standard financial accounting and reporting are not likely to be providing strong accounting support for budgeting, budget officers have welcomed improvements in financial accounting and reporting. Given the centrality of the appropriation process in the formulation and implementation of public policy, accounting support for budgeting deserves critical attention — and investment.

V. ORGANIZATION: Means of Attainment

Paramount Concern: Accounting Support for Budgeting

Budgetary accounting is a form of management accounting. As such, the provision of accounting support for budget formulation and implementation is not subject to the same type of authoritative standards increasingly applied to the practice of financial accounting and reporting, public and private, throughout the world. By all reports, government applications of comprehensive management accounting are relatively rare, and by implication, proper accounting support for budgeting. The following discussion explores the nature of the accounting support problem in sufficient detail to identify desiderata which might be used to define a satisfactory model of budgetary accounting.

Encouraged by multi-lateral international organizations, and also responding to the information requirements of an integrating global economy, governments throughout the world strive to upgrade and standardize their financial accounting and reporting. Because budget processes are strongly conditioned by accounting methodology and staff capabilities, the adoption of standardized financial accounting and reporting has been good news for officials interested in the practice of solution-centered, results-oriented budgeting. However, experience, to-date, indicates that this movement, by itself, does not guarantee that governments are willing to install and maintain the additional administrative and accounting institutions required for the effective practice of solution-centered, results-oriented budgeting.

When derived from standardized financial accounts, independently audited reports can usually provide reliable information about an organization's financial status. Although government officials find standards-based financial reports useful, to interested parties outside, these reports are absolutely indispensable. For this reason, the major multi-lateral international organizations — International Monetary Fund, United Nations and World Bank — have consistently encouraged the adoption of standardized financial accounting and reporting by the governments of the world, stressing the inter-related values of transparency, disclosure and comparability. For the same reason, representatives of the influential investment community have encouraged the adoption of Generally Accepted Accounting Principles (GAAP) by public and private organizations seeking access to the world's capital markets. Responding to these authoritative recommendations, the number of governments practicing standardized financial accounting and reporting, or striving to do so, has been increasing. Given the availability of GAAP-based financial accounting computer software, and the spur supplied by the continuing advance of global economic integration, one may safely predict the eventual standardization of government financial accounting and reporting throughout the world.

In contrast, the constituency for management accounting lies inside, rather than outside organizations. Organizations use well-known management accounting concepts and procedures to record and report information useful to their managers. This extension of accounting practice beyond that required for financial accounting and reporting is not currently subject to authoritative, GAAP-like requirements. Consequently, governments have been free to determine the scope and subject matter of its management/budgetary accounting program. Although not authoritatively standardized, management accounting is a distinct field of practice, supported by literature and formal coursework in educational institutions. Centered on costs, aggregated by product and/or management responsibility, enterprise managers throughout the world make extensive use of management accounting. However, excepting their public enterprises, governments have been reluctant to support their service programs with management accounting.

Within the United States, initiatives affecting governmental accounting began in 1934. In a seminal move, the Municipal Finance Officers Association of the United States and Canada (MFOA) issued the first of its influential series of manuals (known as "blue books") embracing the recommendations of the then newly established National

V. ORGANIZATION: Means of Attainment

Committee on Governmental Accounting (NCGA) for the improvement of government accounting. NCGA suggestions included 1) establishment of a set of separate, but inter-related, "funds" as the basic accounting organization of governmental jurisdictions, 2) adoption of the "double entry" accounting methodology, 3) incorporation of budgetary accounts as an integral component of governmental accounting systems, and 4) recognition of expenditures and revenues on a "modified accrual" basis, except for governmental enterprises which were advised to use the accrual approach.

A notable enhancement of governmental accounting within the United States followed the virtual bankruptcy of New York City in 1974. In response to this event, a broad-based movement, strongly supported by the Government Finance Officers Association (GFOA, formerly the Municipal Finance Officers Association (MFOA), successfully effected a major change in the utility of governmental accounting by establishing "disclosure" and "transparency" as controlling purposes. Although not focused on government, the United States Government reacted similarly to major corporate scandals by adopting the Public Company Accounting and Investor Protection Act of 2002.

In 1984, the Government Accounting Standards Board (GASB) succeeded the NCGA. Summing up at this point, adherence to the standards adopted by the NCGA-GASB has increased significantly within the United States. An important exception to this general adherence concerns requirements for the maintenance of proper fixed asset records. This is regrettable as such records are not only useful in considering capital investment policy, but also facilitate the allocation of capital charges to operating cost centers. It is also regrettable that, despite the heavy promotion of various forms of results-oriented budgeting during the period, accounting support requirements received scant attention.

As noted above, and which will be stressed in the forthcoming discussion of dynamic monitoring in Part 6, the effectiveness of solution-centered, results-oriented budgeting (defined as the efficacious attainment of performance objectives) depends on management's success in employing a process control quartet of implementation instruments. Employed sequentially, the suggested series embraces four instruments of budget implementation: 1) work plans, 2) allotments, 3) formal performance reviews and 4) timely corrective action. Effectively, these instruments must be supported by a) an elaborate, flexible classification and coding scheme and b) accounting procedures facilitating the formal integration of non-monetary performance data and monetary accounting data.

If implemented dynamically, as recommended, this four-phase monitoring sequence enables accountable officials to recognize and diagnose allocation and performance problems in time to take appropriate corrective action before the given reporting period ends. Obviously, the ability of officials to take effective corrective action within any given reporting period is critically dependant on timely recording and reporting of accounting and performance data. The role of timeliness cannot be overstressed, for it is timely corrective action by accountable officials that provides results-oriented budgeting with its managerial muscle. Considering the importance of goal attainment for effective solution-centered, results-oriented budgeting, monitoring systems that do not provide timely recording, reporting and corrective action are fatally deficient. Sad to say, at the present time, the typical budget monitoring system tends to rest on "after-the-period" reporting, when the opportunity to alter a likely undesired outcome has passed — forever!

In institutionalizing the four inter-related instruments of the process control quartet, supportive accounting leadership is indispensable. As noted above, the accounting support for the recommended monitoring sequence should include a) an elaborate, flexible classification and coding scheme and b) accounting procedures facilitating the formal integration of non-monetary performance data and monetary accounting data. Translated into leadership principles, these imperatives require a willingness to 1) make the chart of accounts serve programmatic as well as control purposes, 2) use accounting procedures and records to systematically relate non-monetary performance data to monetary accounting

V. ORGANIZATION: Means of Attainment

data, and 3) establish and maintain reporting practices which keep financial and productivity data flowing to all program units, validated, consolidated and made available on a timely basis. Specifically, the design and operation of the accounting system should satisfy the following criteria:

- To provide for the recording and reporting of budgetary transactions, accounting procedures should incorporate budgetary accounts, recording estimated revenue, appropriations, allocations and allotments, and recording receipts, commitments and disbursements on the same basis as appropriated (cash, accrual, or modified accrual).

- To maintain control of the budget during its execution, accounting procedures should subtract commitments (contingent liabilities, encumbrances, reservations) and disbursements from appropriate appropriation/allotment amounts, indicating the uncommitted balance available to support additional commitments and disbursements.

- To encourage disbursement planning, and by implication, program planning, appropriations/allotments for operations and maintenance should lapse, unless committed by purchase order, at the end of allotment periods, if allotments are used, and most certainly at the end of the fiscal period. Project appropriations (additions to fixed assets) should continue until project completion as "no-year" appropriations.

- To facilitate periodic performance reviews, the accounting system should incorporate "accounts" for recording and reporting performance data in cost center order, specifically, work hours and associated performance measurements and ratios. It is especially important that the accounting system clearly distinguish between "control" and "analysis" classifications by identifying expenditure control with a programmatic classifications, rather than expenditure items.

- To avoid understatements, all expenditure and revenue should be aggregated and reported in gross, rather than net terms.

- To maximize its usefulness, accounting and performance data should be recorded accurately and reported at times required for the effective conduct of the performance review phases of the budget monitoring sequence.

Failure to satisfy all six of the above criteria must be regarded as a serious lapse, having pervasive, deleterious consequences for all dimensions of the budgetary process.

It is instructive (and sobering) to note that accounting professionals clearly perceived the potential impact of results-oriented budgeting on accounting procedures. The following comment in 1954 by James M. Cunningham, a Certified Public Accountant and a former president of the Municipal Finance Officers Association may be taken as representative:

"The adoption of the performance budget by a municipality requires a major change in accounting procedures in order

V. ORGANIZATION: Means of Attainment

to develop the possibilities of the new method to the fullest advantage." Accounting Publication Series, 11-2, MFOA, May 1, 1954.

It is encouraging to note that many governments are increasingly led by officials who understand and support the selected use of the concepts of "management" accounting, including cost centers and concepts of performance measurement. If integrated with supporting administrative institutions, these practices provide a sufficient foundation for the conduct of solution-centered, results-oriented budgeting, provided that the financial accounting system incorporates expenditure and revenue ledgers which permit the maintenance of an elaborate, flexible scheme of cost centers that can reach the lowest levels of supervision throughout the government organization. With this capability, every supervisor can function as a "cost center manager," accountable for the behavior of work time, variable (controllable) costs, related revenues, and, most important, performance. As a practical matter, the introduction and maintenance of solution-centered, results-oriented budgeting, with its heavy demands on the accounting system, cannot be accomplished without the leadership and enthusiastic support of government accountants.

Most assuredly, implementing solution-centered, results-oriented budgeting requires a great deal of cooperation from governmental accountants. Governments wishing to use solution-centered, results-oriented budgeting, or those seeking to do it better, are well-advised to first ensure that requisite administrative and accounting foundations are in place and working smoothly. The attainment of appropriate accounting support is only possible when a jurisdiction's leading finance officials identify with the problems of programmatic and project goal attainment.

However, strong forces work against the expression of a programmatic orientation by finance leaders in every government. Characteristically, finance leaders tend to identify budgeting as a problem of financial "control," and, therefore, define the role of accounting in budgeting negatively and narrowly. According to this line of thinking, budget implementation is accounting, pure and simple. Government leaders subscribing to this philosophy tend to ignore and/or devalue the connection of accounting arrangements to other procedures which assist management in attaining the programmatic purposes of budgeting. Clearly, in governments where the financial control mind-set is dominant, the introduction and maintenance of recommended procedures focused on programmatic and project goal attainment will not rest on strong institutional foundations

To be fair, even if willing, many government accounting units frequently lack the capability to put in place and consistently maintain appropriate budgetary accounting and reporting. Solution-centered, results-oriented budgeting imposes additional operating burdens on a jurisdiction's accounting staff:

- Account classifications proliferate, including identification of fixed and variable costs.

- Transactions and entries increase in number and complexity.

- Reconciliation requirements increase.

- Accounting reports display fewer continuities as accounts and classifications change from period to period to meet changing issues. (This situation may also result in demands for restatement of accounting data to illuminate new issues.)

- Accountants and auditors are given increased responsibility for the entry and integrity of "non-monetary" data (work load, performance indicators and program benefit information)

V. ORGANIZATION: Means of Attainment

and the calculation of relationships of this data to expenditure and revenue information.

Providing the requisite format elaboration and flexibility obviously depends on the sympathetic cooperation of accounting officials. Solution-centered, results-oriented budgets incorporate and display "cost center" arrays and other indicators of program investment, measures of results, and, most crucially, calculations concerning the relationship of program and project investments to measures of results. Consequently, officials wishing to work with the information so provided inevitably find themselves concerned with the composition and integrity of 1) "cost centers," a term applied to aggregations of money or effort applied in programs and projects and 2) related performance data. Depending on one's accounting philosophy, applied financial resources may be aggregated as disbursements, expenditures or expense. Effort identifies work-time designated as hours, days, weeks, months or years. Further, the composition and integrity of monetary aggregations rest on the appropriate classification and faithful assignment of "costs," variously defined (direct, indirect, fixed, variable, etc.), depending on one's management and evaluation purpose.

Concerns about composition and integrity apply to the establishment and maintenance of the cost center aggregations of Performance Budgeting and the decision packages required by Zero-Base Budgeting. Program Budgeting requires that allocations be linked to goals. This is also true of its more elaborate off-spring, the Planning/Programming/Budgeting System. In those frequent cases where goals transcend existing organizational units, goal attainment requires coordinated efforts of more than one organizational unit. This multi-unit situation presents program managers, work unit supervisors, accountants and budget officers with recurring classification, coding and accountability issues.

The introduction of solution-centered, results-oriented budgeting focused attention on the expenditure classification schemes. In seeking to relate allocations to intentions and/or expected results, results-oriented budgeting requires that expenditures be classified by expressive titles.

EXHIBIT 5.2 Budget Classification Concepts

Organization	Accounting	Configuration	Policy	Performance
Ministry	Fund	Class	Goal	Function
Agency	Account	Category	Objective	Cost Center
Department	Object	Component	Service	Responsibility Center
Division	Item	Element	Program	Activity
Bureau	Source	Time	Project	Task
Section	Fixed	Space (Area)		Job
Unit	Variable			

Exhibit 5.2 displays the diversity of classification concepts found in various budget documents. The Exhibit displays 31 concepts for expenditure identification, grouped in five classification "families." Typically, jurisdictions mix their identifiers, drawing terms from more than one classification family. With reference to performance budgets, one does not need computer technology to knit expenditure aggregations together in a single hierarchy of cost center summaries. But, program-style budgets, by design, frequently display summaries incorporating expenditures assigned to the activities of more than one organizational unit. Computer technology makes it possible to expand the number of classifications assigned to any given expenditure or revenue. This capability makes it possible to prepare and execute budgets with multiple connotations, that is, allocations and expenditure can be cross-classified by function, organization, space, time, demography, etc. Knitting multi-dimensional aggregations together requires an elaborate classification and coding scheme.

Computer technology also provides a way to simplify the management of a coding system comprising many digits by assigning a single surrogate code to an inter-related string of code numbers, such as the sequence, 01-1-03-1-0-1-1-001, displayed in Exhibit 2.1, *A Sample Chart of Accounts: Finance Director's Office*. To assign a surrogate code, all strings in a jurisdiction's classification and code system are arranged

V. ORGANIZATION: Means of Attainment

in ascending order, and numbered accordingly. For example, the string noted above might be the 100th in the sequential order, thus, this number could be made to "stand-in" for that string lodged in a computerized "look-up" table. Entering the surrogate code locates the relevant string for entry into the accounting system or other appropriate records with information associated with that string. Using surrogate codes reduce coding effort and the possibility of coding error in entering a long set of inter-related codes in computer files and documents.

As programs frequently involve more than one organizational unit within a government, the classification schemes employed in program budgets are more complicated than those needed by performance formats. Program budgeting brings organizationally segregated, but functionally related, program components together in one summary. Most budget officers agree that this approach is very effective for policy-making, but requires extraordinary management arrangements, crossing normal accountability lines during implementation. Even if jurisdictions can not support program budgets with appropriate arrangements, including accounting support, it is possible to formulate and monitor program budgets by using the "cross-classification," or "cross-walk," technique selectively, on an as-needed basis.

Exhibit 5.3, *A Program Perspective for Family Planning*, displays a budget for a national family planning program. The program embraced a Family Planning Board (FPB), the coordinating agency, and four sector ministries, including the key delivery system provided by the Ministry of Health through its extensive Maternal and Child Health Clinic System. For policy and management purposes, within the FPB and the ministries, family planning costs are identified and coded as an array of cost centers. Additionally, using the cross-classification, or cross-walk technique, the FPB budget officer could prepare a program perspective summarizing the entire family planning budget, including all participating units of government. As shown in Exhibit 5.4, this Program Perspective cross-classified the allocations to the participating institutions to indicate their relative impact on the three key programmatic thrusts of the program.

EXHIBIT 5.3 A Program Perspective for Family Planning

IMPACTS >	Maintaining Current Practitioners	Recruiting Lapsed Practitioners	Recruiting New Practitioners	Total
ORGANIZATION				
Family Planning Board	3,423.2	615.6	3,575.2	7,614.0
Ministry of Health	3,000.0	75.4	835.5	3,910.9
Ministry of Education			392.3	392.3
Youth/Community			1,107.6	1,107.6
Ministry of Agriculture	82.3		400.0	482.3
Total Cost	6,505.5	691.0	6,310.6	13,507.1
PERFORMANCE DATA				
Number of Acceptors	114,000	20,000	43,000	177,000
Cost per Acceptor	57.06	34.55	146.76	76.31
Estimated Births				61,000
Estimated Births Averted				17,700
Cost per Averted Birth				763.31

With the availability of computer technology, the cross-classifications required to support program budgeting can be produced by reference to codes assigned for that purpose, prepared, as needed, for analysis and/or decisions. Computer technology makes it possible to formulate and implement budgets with complex objectives. In contrast to mono-value formats, cross-classified formats permit policy officials to explore more than one dimension of an expenditure proposal, facilitating insight and understanding.

Because they record coded classification schemes and the associated figures, ledgers recording the usage of resources are of the greatest significance to program managers and budget officers. With reference to the use of expenditure ledgers, the location of controls on the incurrence of encumbrances and disbursements is an important issue. The resolution of this issue determines the fundamental design of its expenditure ledger. If the control points are associated with results-oriented "lump-sum" summaries (program, project, activity or task), rather than to expenditure summaries or objects of expenditure, these latter entries will be identified as analytical rather than control identifiers and codes,

V. ORGANIZATION: Means of Attainment

providing information only. In those governments where the leading accounting officials are unwilling to establish controls at a programmatic level (lump-sum), the managerial assumptions of results-oriented budgeting are seriously compromised.

An array of cost centers can be used dynamically for any of the purposes listed in Exhibit 5.4, *Purposes Justifying Significant Cost Centers*. For example, if a specific activity needs management attention, a cost center embracing its elements can be identified and established for research purposes. The research completed, the elements of the cost center in question can be merged into an associated cost center. Organizational and policy changes usually require changes in relevant cost center arrays.

EXHIBIT 5.4 Purposes Justifying Significant Cost Centers

PURPOSE	COMMENT
To identify and organize resource requirements for program implementation.	Requires periodic review of cost center arrays for excessive decomposition, as they may include more centers and levels of aggregation than needed.
To identify costs and work time for performance ratio calculations.	Such calculations justify cost center establishment.
To identify costs for evaluation of resource mix options and alternative production techniques.	Requires commitment to such examinations and resulting changes.
To facilitate cost comparisons.	Requires evidence of decision-related usage of such comparisons to validate cost center design and establishment.
To identify costs for pricing service charges.	Requires commitment to such usage to justify cost center establishment.
To establish accounts related to emerging issues, problems and opportunities. .	Changing circumstance may require cost center modifications through mergers and/or cost reassignments.
To isolate costs which cannot be easily, or accurately, assigned to other cost centers.	Identifies "indirect," "fixed" or "common" costs of supervision, central process units, "overhead" items, etc. Two or more subsidiary cost centers within a cost center probably require a third, "residual," cost center to isolate the common costs of supporting services and/or resources.

As cost centers are the fundamental building blocks of an accounting system supporting solution-centered, results-oriented budgeting, their establishment and adjustment to program conditions merits serious consideration by managers and the accounting staff. Exhibit 2.2, Cost *Center Criteria,* displayed in Part 2, *Instrumentalities,* lists significance, productivity, accountability, reportability and acceptance as considerations when adding a cost center to the Chart of Accounts. A definition of each criterion follows the display of Exhibit 2.2 in Part 2.

In practice, governments discriminate among cost centers in the application of the specifications displayed in Exhibit 2.2, especially with reference to the criterion of accountability. Theoretically, every supervisory official (agency heads down to supervisors at the base of agency hierarchies) merits consideration as an accountable cost center manager. However, organizational complexity (the mix of divisions, bureaus, sections, etc.) frequently conditions the allocation of the management duties defining accountability. Multi-unit, multi-level agencies will surely have a number of supervisors overseeing the work of other supervisors until the "front line" supervisor is reached. Certain of these supervisors of supervisors may be organizationally (and perhaps physically) remote from the sites and scenes of actual production. Cost centers established to aggregate their expenditures tend to serve analytical rather than budget control purposes. As indicated by the following list, a truly accountable cost center manager would:

- Appoint the staff funded by the cost center.
- Supervise staff funded by the cost center.
- Discipline staff financed by the cost center.
- Certify work time and authorized absences for payroll purposes.
- Authorize requisitions and/or purchase orders.
- Certify receipt of purchases for vendor payments.

V. ORGANIZATION: Means of Attainment

- Formulate cost center budgets, work plans and allotment requests.
- Re-allocate cost center budgets, when necessary.
- Maintain and use output measurement records.
- Monitor and report performance.

Certainly an impressive and imposing list of duties! In practice, governments tend to distribute, rather than concentrate, these duties within their hierarchical formations. The assignment of supervisory duties is everywhere subject to laws, administrative traditions, hierarchical imperatives and official self-interest. In governments with centralized human resources and procurement agencies, strong civil service regulations, and collective bargaining agreements with employee unions, supervisors will tend to lack effective authority with reference to certain of the duties listed above. With reference to budgeting, higher ranking officials often desire to retain the power to re-allocate budgets of subordinate units during the fiscal year.

By the intrinsic logic of the efficacy triad, front-line supervisors should be deemed the most accountable. However, in the work-a-day world, front-line supervisors are usually not given much discretion. One might say that "bucking" key operating decisions "upwards" is the general rule in public agencies. Suffice it to say that, in assigning the duties listed above, governments should bias their distribution in favor "front-line" supervisors, that is, those who oversee the work of those who actually produce services and products.

In addition to permitting an elaborate and flexible format, expenditure ledgers should be designed to assist cost center managers with the implementation of their budgets and the associated work plans. This includes the following facilities:

- Recording and timely reporting of work hours charged to activities/tasks listed in work plans, maintained as subsidiary ledgers. (Because work plans are fundamentally based on work time calculations, this facility is of even greater value to cost center managers than variable cost reporting.)

- Recording and timely reporting of the variable costs of activities/tasks listed in work plans.

- Permitting cost center managers to enter budget reservations into the accounting system as contingent liabilities, especially requisitions for goods and services which have not yet reached the status of encumbrances, that is, contracts and purchase orders. (Because it tracks the status of obligations from source to settlement, this arrangement is especially useful in jurisdictions with centralized purchasing units with their inevitable service queues. The ability to reserve portions of available budget balances also facilitates the planning of operations.)

With regard to solution-centered, results-oriented budgets, government accountants tend to agree that management accounting systems would provide the best accounting support. However, in contrast to profit-oriented enterprises, governments lack compelling incentives to invest in this expensive elaboration of their accounting systems, especially for the service programs funded by general revenues. In view of this reluctance, alternatives can be employed. As noted, subsidiary ledgers administered by supervisors can be used to record and control work plans, deemed essential management instruments. In the discussion of Exhibit 5.3, *A Program Perspective for Family Planning,* it was suggested that the "cross-classification" technique could be used on an as-needed basis. Similarly, when cost estimates, especially statements of total,

V. ORGANIZATION: Means of Attainment

or "full" cost are required to make important decisions, cost finding procedures can yield acceptable results. As research and analysis, rather than accounting, cost finding requires the assembly, evaluation and adjustment of relevant information drawn from various sources, including data provided by the formal accounting system.

2. Leadership: Unified and Accountable

Historically, the key organizational deficiency of government finance has been fragmented leadership, defined as an undesirable distribution of finance management authority. Countless jurisdictions throughout the world lack unified finance leadership short of the chief executive's office, especially with reference to budgeting and revenue collection, not to speak of rivalries between finance ministries, central banks, and planning agencies controlling access to external finance and funds.

Using the United States as a case in point, at the beginning of the 20th century, organizational arrangements for finance work typically embraced elected finance officials, multi- member boards exercising finance functions, and, frequently, numerous appointed finance officers, function by function, reporting variously to boards, legislative bodies and/or senior officials. The prescription for this fragmentation called for the concentration of finance supervision in a finance director reporting to a chief executive. Although this prescription had been adopted by many governments by the beginning of the 21st century, integrated finance establishments have by no means supplanted the fragmented approach to finance organization, particularly in the larger jurisdictions. The incomplete realization of the integration ideal represents an important item of unfinished business for those interested in the efficient and effective management of government and its finance in the United States.

Looking back, the concept of comprehensive finance establishments was rooted in turn-of-the-20th century campaigns to free American governments from corruption — and cannot be truly understood apart from that struggle, and its theory of public administration.

Managerial Thought for Public Finance Officers

In this theory, "good" government, defined as public accountability, is better served by a concentration of authority, rather than its dispersion. The idea of concentrating the supervision of finance work in an integrated finance establishment appeared as a necessary and logical extension of this theory. Facing entrenched corruption, the turn-of-the-20th century reformers sought to concentrate administrative authority in chief executives as the best means of ensuring government accountability. They also saw, as a practical matter, that the financial aspects of administration should be concentrated in the hands of an officer reporting to a strong chief executive to make that office effective.

Seizing on the strategic fact that finance cuts across all programs, the advocates of integrated finance establishments expected incumbent chief financial officers to exploit the advantage of their position to 1) enforce government policies by means of finance-related controls; 2) represent and enforce the values of economy, efficiency and effectiveness throughout the government; and 3) provide policy advice on issues facing the government. The reformers also recognized that the intrusive power of finance reaches into every nook and cranny of government. The organizational and procedural arrangements for the exercise of this power provide a basic system of order, and a prime vehicle for regulating the execution of governmental policies. Looking outward, the exercise of a government's fiscal power regulates its relationship to the financial and economic marketplace, affecting the arithmetic of the community. In various degrees, this relationship is most precisely formulated at budget time, when, in addition to defining its service agenda, appropriation decisions invoke collateral decisions on taxes, service charges and loans.

In addition to programmatic and agency proliferation, social and economic trends since World War II have significantly altered the conditions of official service in governments throughout the United State. First consider this general observation about the current environment of government agencies.

V. ORGANIZATION: Means of Attainment

- In differentiated modern society, the values of accountability and responsibility are at war with one another. In this context, "accountability" refers to authoritative action exercising the discretionary powers of an office in accordance with law and/or a code of official conduct. "Responsibility" refers to authoritative action subject to correction by those subject to it. If one is totally responsible, one has no authority. (On the contemporary scene, the distinction between accountability and responsibility can be clearly seen in the controversy over the review of police action by citizen boards.) As the complexity of modern society increases, administrative organizations differentiate in an effort to respond, that is, satisfy the demands of a steadily growing array of sub-groups, sub cultures, and differentiated environments. Under the impact of differentiated interests, official response to stimulus tends to replace the reasoned exercise of authority.

In particular, social and economic trends since World War II have significantly affected finance establishments in significant ways. Consider the following observations:

- Increasing real wealth encouraged and permitted the leaders of government to promote programmatic values. As a result, service programs proliferated and expanded, willy-nilly, straining the power of chief executives to direct and coordinate operations by traditional means. Seeking accountability, many governments responded to growing coordination problems by establishing "super" departments, including departments of management or administration under the control of an executive appointee. In many cases, the government's chief financial officer is required to report to this appointee instead of the chief executive.

- Improvements in budgetary technique, deemphasized he accounting nature of the format and process in favor of its policy-making and managerial aspects. This often resulted in a shift of important budget duties from chief financial officers to a member of the chief executive's immediate staff, or to the aforementioned departments of management or administration.

- Computerization, in most cases originally introduced into government by alert and progressive finance directors, grew to the point where the system-wide applications and implications led some governments to reduce or eliminate the supervisory role of chief financial officers for this fabulous technology, an ironic twist.

Before turning to a discussion of a most important issue of internal finance organization, the placement and role of the budget function, we should note that government leaders confront an organizational problem of considerable complexity in maintaining liquidity and efficacious revenue collection procedures. Cash management is by no means a costless activity, nor should it be considered as a treasury sideline, based on ad-hoc decisions, guesswork and "rules of thumb." To maximize investment potential, cash must be a prime subject of

V. ORGANIZATION: Means of Attainment

government-wide managerial thinking, planning and collaboration. Many variables are involved, such as, vigorous collection of receivables, prompt deposit of cash, and accurate disbursement forecasting by all service program managers. Recognizing that important variables lie in hands outside the treasury, governments can best provide a high order of finance leadership for cash management by vesting this function in their chief financial officer. A government may gain as much, or more, from this leadership assignment as it might from the exercise of pure investment savvy. Furthermore, as the requirements for a separate treasury office disappear under the impact of computerization, governments with integrated finance establishments can assign the treasurer's duties to the chief financial officer without weakening internal controls.

Financial management is commonly regarded as a staff or auxiliary function, a type of undistributed "overhead" cost. As undifferentiated overhead, finance establishments receive a direct appropriation. As a result, the "users" of financial management services, that is, the various programmatic units producing governmental goods and services, have virtually no influence or control over the cost, volume or quality of financial management outputs. Indeed, because financial management activities are frequently conducted by central process agencies, (e.g., accounting, accounts receivable and payable, and procurement) poor performance by these agencies can have a substantial adverse impact on programmatic performance. Consider the following:

1) Failure to pursue delinquent accounts receivable reduces the overall availability of funds for programmatic activities.

2) Delays in procurement of services and supplies reduce program effectiveness, and in periods of inflation, increase program costs.

3) Delays in processing accounts payable reduce vendor willingness to compete for a jurisdiction's business, and tend to increase prices, thus adding to program costs.

4) Failure to invest idle funds reduces overall availability of funds for application to program activities.

Obviously, the relationship between government arithmetic and the arithmetic of the community is most precisely formulated at budget adoption time, when, in support of its adopted service agenda, government leaders make collateral decisions on taxes, fees, service charges and loans. In addition to financial conceptions, the budget formulation and adoption process requires the application of socio-economic thought. This requirement encourages public finance officials to assemble and interpret pertinent information on the socio-economic environment of their jurisdiction. In this endeavor, they also rely on data developed during the conduct of finance-related activities, putting a premium on the integrity, relevance and timeliness of this data.

The discussion concerning the responsibility of public finance managers for the productivity of money in Part 3 pointed out that the quality of a jurisdiction's finance management is insolubly linked to applying the values of the efficacy triad to the use of its capital. Success in attaining this goal requires the application of formal allocation criteria to proposed investments in projects and programs. Overall responsibility for assessing the productivity of money is usually assigned to budget units. To budget is to ration scarce resources among competing purposes. To budget well is to ration scarce resources among the most meritorious competing purposes As such, budgeting is certainly not finance or accounting; yet budget officers are absolutely dependent on finance and accounting activity for information, structure and process. For some, this dependency, and the

V. ORGANIZATION: Means of Attainment

consequent staff interplay, provides sufficient rationale for locating the budget function within the ambit of an integrated finance establishment. For others, the symbiotic advantages of placement within an integrated establishment are less advantageous than an identification of the budget function with the chief executive's office. Is there a solid institutional answer to the placement question?

For the organizational placement of its budget office, government jurisdictions have adopted one of the following four possibilities:

1) Chief budget officer reports to the chief financial officer. (Probably the most common arrangement.)

2) Chief budget officer reports to the chief executive. Budget office is incorporated within the chief executive's office. (e.g.: Office of Management and Budget (OMB), United States Government.)

3) Chief budget officer reports to the chief executive. Budget office enjoys ministry or departmental status.

4) Chief budget officer reports to the head of multi-function administrative services organization enjoying ministry or departmental status. .

Every well-ordered government expects sound advice from its budget staff, such advice embracing economic and financial considerations, resource availability, operational feasibility and reliable estimates for programs and projects deemed meritorious. Ideally, this advice should reflect the application of formal allocation criteria, including reasoned judgments on program and project efficiency and effectiveness. Budget work is reflective work. It is best done by disinterested persons, endowed with an analytical cast of mind.

In terms of the specifications outlined above, what are the hazards of a non-finance placement of a budget office? The following comments trace the likely ramifications of direct supervision of a budget division or department by a chief executive:

> First, chief executives, and their aides, are typically immersed in the concerns of the day, fending off attacks, checking things out, "fighting fires," etc. Considering the unremitting pressure, it is not surprising that chief executives reach for additional staff resources. Lacking a buffer to regulate its involvement, the budget staff is easily drawn into the hot-house atmosphere of a chief executive's office, with predictable and deleterious affects on the objectivity of its advisory output. To do its best work, a budget unit needs relative detachment and a relatively remote time horizon.
>
> Second, a chief executive's relationship with program leaders, while fundamentally hierarchical, is frequently grounded on consultation and reciprocal loyalty. The reflective work of budget units is often seen as threatening by those affected. Those who observe close relationships tend to impute subjectivity. People who are thought to have the "king's ear," so to speak, find it difficult to maintain a reputation for objectivity. Recommendations produced by budget units closely identified with a chief executive's office may be perceived to represent the chief executive's true position, even if the chief executive disavows them as damaging important relationships with political forces or the department head(s) concerned. To an extent not usually appreciated, even by practitioners, budgeting is a search for truth. Effective budget work depends on a deserved reputation for the employment of evidence, logic and objectivity. Budget officers should not

V. ORGANIZATION: Means of Attainment

be placed in administrative environments which can not, by their very nature, protect the credibility of analytical work.

Finally, it is highly unlikely that budget units reporting to chief executives, or their executive aides, can get the depth and breadth of supervision required to review an agenda of reflective work, and give that work proper encouragement as it progresses.

The assignment of budget officers to a department of administration, or to some such organization embracing centralized process agencies, and, perhaps some, or all finance functions, at least provides a buffer between the budget staff and the chief executive's office.

On balance, however, if the jurisdiction has a comprehensive finance establishment, the budget unit should be placed under the supervision of its director, with the understanding that the chief executive determines the analytical agenda in consultation with the chief financial officer and the budget director. This placement maintains the required "administrative space" between the executive office and the work of the budget unit. In this regard, it is important to note that chief financial officers are usually the most competent officials in government to review proposed policy and procedural proposals, including budget recommendations, for administrative and financial feasibility. It is the only office within government where program and financial values consistently intersect.

Of course, the effectiveness of this recommended arrangement depends on the orientation of the chief financial officer, who must habitually express an enthusiastic interest in analytical and planning values, in addition to the values of coordination and control traditionally manifest in finance work. By not having a budget unit within their purview, finance directors find it very difficult to muster the analytical talent needed to assess the productivity of the capital applied to government operations, much less to discover and support those uses for capital producing the highest rates of return for the community as a whole.

3. Staff: Qualified by Education and Experience

Institutions thrive and spread when they offer the best way to serve important values and attain desired goals. Traditionally, public finance establishments have been seen by officials and citizens alike as coordination and control agencies. Also, in general, finance establishments have not been marked by high degrees of professionalization. One does not readily find economists, sociologists, etc., serving in public finance establishments. Until the advent of electronic technology in finance work, staff shortcomings were magnified by low capital/labor ratios. However, today and for the foreseeable future, governments need finance establishments which not only efficiently assess and collect revenue, keep books, pay bills and husband resources, but that can assist them to pre-figure their social, economic and fiscal future. Intrinsically, the tasks required for socio-economic analysis and related fiscal planning demand more talented and imaginative leadership than do the tasks associated with coordination and control.

Governments which persist in maintaining fragmented finance organizations are bound to experience serious difficulty in recruiting and retaining the requisite talent. Governments with a comprehensive finance establishment, on the other hand, can offer positions with enough scope, prestige and continuity to attract and retain the requisite talent, and provide that talent with ready access to resources and information needed for analytical and planning work. In this connection, in many governments burdened with multi-headed finance establishments, one notes that frustrated chief executives frequently try to provide a base for finance leadership by appointing a special assistant for fiscal affairs. Predictably, this assistant, weary of begging needed information and cooperation from relatively "independent" controllers, treasurers, collectors, assessors, etc, (who may not be on very good terms with

V. ORGANIZATION: Means of Attainment

one another, or with the chief executive), leaves for a more lucrative job, probably with some finance-related firm. In addition to suffering a damaging discontinuity in policy development, the government loses the knowledge acquired by the special assistant. On the evidence, such ad hoc arrangements are no substitute for a solid institutional approach to the requirements of finance leadership.

It is axiomatic that job design influences recruitment, that is, a known demand for certain skills calls forth a supply. The amazing spread of the council-manager form of government in the United States is a telling example. The availability of a sufficiently honored city manager career stimulated and sustained a supporting recruitment system. Indeed, the osmotic effect of the council-manager plan produced an informally organized non-partisan urban career service. If finance establishments are to emphasize analytical and planning values, in addition to the traditional values of coordination and control, there is every reason to believe that the very design of the job will have the desired osmotic effect of attracting persons with the requisite temperament and skill.

It seems abundantly clear that any serious attempt to enhance analytic and planning values in finance establishments will have rather profound affects on current organization and procedural arrangements. Certainly, one can foresee the employment of a mix of talents and knowledge not ordinarily found within finance directorates, such as, more highly qualified accountants, economists, sociologists, mathematicians, industrial engineers, scientists and other minds of analytical bent. Collaterally, changes will be required in the divisional breakdown of finance units, and in the procedures required to expand and protect a database useful in the evaluation of program benefits.

4. Staff Deployment: Flexibly Assigned According to Issues, Problems and Tasks

Characteristically, finance establishments are organized for the conduct of activities employing specialized staff. These activities, such as, budgeting accounting, revenue collecting, etc., are usually assigned to organizational units, variously titled, and, thus, provide the primary basis for the distribution of authority within finance establishments. These units may be segmented internally by groupings with one or more levels of supervision. These divisions typically experience peaks and troughs in work volumes, yet organizational rigidities inhibit teamwork and fluid deployment to meet performance targets. Respecting the grouping of finance activities for supervisory purposes, one finds a variety of combinations, such as, a common supervisor for revenue collection and treasury units. Basically, no one can point to a common form for the internal organization of finance establishments.

Organizational rigidities, based on the "checks and balances" theory of financial control, also inhibit the introduction of procedures fostering the continuous assembly of outputs. Additionally, staffing inadequacies, low capital/labor ratios, inadequate accounting and a control rather than service orientation of finance staffs, inhibit finance managers who would like to address vigorously all four of the prime concerns of finance management, especially the concern for the productivity of money.

Key finance activities are highly susceptible to routinization and continuous assembly of outputs. It seems entirely possible, then, to establish a single directorate-wide work force under unified leadership to maintain performance standards in data entry, data integrity, and data output for all routine operations. This group could be supplemented by another establishment-wide work force assigned to improve routine operations on a project-by-project basis, and expand the database to meet analytical and planning specifications. A third directorate-wide work group could be established to marshal intellectual resources for production of the desired analytical and planning outputs, such as, social and economic reports, in addition to an expanded annual financial report, and "disclosure" documents which "model the future" of the community for the investing public.

V. ORGANIZATION: Means of Attainment

Budget formulation and adoption time is one of two major "peak-loads" occurring in finance work. The staff of the finance establishment is keenly tested during the run-up to budget adoption. If deadlines are strictly enforced, "closing the books" at the end of reporting periods is another peak load testing the competency and dedication of finance workers. Additionally, if the jurisdiction practices "dynamic" monitoring, as recommended herein, peak loads will occur at the two-thirds point in each quarter. Revenue collection may feature peak loads due to payment deadlines.

Peak loads are a vexing problem for officials interested in relating expenditures to workloads and goals, a concept which is (or should be) a fundamental management preoccupation, a cardinal principle of good budgeting, and a fundamental element of efficacious management. Finance establishments are not alone in coping with peak loads. A typical fire suppression service provides an example of an organization built up to meet fire potentials which occur randomly. Police manpower can be more closely correlated with everyday service demands, but significant peaks and troughs of activity may occur by area and by time. In these cases, staffing allotments reflects an effort to meet peak loads, meaning that periods of low productivity are inevitable, unless a flexible mix of resources can be devised which varies with workload fluctuations. But, in contrast to the relative rigidity of public safety resources in the face of workload fluctuations, finance officials have the freedom to employ a combination of flexible staff assignments, contractual services, temporary help and overtime payments to help meet demands with a modulated response. The difficulties of adjusting, or modulating, budgets to varying demands, seasonal and otherwise, are well known. Budget review officials often show keen interest in correlations, particularly the relationship, or lack of one, between "regular" payroll expenditures and fluctuating workloads. It is only prudent to anticipate these questions by making the study of peak loads a special focus of management concern.

5. Technology: "State-of-the-art" capitalization of production, supported by depreciation policy

Capitalization of Production

Capitalized finance work, is now an entrenched feature of contemporary public finance establishments. It was not always so, attested by the image of Scroge's countinghouse protrayed by Charles Dicken's in his classic tale, "Christmas Carol." The question today, and in the future, is not when and if finance work will be infused with technology, but how quickly one can replace what one has with that which is state-of-the-art. In other words, leading public finance officers, considered as managers, must now be ever alert to the productivity implications of capital/labor relationships, and be nimble in making adjustments. . .

> *An author's aside: Before the advent of computers, public finance officers were only incidentally concerned with their equipment, much less with taking a capital/labor ratio approach to the efficacy of finance work, or government work in general. In this, they were not alone as the typical government official, unlike their enterprise counterparts, did not stay up nights worried that competitors would get an edge by adopting the latest productivity-enhancing technology. Reflecting my experience, public officials tended to be defensive about adopting work-related technology. In an incident in point, once, after installing a computer-based tax receivables system, I invited a group of tax collectors to a review. Although duly impressed, the group's leader remarked to my staff, "This is all good, but don't forget your pencils" In another incident, an entrepreneur of my acquaintance, seeking to access the government market, commented that, "The typical government official contemplating acquiring an innovation is reluctant to do*

V. ORGANIZATION: Means of Attainment

so, unless referred to others who have already done so. In contrast, the typical enterprise official is eager to be first."

Obviously, when one must be interested in the replacement of obsolete, or less efficacious equipment, one thinks of the advantages of applying the concept of depreciation. I have highlighted the utility of this important (and neglected) accounting concept at many points in this essay, especially with reference to the deployment and upkeep of public capital in Part 4. Its role in supporting efficacious finance work, as well as government work in general, is emphasized again at the end of this commentary on capitalization of production.

In historical perspective, the influential advocates of comprehensive finance establishments advanced "coordination" and "control" values as the principal rationale for a hierarchically integrated finance organization. By providing a single authoritative source, this hierarchical integration was also seen as a way to reduce conflicts and contradictions in advice and information supplied by finance officers to policy-making officials. As their experience did not embrace computers, the early advocates of hierarchical integration did not envision the collateral issue of "data integration," and its organizational and procedural implications. Since then, the organizational and procedural consequences of computers have become clearer. The power and speed of computers increased exponentially, the relative price of computer power decreased significantly, integrated financial software become readily available and widely used, a very useful "spreadsheet" software was invented and spread rapidly, compact "personal" computers invaded office after office, and could be tied together in area networks, and, with the advent of the laser printer, anybody could compose and produce first class, illustrated documents. Consequently, finance employees work less at traditional tasks, such as, posting, transcribing, calculating, stamping, logging, listing etc., as computers do more processing and manipulation. Collaterally, finance employees increasingly work at "controlling" the status and flow of computerized data.

Because they extend the reach of the human nervous system, and expand the human memory, computers are revolutionizing work. And mark this: Even more than organizations, computers empower persons. In a thoroughly computerized environment, the concept of supervision, which traditionally defined a hierarchical relationship, seems more appropriately applied to data, rather than persons. Endowed with access to computer resources, including software which facilitates data storage, transfer and manipulation, finance workers become creative personnel, if you will, supervisors of data bases, and, as such, are beyond the reach of traditional, person-on-person, techniques of supervision.

As many finance officials who have installed computers will testify, there are no technological shortcuts to lower costs and increased efficiency, despite the claims of equipment manufacturers. Simply grafting computer technology onto existing procedures is quite common. Underuse and/or overuse of computers is also common. There is simply no substitute for disinterested analysis of procedures prior to decisions about equipment acquisition. Indeed, the advent of inexpensive, desk-size computers, sharply increases the potential for idiomatic, repetitive recording or usage of data - the practice which we have identified as a major cause of inefficiency in finance work, computerized or not. Where reliance on a single, centralized computer facility tended to force finance officials into various degrees of data integration, decentralized computer resources provides no such incentive. Indeed, the tendencies run the other way.

It is obvious that the ideal of integrated data management will be more, not less, difficult to achieve in an organization which provides its staff with decentralized computer resources. The availability of small, powerful computers will produce an irresistible demand for such decentralization. Only strong, continuous planning for integrated data management, via coordinated file structures and coding protocols, can offset the inherent waste and duplication which will inevitably accompany a planless distribution of these fabulous resources. Nowhere is the tendency to think about procedures in planless, segmental ways

V. ORGANIZATION: Means of Attainment

better illustrated than in the haphazard introduction of micro-graphic technology by governments. One frequently hears of a microphotography applied to large volumes of inactive records. Far less frequently does one hear of a jurisdiction which applies micro-graphic technology in daily operations. Rarer still is the jurisdiction which has developed a comprehensive records management plan which balances, and integrates, where possible, the use of "hard-copy," micro-graphic, and computer records.

The Supporting Role of Depreciation

Ready cash is the best form of support for a state-of-the-art approach to capital replenishment. In my Part 4 discussion about reducing the cost of public debt, I pointed out that few leaders of governments of general jurisdiction in the United States support the application of the concept of depreciation, fearing its financial and budgetary implications. Yet, with reference to an existing capital stock, the advantages are significant and plain to see: Funded depreciation fosters a) capital project planning, b) timely capital replacements, and c) accurate costing of services, useful in setting service charges. Reserved depreciation allowances can promote timely acquisition of new or replacement assets, facilitating executive and legislature action. Additionally, depreciation allowances can be linked to deferred maintenance liability accounts to stimulate needed infrastructure maintenance.

As I advanced previously, governments should authorize 1) an annual program of investments in public facilities which equals or exceeds annual depreciation allowances, and 2) an annual program of investment which attains and maintains capital/labor ratios required for efficacious work.

I am not going to re-argue the case I have made for funded depreciation in public finance, except to re-state, for the reader's convenience, some of the technology-related benefits conferred by applying the concept:

"... depreciation allowances, if funded, would help governments mitigate the damage caused by capricious capital budgeting, especially regarding facilities and equipment replacement. Government facilities are typically littered with abandoned, obsolete and inefficient equipment. In contrast to business leaders, government officials are not known for their concern about capital/ labor ratios. No less than in business, efficacious work is fostered by providing employees with state-of-the–art equipment. Funded depreciation can free the equipment replacement process from the vicissitudes of capital budgeting, as reserves can be deployed on rational, timely schedules. Moreover, depreciation entries, as an instrument of cost recovery, provide information useful in determining the true cost of services, placing service charges on a sound basis."

VI. MANAGEMENT: Pursuit of Attainment

... explores proven pathways to the attainment of desired ends by an aggressive, accountable management of resources.

As the reader will recall, at the close of my introductory remarks, I stated that my vantage point was that of a chief financial officer supervising a comprehensive public finance establishment, including a unit responsible for the jurisdiction's budget function. Consequently, the following commentary on the ways and means of goal attainment in public finance work presupposes a government of general jurisdiction with a chief financial officer accountable for the conduct of 1) the recommended anticipatory process, and its documentation, and 2) budget formulation, and its implementation.

However, although my focus is on governments of general jurisdiction, I am confident that my commentary will interest finance officials serving governments of limited jurisdiction, including, in the U.S.A alone, thousands of special districts providing utilities, public education, etc.. Many special districts are formidable public institutions with substantial financial management requirements. . First, a few words about the concept of *management*—a popular term for the behavior of persons coordinating the factors of production. Historically, it is a relatively new concept. It is applied to behavior not as well described by kindred terms, including, most notably, supervision, oversight, administration and entrepreneurship. *Managers* seek the attainment of desired ends by aggressive, accountable coordination of resources. (An interesting question for the reader: Join me in thinking about why in baseball we have managers, but in football we have coaches?) Bringing to bear their implementation experience, managers also contribute to the formulation of the ends sought. Throughout this commentary, I have assumed that public finance officials entrusted with supervisory responsibilities consider themselves "managers," and accept the intellectual and behavioral implications of that identification.

At the dawn of the Industrial Revolution, the classical economists identified land, labor and capital as the key factors of production. Applying entrepreneurial savvy, proprietors put these factors into productive alignment. However, the rise and spread of formal organizations, especially enterprise corporations, required a more institutionalized approach to the coordination of specialized work. Compared to the subjective, charismatic and idiosyncratic dispositions associated with "entrepreneurship," management is 1) an objective "structural" condition which can be deliberately established and maintained within organizations, and 2) a skill which can be defined and taught to persons of appropriate aptitude. Today, the term, "management," not only has joined the classic trio of productive factors, but is deemed the most important agent in the performance of complex social and economic organizations.

Applying criteria of effectiveness, efficiency and economy as they go, "managers" strive to "get things done." Further, if this managerial injunction is expanded to read "get the right things done right," the criterion of appropriateness adds a moral dimension to the dynamic role of managers. To secure the dynamism suggested by the term, thousands of local settlements in the USA have adopted the council-manager form of government. However, we must also acknowledge that the dynamic dispositions associated with the term probably account for the failure to use the term, "manager," as a common position title in government hierarchies, where it seems reserved for use in public enterprises, if at all. Rarely does one find systematic use of the term, "manager' in official position descriptions, where hierarchical and functional titles are

VI. MANAGEMENT: Pursuit of Attainment

preferred. Certainly, this generalization applies to the position titles used to allocate authority and duty in public finance establishments.

As generally cited in management literature, at every level of supervision, managers "manage" by engaging in four inter-related activities designed to define (and energize) the work environment:

1) Planning (setting goals)
2) Organizing (allocating authority, accountability and responsibility)
3) Directing (prescribing procedures and assigning duties)
4) Controlling: (measuring and adjusting performance)

When these inter-related activities are dynamically conducted, the resulting coordinated effort produces goal attainment. It is effectiveness which provides managers with their *raison d'etre,* their reason for existence. However, the concept of management involves more than a single-minded focus on effectiveness, defined as goal attainment. Our management model also embraces the criteria of efficiency and economy, giving us an efficacy triad. These additional criteria indicate that the *manner* of goal attainment is also important.

In Part 2, *Instrumentalities,* I pointed out the management importance of *data about finance data,* indicating that such "meta" data provided the raw material of managerial thought applied to finance work. Ensuring the availability of relevant, accurate metadata is, in itself, a fundamental act of management, a condition precedent for subsequent management acts. Clearly, creating and using metadata is a defining characteristic of managers interested in getting the right things done right.

The expression of appropriate management thought should not be left to chance, or to the initiative of individual officials. *It can, and should, be deliberately cultivated by means of procedures requiring the application of management thinking.* This thesis is anchored by an axiom of organizational life that efficacious performance effervesces most frequently when consciously (on principle) cultivated by management leadership and design. This axiom locates the "cause" of organizational efficacy in the environment established and maintained by and for managers. It is administrative institutions which establish enduring conditions promoting efficacious work in pursuit of goal attainment. In this regard, Exhibit 1.1, Section D. *Foundations of Efficacious Public Finance Management,* listed preferred practices. Keyed to the budget cycle, practices 1 through 4 provide public finance officials with a series of opportunities to apply management thought. For the reader's convenience, Exhibit 6.1 reproduces this list of preferred practices.

EXHIBIT 6.1 Foundations of Efficacious Public Finance Management

D	MANAGEMENT	PREFERRED PRACTICE
1	Preliminary Work	Fiscal and budgetary perspectives.
2	Resource Acquisition	Revenue mobilization methodology.
3	Resource Utilization	Solution-centered, results-oriented budgeting.
4	Controls	Dynamic monitoring.
5	Management Motivation	The will-to-achieve.

With varying degrees of commitment and proficiency, governments engage in some or all of the first four listed practices. The importance of institutionalizing these preferred practices cannot be overstated. Activated at strategic points in the budget cycle, they function as cues, sparking appropriate managerial behavior, that is, action seeking desired objectives by 1) coordinating the use resources and 2) expressing the values of the efficacy triad. Each practice has a natural foundation in government work and can have an ideal development, *provided* accountable officials throughout the government possess and express appropriate motivation and talent. This critical proviso spotlights the determinant role of leadership, and skill.

VI. MANAGEMENT: Pursuit of Attainment

EXHIBIT 6.2 Budget Cycle Components

ANTICIPATORY PROCESS		BUDGETING	IMPLEMENTATION			
Current Fiscal Year, Months 6-8		Last 4 Months	Quarter 1	2	3	4
STUDIES	STATEMENTS	FORMULATION				
- Survey of Issues, Poblems and Opportunities. - Selection of Initiatives.	- Statement of Fiscal Capability - Resource Mobilization Methodology - Fiscal & Budgetary Perspective - Budget Call	1) Rationale 2) Goal Statement 3) Collaborators & Affected Parties 4) Conditions of Performance 5) Work Plan 6) Budget 7) Alternatives **ADOPTION**				
			- Work Plan - Allotment - Performance Review - Corrective Action	" " " "	" " " "	" " " "
			ANTICIPATORY PROCESS, Months 6-8			

Exhibit 6.2, *Budget Cycle Components*, places the preferred management practices within the major phases of a typical annual budget cycle in a government of general jurisdiction. As noted, a recommended program of decision-related research initiates an anticipatory process which culminates in the chief executive's call for budget estimates. Ideally, the process is designed to identify potential budget initiatives related to issues, problems and opportunities facing the jurisdiction. The process of settling on these initiatives is conditioned by the results of simultaneous inter-related reports concerning fiscal capability, and the prospects for mobilizing resources. Consequently, this integrated anticipatory process culminates with the development and publication of

a Fiscal and Budgetary Perspective identifying significant proposals, if any, recommended for adoption in the upcoming budget.

Also note that the fiscal year has been divided into quarters establishing periodic checkpoints for the exercise of formal, periodic performance reviews. As dynamic, rather than static events, these performance reviews should be conducted two-thirds through each quarter, providing a month for corrective action in those cases where the review indicates probable failure to attain projected goals by the quarter's end. This emphasis on dynamic monitoring rests on the belief that performance reporting after the reporting period is over is an ineffective ritual, serving an archival rather than management function.

To be conducted effectively, a jurisdiction-wide anticipatory process requires vigorous, thoughtful management, best provided by the government's finance establishment. By function and knowledge, the jurisdiction's chief financial officer is the appropriate official to organize and supervise the process, and produce the annual fiscal and budgetary perspective, and the draft of the chief executive's budget call. The day-to-day management of the research process should be assigned to budget officers familiar with the various subjects under review.

This assignment of management responsibility raises an important question concerning the role of planning agencies in the anticipatory process. Typically, governments of general jurisdictions establish planning agencies. Where established and professionally staffed, the intellectual contribution of these agencies significantly influences official thinking about the future. Obviously, available planning agency data, analyses and recommendations should strongly condition the formulation of fiscal and budgetary perspectives. Of course, this injunction assumes the existence of a harmonious, respectful relationship between the finance establishment and the planning agency. Reportedly, however, many finance officials are rather wary of planning agency activity, and vice versa. Mutual suspicion is usually rooted in an environment of competition and conflict. The reasons for mutual worries are understandable, given the fact that, inevitably, planning agency thinking

VI. MANAGEMENT: Pursuit of Attainment

has finance and budgetary implications, the thrust of which may not be appreciated by finance officials. Consider the following typical circumstances: Planning agencies play a dominant role in the composition of capital investment plans. Moreover, in many nations, planning agencies establish and maintain key relationships with donor agencies, including the multi-lateral financial institutions. If so, this connection provides planning agencies with a formidable power base. Further, planning agencies with responsibility for economic analysis are usually responsible for defining the relationship of prospective budgets to prospective estimates of Gross Domestic Product. This work usually results in a recommended "budget constraint." Representing a key variable in the determination of fiscal policy, the recommended constraint usually gets serious consideration during the formulation of prospective budgets.

Given the range and the financial import of these planning activities, it is not surprising that many finance officials are wary of planning agencies. On the other hand, planning officials may not eagerly seek and maintain consultative relationships with finance officials, who they may view as representing an institutionalized "No!" (It must be admitted, however, that true "program-oriented" finance officials are relatively rare.) Planning officials may regard the result of such consultations as "prior restraint," that is, pressure impinging on independent staff thinking and objectivity. This type of situation can be exacerbated when finance and planning officials pursue their work in relative isolation from one another. If so, they are more likely to be surprised and upset when recommendations surface during the anticipatory phase of the budget cycle. Regarding this prospect, knowledgeable observers have noted that competition and conflict are inherent factors in the finance-planning relationship, but, with disclosure and transparency, can produce better-considered decisions. Dynamic monitoring, as herein recommended, provides a handy institutional vehicle for enhancing disclosure and transparency across organizational lines. A dynamic monitoring process can be structured so that finance establishment and planning agency representatives participate in each other's periodic, formal performance reviews. Knowing what each other is doing during the fiscal year may help reduce tension between the staffs of these two important governmental units. Dynamic monitoring is discussed in some detail later on.

1. Preliminary Work: Fiscal and Budgetary Perspectives

Rationale and Methodology

Strictly speaking, the future is unknown, and, unknowable. Yet, pragmatically, we continuously count on regular recurrences, *ceteris paribus*. This tacit assumption of regularity has profound affects, for it emboldens us to anticipate and to plan. It has been wisely said that the assumption of regularity gives us the nerve to anticipate and plan, and most important, to act! As a case in point, budget adoption represents a legislative act of faith that desired programmatic values can be realized at a future time. Although this faith is usually braced by a predictable application of administrative and accounting controls, unforeseen contingencies usually require allocation adjustments during implementation. Legislative adoption of supporting statements of estimated revenue is also an act of faith, with a lower probability of realization. Clearly, given the importance of attaining revenue targets, governments are well advised to invest in proven ways and means of revenue mobilization, as will be recommended, to maximize collections in the face of inevitable revenue contingencies. In sum, although plans are manifestly fallible, conceived in terms of design and control, government leaders are well advised to engage in anticipatory exercises, thus institutionalizing leadership thinking about the future. Due to the intrinsic difficulties of prediction, a weak, haphazard approach to anticipating future events will surely waste time and resources, and, quite probably will have regrettable consequences.

Based on the results of a jurisdiction-wide survey of problems, issues and opportunities, an annual fiscal and budgetary perspective, preceding the formulation of the annual budget, serves to counter the

VI. MANAGEMENT: Pursuit of Attainment

conservative bias of the budget process by highlighting important considerations which should condition the budget for the coming year. Minimally, a well-crafted perspective would include an authoritative statement concerning the jurisdiction's fiscal capability based on a recommended revenue mobilization methodology. An annual perspective may be expected to condition budget deliberations, especially if the jurisdiction is committed to compliance with a "budgetary constraint," limiting deficit spending. Surely an honest assessment of the issues, problems and opportunities facing the jurisdiction should influence decisions about the distribution of available resources.

Governments are the key institutions for selecting and attaining desired community goals. However, government leaders vary in their willingness and capability to fulfill this expectation. As recommended herein, perspectives reflect the results of organized thinking about the efficacy of present and possible future policies and programs. As indicated below, thinking about the future takes three forms. The first mode of thinking about the future assesses the future consequences of current action. The second mode assesses the future consequences of current inaction. The third mode centers attention on the future consequences of future action, the most popular conception of planning, that is, doing something in the future to affect the future. Officials who participate in the development of annual fiscal and budgetary perspectives will undoubtedly find themselves engaged in all three modalities of thought. These three modes of thought provide a format for process controls, useful in monitoring the status of work on each issue, problem, or opportunity being considered during the development of a fiscal and budgetary perspective. A brief evaluation of each mode follows:

1) At the negative pole of a capability spectrum, one places those governments which pursue minimum service and regulatory policies, their leaders taking a rather fatalistic position on social and economic situations. The officials of these

governments are not likely to invest in developing fiscal and budget perspectives.

2) Those governments which strive to attain and maintain themselves in a harmonious balance with social and economic formations and forces in their environment may also, circumstances permitting, strive to establish desired future states and situations. Should these governments adopt formal fiscal and budget perspectives, their leaders will find that their ability to take advantage of opportunities, as they arise, will be significantly enhanced. Indeed, they may find that introduction of formal fiscal and budget perspectives produces a significant change in the fundamental relationship between the government and its citizens, with citizens expecting a stronger more efficient and effective management of services and regulations

3) Governments that formulate multi-year capital investment programs and practice solution-centered, results-oriented budgeting have already introduced processes consistent with the logic of trying to anticipate and control the future. The same may be said for governments which develop and implement land use plans and zoning. Officials of governments which already try to exert positive leadership in defining and realizing community goals will find that the formulation of fiscal and budgetary perspectives provides a comprehensive core process enhancing the effectiveness of all its policy and management tools, especially budgeting. .

VI. MANAGEMENT: Pursuit of Attainment

EXHIBIT 6.3 Developing Fiscal and Budgetary Perspectives

1.0 ORGANIZATIONAL REQUIREMENTS
  A. Adopt a research agenda, initiating the budget cycle.
  B. Organize, specifying the role and responsibilities of staff assigned to research teams, with budget officers serving as their secretariat.
  C. Communicate and Document, stressing consultation, clearance, disclosure and transparency.
  D. Control the research process, via dynamic monitoring.

2.0 PROCESS
  2.1 Survey Issues, Problems and Opportunities
    A. Conduct Public Forums
    B. Convene Technical Conferences
    C. Commission Technical Papers
  2.2 Formulate and Document Fiscal Capability
    A. Estimate resources and formulate a Mobilization Methodology
    B. Formulate a Multi-year Fiscal Capability Statement
  2.3 Formulate and Document Proposed Initiatives
    A. Select key issues, problems and opportunities
    B. Formulate proposed initiatives:*
      1) Define program rationale
      2) State goal(s) in a multi-year perspective
      3) Identify collaborators and affected parties
      4) Identify conditions required for goal attainment
      5) Formulate preferred solution(s) and tentative multi-year budget
      6) Identify alternatives considered, but rejected, and rejection rationale
  2.4 Complete and Submit Fiscal & Budgetary Perspective

* Proposed initiatives need be detailed to the extent required to establish them as candidates for budget consideration..

As my experience accumulated over the years, I came to favor the term, "perspective," rather than "plan" to identify the product of the anticipatory process, herein recommended. The term, plan (often coupled with "strategic"), suggests a narrowing of options, a series of precise steps and the specification of the "one best way" — characteristics which tend to vex political minds which crave options and prize discretion. In contrast, a "perspective" suggests a point of view—a presentation of related facts, opinions and possible happenings, displayed in a context of appropriate depth and latitude. The organizational and programmatic steps in perspective development are outlined in Exhibit 6.3, *Developing Fiscal and Budgetary Perspectives.*

Perspectives confer the following advantages: 1) Formulation of fiscal and budgetary perspectives, as recommended, tends to promote organizational cohesion by improving inter-agency communication. 2) Educational impacts of well-executed perspectives on officials and other interested and affected parties can be significant, and, indeed, this potential effect provides perspectives with sufficient rationale.

However, the strongest rationale for establishing an anticipatory organization and process, as outlined by Exhibit 6.3, *Developing Fiscal and Budgetary Perspectives,* lies in its stress on decision-related research, conducted outside normal budget and law-making channels. The dearth of decision-related research on public problems is a grave weakness of contemporary governance, world-wide. As the tide of science-based technological innovation sweeps onward, governments find themselves enmeshed in internal and external complexities which simultaneously demand new policy decisions, yet obscure potential consequences. These complexities confront officials with challenges to their knowledge, their experience and their will. In the web of interactions defining the complexity of modern life, "public problems" are increasingly difficult to properly define, let alone "solve" by legislative and administrative action. In many cases, the critical variables in the situation are beyond the reach of government. Significantly, the spread of wireless and internet-based communication has increased the volume of transmissions and information about public issues, without noticeably enhancing the effectiveness of public decision-making processes. If anything, the increase in the total flow of fact and opinion is tending

VI. MANAGEMENT: Pursuit of Attainment

to produce a daily plebiscite on what is "true" and "good," undermining the role of analysis, synthesis and deliberation in shaping public policy. The anticipatory process outlined by Exhibit 6.3 has features which institutionalizes systematic discussion and reflection on complex matters by qualified parties. As noted in Exhibit 6.3, the process of developing perspectives begins with a survey of issues, problems and opportunities, conducted by means of public forums, technical conferences and technical papers— a process designed to encourage the vigorous participation of non-politicized, non-bureaucratized parties. This helps to counterbalance the biases of legislators, administrators, and the influence of special pleaders who work tirelessly for their client's interest in the political background.

An anticipatory process is a complex undertaking. Consequently, when making organizational and procedural arrangements, the accountable officials are advised to recognize and respect this complexity. If not, the process will be ineffectively conducted and poorly related to key policy and management processes. Respecting the complexity, the accountable officials should consider the following factors:

> First, the process requires the cooperation of many parties, willing and unwilling, within and without government. (Many career-conscious officials regard assessments and projections as risky business, best avoided, if at all possible.) To adequately define issues, problems and opportunities, and formulate likely solutions requires a strong institutional commitment to research, consultation with affected parties and inter-agency collaboration. Minimally, the research agenda should include a) public forums, b) technical conferences, and c) technical papers. Moreover, the research requires valid, relevant data, and dedicated researchers, impossible to obtain and maintain without clear and steady institutional commitments. Furthermore, as the implementation of recommend

initiatives will require legislative support, organizational arrangements should include reporting commitments and the constructive involvement of policy leaders. Finally, the timely development of perspectives requires management attention and persistence, best expressed through dynamic monitoring of the process.

The anticipatory process should be completed no later than the end of the eighth month of the current fiscal year. This timetable permits the annual "call for estimates," initiating the budget formulation process, to reference the results of the anticipatory effort. Indeed, if it has been conducted as recommended, accountable program officials have been key participants and contributors to the process. Consequently, no accountable program official should be surprised by the contents of the "call for estimates." This procedure encourages program leaders and cost center managers to consider the proposed initiatives, and, if acceptable in concept, refine them as needed for incorporation in their budget requests. Ideally, the concerned program officials are free to modify or reject the proposed initiatives. Objection and rejection are always possibilities in an open process which is designed to elicit and respect facts and considered opinions.

The communication and documentation requirements for consultation, clearance, disclosure and transparency provides a necessary, but insufficient, foundation for effective implementation of any recommended initiatives. Effective implementation of programmatic initiatives requires the integrated employment of four key instruments: 1) work plans; 2) allotments; 3) dynamic monitoring, that is, periodic "before-the-fact" formal performance reviews; and 4) corrective action in cases of impending failure to attain stated goals. These instruments of implementation apply to the research program conducted during an anticipatory process. The requirement of dynamic monitoring is listed in Exhibit 6.3. At a later point, these instruments of implementation are explored in detail.

VI. MANAGEMENT: Pursuit of Attainment

Generally, even under the best of circumstances, government leaders find program and project implementation beset with difficulties. Indeed, observers familiar with the concept and practice of strategic planning frequently mention implementation failures. As a case in point, the following advice concluded a study of the failure of an economic development program in Oakland, California:

"The great problem, as we understand it, is to make the difficulties of implementation a part of the initial formulation of policy. Implementation must not be conceived as a process that takes place after, and independent of, the design of policy. Means and ends can be brought into somewhat closer correspondence only by making each partially dependent on the other." Pressman, Jeffrey L. and Wildavsky, Aaron B. *Implementation.* Berkeley: University of California Press, 1973. p143

The intrinsic difficulties of government program and project implementation deserve formal recognition and respect by officials supervising an anticipatory process. Emphatically, implementation should be the *first and abiding* concern of officials formulating program and project proposals. Consequently, before channeling time and effort selecting and formulating proposed programs and projects, the assigned research teams must weigh the possibilities of implementation, especially the vital matter of financial support for proposed initiatives. The following practices deserve consideration:

- Involve implementing officials, and interested and affected parties, in the anticipatory process. This is especially important in the initial survey phase, despite the risk that involving "beneficiaries" may unduly bias the research process.

- Conduct the anticipatory process before the start of the annual budget cycle, requiring the submission of the Fiscal and Budgetary Perspective to the chief executive prior to the call for budget estimates. Initiatives favorably noted by the call for estimates obviously have a high probability of adoption, and eventual implementation.

- Require the jurisdiction's chief financial officer to provide a multi-year fiscal capability statement early in the anticipatory process, estimating the resources available to support proposed initiatives. The concept of available resources embraces estimated 1) revenue growth, 2) uncommitted balances, and 3) borrowing power.

- Employ a selective approach to proposals, applying the criterion of implementability, referenced to the multi-year fiscal capability statement. Concentrating on implementable initiatives conserves analytical time and effort and tends to produce better proposal designs.

- Employ the jurisdiction's budget staff as the research secretariat, responsible for organization and conduct of the process, and the composition of the Fiscal and Budgetary Perspective. This procedure draws budget officers into program development at formative stages, reducing the chances of arbitrary revisions during budget formulation.

VI. MANAGEMENT: Pursuit of Attainment

The Foundation: Fiscal Capability

Obviously, fiscal and budgetary perspectives will be critically shaped by resource availability. By organizational logic, the jurisdiction's financial staff should define fiscal capability. When competently defined, fiscal capability effectively limits the scope and, possibly, the direction of decision-related research. A research team investing precious time and effort in considering proposed programs and projects that, no matter how meritorious, will require resources beyond the boundary of defined fiscal capability risks its credibility with officials, and the public, alike. It is also obvious that to be of maximum utility, statements of fiscal capability should be formulated very early in the research process, or, even better, preceding it.

EXHIBIT 6.4. Multi-Year Fiscal Capability Worksheet

	GENERAL FUND	Current Year Estimate	Budget Year	Budget Year + 1	Budget Year + 2
1.0	**RESOURCES**				
1.1	Prior Year Balance (Surplus or Deficit)				
1.2	Base Revenue Projections* (List Sources)				
1.3	Subventions, Grants, Donations, etc.				
1.4	Other Resources				
	TOTAL				
2.0	**RESOURCES APPLIED** **				
2.1	Operating and Maintenance Expenditures				
2.2	Debt Service				
	TOTAL				
3.0	**ESTIMATED BALANCE (Plus/Minus)**				
4.0	**ADD CONTINGENT RESOURCES** ***.				
	TOTAL				
5.0	**ESTIMATED BALANCE (plus/Minus)**				
6.0	**ESTIMATED BORROWING POWER**				

Notes:
* Base projections do not reflect any proposed rate adjustments, change in management practices, or new taxes, service charges, fees, etc.,
** Capital Investments are assumed to be charged to a Capital Investment Fund, or some such separate accounting entity. Additionally, Capital Investments should not be incorporated in this table as their very authorization may depend on the amount of available funds (surpluses) and/or financing (borrowing power) determined by the entries and calculations reported by this table.
*** Estimates assume the implementation of revenue policy and management proposals formulated by a Revenue Mobilization Team.

At this point, consult Exhibit 6.4, *Multi-Year Fiscal Capability Worksheet*. It presents a model worksheet for assembling and displaying financial estimates over a multi-year span. (The Worksheet assumes the entry of estimates formulated by the staff assigned to the mobilization of resources.) With regard to financial estimates, it is essential that the Fiscal Capability Statement provide a commentary clearly disclosing the assumptions that conditioned its projections. Requiring careful and thoughtful consideration, and composition, this commentary on assumptions represents a key contribution to a jurisdiction's fiscal and budgetary perspective.

Assuming that a jurisdiction uses a general, or consolidated, fund as its prime accounting entity, and that its capital investments are recorded and controlled by means of a separate accounting entity dedicated to that purpose, the general fund financial capability statement should not include projections for funding and/or financing prospective capital projects. The model worksheet provides three columns to register projected revenues and service expenditures for the upcoming budget and the following two fiscal years. If desired, the projection can be extended to cover more than three future years, although this step is not recommended. (With tolerable degrees of error, government officials may be expected to project revenues and expenditures for a two-to-three year period, but no longer.) Also, if desired, the model can be expanded to display the experience of prior years. However, from my point of view, historical experience should be excluded because its inclusion tends to encourage "mechanical" approaches (extrapolation) to projection, a tendency to be resisted. The problem of projection techniques will be addressed momentarily.

Line 1.1 registers the estimated surplus or deficit carried forward from prior year operations. Of course, at the time of its calculation at about the mid-point of the current year, the estimated surplus or deficit figure carried forward as available for funding the Budget Year will be the amount derived from the difference between estimated current year revenues and expenditures, posted on Line 3. The same procedure

VI. MANAGEMENT: Pursuit of Attainment

applies to the two ensuing years. Significantly, the worksheet displays revenues under two aspects, one projecting the "status quo," (line 1.2), the other, possible changes in revenue policies and rates (line 4.0). Line 1.2 records revenue estimates for all four years referenced by the worksheet. Revenues for the Budget Year and the two following years are to be projected using *current policies and rates,* with the proviso that they may be adjusted for anticipated changes in economic conditions which might affect collections. These calculations provide a revenue base for the Budget Year and two following years. It should be noted that revenues are "dependent" variables, that is, the amount collected is a "resultant," traceable to the behavior of "controllable" and "uncontrollable" environmental, policy and managerial variables. Consequently, the staff assigned to revenue mobilization must examine the context of each revenue, then formulate projections which 1) reflect the influence of "uncontrollable" factors (population, inflation, economic activity) on that revenue for the Budget Year, and the ensuing two years.

Lines 1.3 and 1.4 provide for the entry of estimates of subventions, grants and donations from other governments and parties, and funds flowing from miscellaneous sources not already entered in the table. As they are generally difficult to predict, conservative estimates are definitely in order here.

Under Line 2.0, Resources Applied, sufficient space should be provided for estimates for operating and maintenance expenditures assigned to a jurisdiction's General Fund, identified by function, agency, etc. In best practice, these estimates are formulated by the accountable program officials. In this connection, it should be noted that not all program officials will be comfortable with the responsibility for preparing projections, especially if they reach too far forward into an uncertain future. These officials should base their projections on current programmatic concepts and production techniques, and expected economic conditions. Obviously, these estimates, although projecting a programmatic the status quo, may require adjustment for anticipated changes in economic variables, such as wage and price changes which increase costs without changing production concepts or techniques. At this point in the anticipatory process, significant programmatic changes are contingent variables, subject to consideration in the upcoming budget process. Line 2.2 provides for the entry of the annual cost of servicing outstanding debt.

The worksheet provides two "bottom line" numbers which are of vital interest to research teams and the involved program officials contributing to the anticipatory process. Line 3.0, identified as Estimated Balance, registers the amount derived by subtracting applied resources (expenditures) from resources (revenues, etc.). This calculation results in a surplus or deficit. As previously noted, surplus amounts may be made available to finance initiatives explored during the anticipatory process. Entries identified as Contingent Estimated Balance on Line 4.0 reflect the addition of resources which might be made available through revenue policy and rate changes. However, as the proverb warns, "there is many a slip between the cup and the lip," initiatives to be supported by these additional resources should also be identified as contingent on adoption of the recommended changes in revenue policies and rates. Line 4.0 records the incremental revenue effects of recommended policy and management actions (adoption of new forms of revenue, intensified enforcement, expansion of coverage, rate revisions, etc.) having a predictable impact on the timing and amount collected in the Budget Year and the two ensuing years. Obviously the adoption of these recommendations increases the support which might be made available for the funding or financing of initiatives to be considered during the anticipatory process.

Line 6.0 permits the registration of the results of calculations related to potential borrowing, after the addition of additional resources. In this model, uncommitted balances, or portions thereof, are used as indicators of amounts available to pay annual loan principal and interest on new debt. Of course, the total new debt which can be supported by these amounts depends on the amortization schedule, the interest rate

VI. MANAGEMENT: Pursuit of Attainment

and the debt coverage ratio policy of the government. If surpluses are forecast, and the amounts can be assumed to continue to be available for a specified term, they can be deemed to be an *estimated uncommitted balance*, identified as "Y" in the following useful formula. Officials can use this formula to calculate *Borrowing Power* by dividing the estimated uncommitted balance (Y) by the following variables, appropriately combined as indicated:

$$\frac{Y}{(1/n + i) \times DCR} = X \text{ (Maximum Amount of Loan)}$$

Where:
n = Term of Debt in Years
i = Prospective Interest Rate
DCR = Minimum Debt Coverage Ratio

The form and content of Multi-Year Fiscal Capability Statements is, of course, subject to modifications reflecting differences in circumstances and budget and accounting concepts from jurisdiction to jurisdiction. Also the anticipatory process will undoubtedly produce proposals which alter the assumptions used to project revenues and expenditures. Indeed, it may be expected that the survey phase of the anticipatory process will address questions related to the efficacy of existing local government services and potential capital expenditures, matched to funding and/or financing requirements. (See the discussion in Part 4 concerning my recommendations for the "monetizing" multi-year Capital Improvement Programs.) Consequently, the resulting Fiscal and Budgetary Perspective should include an updated Multi-Year Fiscal Capability Statement, complete with entries recording the estimated impact (plus or minus) of research team recommendations.

Further Thoughts on the Anticipatory Process

Thus far, the discussion has centered on resources that pass through the government treasury: revenues, loan receipts and disbursements. Of course, cash resources are important, but the scope of an anticipatory process should embrace the entire government environment, private as well as public. Indeed, its wide scope is a distinguishing feature. Research teams cannot successfully address economic issues, problems and opportunities without considering the deployment of private resources. From a strategic point of view, it does not matter who provides the good that is sought, as long as it is provided in a manner that is satisfactory to the accountable officials. Without doubt, the anticipatory process can, and should, be used to encourage private parties to cooperate with one another and with the government to attain desired community goals. Finally, research teams may also recommend program and/or procedural changes that have much strategic merit, but do not have budgetary implications to any significant degree.

As noted, to be useful in the budget process, findings and recommendations developed through an anticipatory process must be submitted to the chief executive's office in time to influence the content of the annual call for estimates. The amount of time and effort devoted to the formulation of initiatives necessarily varies, depending on the complexity of the nature of the issues, problems and opportunities addressed. The starting date must provide sufficient time to (a) establish the assigned teams, (b) set a research agenda, (c) assemble and verify required data, (d) conduct the research, (e) formulate initiatives and (f) compose a report of findings and recommendations. Governments developing fiscal and budgetary perspectives for the first time are well-advised to start at least six months prior to the issuance of the call for estimates. The conduct of an initial anticipatory process will undoubtedly require more staff time over a longer period than that required once the assigned teams gain experience with the process. Once the process is thoroughly institutionalized, experienced staffs should be able to formulate the annual update in approximately 3 months. Thus,

VI. MANAGEMENT: Pursuit of Attainment

a starting date of no later than the beginning of the third quarter of each fiscal year is recommended.

The formulation of fiscal and budgetary perspectives requires the cooperation of many parties, starting with the chief financial officer's submission of research agenda proposals to the jurisdiction's chief executive for suggestions and concurrence. Prior to approval, the chief executive should consult with legislative leaders about the proposed agenda, taking their suggestions under advisement for consultation with the assigned staff. Documentation of the process should not be left to chance, or to the inclinations of the assigned staff. (Lost or misplaced documents, computer file accidents, unintelligible work papers, etc., are ever-present hazards in any research effort.) To obtain and maintain the required cooperation, the jurisdiction's leadership must actively support the assessment process. The jurisdiction's chief executive can appropriately express this support by these steps:

1) Announce the establishment of assigned teams, the research agenda and timetable.

2) Conduct a review of the work in progress one month prior to the due date for submission of proposed initiatives.

3) In concert with legislative leaders, conduct a public review of the recommended initiatives prior to issuing the call for estimates.

With all key officials participating, the recommended management review (Step 2) and public review (Step 3) will serve to advise all interested parties, including the public, about emerging recommendations and projections, and their implications for the jurisdiction's service and development plans. The management review is important as it provides a forum for defining and solving any remaining problems in completing the fiscal and budgetary perspective.

To merit legislative and public support for its recommendations, the assigned staff must do quality work. As a general rule, quality work requires concentration on key tasks and topics. In conducting its work, the assigned staff must balance its desire to do in-depth research on outstanding problems, issues and opportunities against the need to produce proposed initiatives for next year's budget. Essentially, the consideration of creditable initiatives, year after year, requires a consistent approach to the annual research agenda. First, staff and time constraints will not usually permit the assigned staff to conduct a comprehensive annual program of in-depth studies — and do it well. Second, even if the assigned staff could conduct comprehensive studies each year, the submission of more recommendations than the policy leaders of the jurisdiction are willing to consider would (a) waste valuable time, (b) frustrate the assigned staff, and (c) tend to reduce the credibility of the fiscal and budgetary perspective process.

Typically, officials are executing a current year budget when it initiates the formulation of next year's budget. In many cases, the current year budget will be a source of concern. Unanticipated events, unavoidable delays and revenue shortfalls are to be expected. If they are serious, and deemed uncorrectable during the remainder of the current year, these current year implementation problems should be addressed, and therefore listed at the top of the research agenda as "Unfinished Business."

Proposed priority initiatives have the best chance of effective and efficient implementation if the proposed programs and projects are 1) within the limits of estimated available resources, and 2) incorporated in annual budgets by means of regular budget processes. This latter requirement clearly establishes managerial accountability for implementation. This may include special organizational arrangements for implementation, such as, project teams and inter-agency "task forces."

The proposal format for initiatives outlined in Exhibit 6.3, *Developing Fiscal and Budgetary Perspectives* may appear intimidating, but addressing these topics in some detail provides assurance that a proposed initiative is well conceived and worthy of inclusion in the upcoming budget. This proposal format is similar to that recommended for formulating and documenting budget requests. A description of

VI. MANAGEMENT: Pursuit of Attainment

recommended proposal elements is provided in a section below devoted to solution-centered, results-oriented budgeting.

In summary, what outcome justifies an investment of a jurisdiction's resources in the development of an annual fiscal and budgetary perspective? "Effective implementation of efficacious programs and projects" is the short answer to this important question. Weak, ineffective policy and program implementation is acknowledged to be a key problem in government jurisdictions everywhere in the world. Indeed, at the time of this writing, the world's governmental landscape appears littered with inefficient, uneconomic and ineffective projects and programs. Obviously, as currently conducted, the budget process does not present a strong defense against the authorization and re-authorization of inefficacious programs and projects. Regrettably, budget formulation and adoption processes tend to perpetuate, rather than challenge, an existing distribution of resources, including inefficacious programs. Experience indicates that the programmatic distribution of resources usually changes only incrementally from year to year. Without a strong anticipatory process, as recommended, a customary "bottoms-up" approach to budgeting tends to cultivate justification, rather than foster objective judgment. How could it be otherwise with a process which gives program managers at all levels an annual opportunity to express their deep self-interest "in keeping what they have and getting more."

Projection Methodology

A brief discussion of projection techniques closes this commentary on Fiscal and Budgetary Perspectives. Those who use mechanical projection techniques tend to rely on spread sheet software to extrapolate past experience into the future, with insufficient consideration of policy, management or environmental factors which affect the expenditures and revenues in question. Methods, such as, "regression," and the application of percentage rates of change and fixed amounts to base amounts, are widely used in preparing multi-year financing plans. Statistical software facilitates the application of the "least squares" method of projection.

This method establishes a "trend line" for past events which can be used to chart future events of a similar nature. Although fast and easy, such methods of extrapolation are not preferred for the following reasons:

- For many reasons, public expenditures and revenues tend to vary, period-to-period. In most cases, the causes of this variation are unique in time and place, and will not recur. Consequently, a "trend line" fitted to unique past experiences does not provide an solid basis for projection.

- Even if variations in expenditures and revenues are relatively constant in past periods, extrapolation of this experience is only permissible if future conditions are expected to duplicate the past. Few situations meet this specification.

Most important, however, mechanical approaches to projection negate the management premise of the resource mobilization process next considered, which features deliberate adoption and implementation of actions based on research into revenue-influencing factors. This point deserves re-emphasis: Reliance on mechanical means of projection should be resisted by government leaders because their use sheds no light on what should be done to produce future revenues.

2. Resource Acquisition: Revenue Mobilization Methodology

As noted, the recommended anticipatory process initiating the budget cycle requires formulation of a resource mobilization methodology—a critical procedure requiring jurisdiction-wide cooperation. The required coordinated effort is crucially dependent on strong, continuous leadership best provided by the jurisdiction's chief financial officer.

VI. MANAGEMENT: Pursuit of Attainment

At budget formulation time approaches, government leaders must assess its capability to fund and, if loans are required, finance contemplated expenditures. By observation and report, the quality of this assessment varies significantly from year-to-year among jurisdictions. Apparently, government leaders invest in systematic revenue research only when inescapable "shortfalls" loom, and even then, tend to limit their exertions to closing a looming revenue-expenditure gap, or forego such exertions entirely in favor of borrowing money. Ironically, despite its transcendent importance, many officials seem to regard revenue mobilization as a rather pedestrian (even distasteful) process, necessary to be sure, but not attended by the interest and excitement associated with expenditures. Typical points of weakness include:

- The failure of governments to require chief revenue collection officials (who, wary of the viciousness of revenue politics, typically bury themselves in their collection routines) to provide systematic, jurisdiction-wide leadership and technical support for revenue policy and management research.

- Budget officers too preoccupied (fascinated would be a better word) with expenditures to give revenues the attention they deserve.

- The well-nigh universal failure of governments to require their program managers to pursue revenue potentials with the same intensity they devote to the formulation and advocacy of desired expenditures.

Revenue mobilization procedures are not nearly as rationalized, or consistently applied, as those invoked for expenditures. Most tellingly, the literature concerning revenue mobilization procedures is sparse, indeed, compared to the volumes available on expenditures. This brief recital of acknowledged deficiencies in the revenue mobilization process serves to introduce and justify the remedy suggested here, that is, the institutionalization of procedures for the mobilization of resources, using the formulation, adoption and execution of an annual Resource Mobilization Methodology (RMM) as its linchpin. Further, as revenue estimates are required to complete fiscal capability statements, the formulation of an annual RMM is a key step in the development of an annual Fiscal and Budgetary Perspective.

The following discussion of resource acquisition goes beyond RMM composition and implementation to include securing a) maximum returns on the investment of cash-on-hand and b) enlisting program managers in revenue mobilization.

RMM Formulation

Resource mobilization is hard, exacting work. For jurisdictions of general jurisdiction, it is a test of their management capabilities, that is, their power to attain desired ends by coordinating the application of resources. Doing it well requires persistent executive support, continuous coordination of efforts, a firm policy and management action plan and, then, relentless monitoring. Contrasted with expenditure formulation, which is infused with the interest of motivated officials and interested parties, the mobilization of budgetary resources requires a more principled management commitment to its institutional underpinnings. These underpinning include (a) clear, unequivocal expressions of executive interest, (b) adoption of research agendas and work plans, (c) assignment and supervision of researchers, and (d) periodic performance reviews. If properly institutionalized, as recommended, the resource mobilization process will provide government officials with well-grounded opportunities to 1) foster equity among those required to pay taxes, fees and service charges, and, 2) secure sufficient resources to fund or finance needed and desired programs and investments.

To be perceived as fair and effective, governments must actively strive for revenue equity and revenue sufficiency. Governments expressing

VI. MANAGEMENT: Pursuit of Attainment

these important public values (1) promote civic morale and cohesion, and, simultaneously (2) nurture financial support for beneficial programs and projects. Certainly, the maintenance of equitable revenue policies tends to make it easier to secure public support for measures which pay for needed and desired services and investments. In turn, governments which provide quality services tend to find citizens more willing to pay taxes, fees and service charges, making it easier to adopt revenue measures clearly related to valued service benefits. Thus, revenue equity and revenue sufficiency are complementary values, the struggle to attain one assisting in the struggle to attain the other. Conversely, an acknowledged deficiency in striving for either one of these values cannot help but impede the attainment of the other. Officials who strive for revenue equity and sufficiency will find their work facilitated by the annual production and execution of a Revenue Mobilization Methodology. The suggested process has an exceptionally strong rationale. It merits institutionalization, and leadership commitment.

Obviously, the revenue situation conditions the size and shape of service programs and public investments. Reciprocally, the size and shape of service programs and investments frequently affect revenue potentials, especially when service costs are partially or fully charged to service beneficiaries. Moreover, the implementation of revenue recommendations, itself, may require resources, and, thus, have budgetary implications. When revenue projections are incorporated in annual funding and financing plans, the supporting policy and management actions become significant monitoring considerations for those officials responsible for managing the jurisdiction's cash. Certainly, the ever-present disposition to delay the implementation of revenue recommendations (increases in service charge rates, for example), will reduce anticipated available cash, and depending on the overall situation, may disrupt expenditure plans. For these reasons, resource mobilization activities should be closely coordinated key management processes, notably budgeting, accounting, performance monitoring and the management of cash.

Recognizing the complexity of revenue collection, the following factors merit consideration: The collection of government revenues requires the collaboration of many parties, willing and unwilling, within and without government. Understanding the problem presented by each source of revenue, and achieving a satisfactory procedural solution, requires a strong institutional commitment to (a) thorough research, (b) consultation with interested and affected parties and, (c) inter-agency collaboration. Moreover, revenue research requires valid, relevant data, and dedicated researchers, impossible to obtain and sustain without clear and steady institutional commitments. Furthermore, as revenue recommendations usually require legislative support, organizational arrangements should include commitments to quality reporting and the constructive involvement of policy leaders. Finally, the timely formulation and implementation of revenue measures require management attention and persistence, best expressed through work plans and formal performance reviews.

RMM formulation and implementation requires the cooperation of all officials who have revenue collection responsibilities, usually a numerous group in governments of any size. To obtain and maintain the required cooperation, the jurisdiction's chief executive must actively support the RMM process. This support includes 1) establishing a RMM Team, 2) setting its research agenda and timetable, 3) conducting management reviews of RMM recommendations, when in draft form, and 4) conducting public hearings on draft RMM recommendations in concert with legislative leaders. With all significant revenue-related officials participating, the management reviews (Step 3) and public hearings (Step 4) serve to advise all interested and affected parties, including the general citizenry, about emerging revenue measures and projections, and their implications for the jurisdiction's service and development plans. These reviews provide a forum for defining and solving any remaining problems in completing the RMM Report.

With reference to team membership, a caution is in order. Avoid reliance on "position" as the criterion for assignment to the RMM Team, as this provides no guarantee of analytical skill or aptitude for research work. Jurisdictions of any size will have several officials who could

VI. MANAGEMENT: Pursuit of Attainment

be likely candidates to lead a RMM Team. Possibilities include a tax or revenue collector, treasurer, cash manager, chief financial officer, or budget director. The choice of team leader should fall on the technically qualified official deemed most likely to elicit the required cooperation from all officials who have revenue collection responsibility. Further, active participation of the jurisdiction's cash manager and treasurer (often the same official) in the RMM process is the best guarantee that its results will factor into the jurisdiction's cash flow forecasts. (At this point, it is worth noting that the cash management process, itself, may produce significant investment income.)

Archives. In conducting research on specific revenues, the assigned staff will draw on many sources of data. To facilitate its work, the staff requires ready access to files of basic data on all revenues, with these files kept updated. Minimally, the basic data files should include information on the following topics:

1. Name of Revenue
2. Legal Citation
3. Philosophical Basis (including observations about revenue equity/fairness)
4. Source(s)
5. Rate(s)
6. Collection Performance/Projection
7. Collection Effectiveness
8a. Collection Cost
8b. Service Cost (Useful in setting service charges)
9. Collection Efficiency

Additionally, pertinent information bearing on revenue collection (reports, articles, etc.), properly sourced, dated and filed, should be readily available. If regular accounting reports do not provide the data required for relating collection and service costs to revenues (data elements 8a and 8b listed above), the RMM Team must press for the maintenance of records which permit costs, direct and indirect, to be identified and assigned to revenues. Additionally, work hours should be so recorded when they can be clearly associated with the collection of specific revenues.

Work Plans. As pointed out at many points in this essay, and repeated here for emphasis, formal work plans and dynamic monitoring provide the best response to efficacy concerns. Consequently, in conducting its work, the RMM Team should apply the instruments of implementation to itself. As prime management instruments, work plans should be associated with the immediate supervisor responsible for the conduct of the assigned activities and tasks. Exhibit 6.5 provides an indicative example of a RMM Team work plan embracing activities/tasks, measurements of effort (work hours), outputs and checkpoints (milestones).

EXHIBIT 6.5 An Indicative RMM Team Research Work Plan

ACTIVITIES/TASKS	Month "A"	Month "B"	Month "C"	Total
1. Review Prior Recommendations Document Conclusions	Work Hours Due Date			Hours
2. Update Basic Data Files Task Completed	Work Hours Due Date			Hours
3. Study of Revenue Management Draft Completed	Work Hours	Work Hours Due Date		Hours
4. Study of Revenue "X" Draft Completed	Work Hours	Work Hours Due Date		Hours
5. Study of Revenue "Y" Draft Completed		Work Hours Due Date		Hours
6. Study of Revenue "Z" Draft Completed		Work Hours Due Date		Hours
7. Revenue Projections Task Completed		Work Hours	Work Hours Due Date	Hours
8. Composition of RMM Report Report Submitted		Work Hours	Work Hours Due Date	Hours
Performance Review	Due Date	Due Date	Due Date	Hours
Unallocated Work Time	Work Hours	Work Hours	Work Hours	Hours
Total Work Hours	Work Hours	Work Hours	Work Hours	Hours
Add Authorized Leave (Hours)	Hours	Hours	Hours	Hours
Total Paid Hours	Hours	Hours	Hours	Hours

VI. MANAGEMENT: Pursuit of Attainment

All supervisors charged with revenue collection duties should formulate work plans. These statements provide a basis for monitoring revenue collection activity. The monitoring process must not be left to chance and circumstance. Periodic performance reviews are required to evaluate the status of assigned activities/tasks, and to authorize corrective action to maintain progress, when indicated. The staff of centralized revenue collection units and the staff of revenue-collecting program units should be provided periodic opportunities to report (a) performance for the latest completed milestone period, (b) revised estimates for the current period, and (c) projections for the coming period.

Research Considerations. Clearly, I favor an analytical approach to calculating resource estimates. This requires that a RMM Team, and assigned staff, assemble data and knowledgeable opinions about the various factors likely to affect the amounts collected at various times in the future. Likely considerations are listed in Exhibit 6.6, *Worksheet: Revenue Projection Factors.* The required information must be diligently sought from appropriate agencies, public and private, and carefully documented for inclusion in the RMM files. When used in making projections, sources should be duly noted, and dated.

EXHIBIT 6.6 Worksheet: Projecting Revenue by Factors

	Revenue: _____ Date: _/_/_	Budget Year Estimate
	FACTOR	
1	Base Estimate	
2	Changes in Coverage: A) Subjects & Objects B) Remittances C) Delinquency	
3	Population Change	
4	Per Capita Income Change	
5	Change In Currency Value (Inflation, Deflation)	
6	Rate Changes	
7	New Developments	
8	New Revenue Sources	
9	Procedural Changes	
	TOTAL	

A brief discussion of each factor follows:

1. ***Base Estimate.*** Projected revenue for the upcoming budget year rests on a base amount to be entered on Line 1 of the Worksheet. As the factorial approach requires calculations of the plus or minus impact of likely changes affecting the current year situation, the base amount should be latest estimate of revenues to be collected in the current year.

2. ***Coverage***. This factor refers to plans to expand the effective coverage of revenue collections, that is, bring the actual collections of a revenue closer to the potential of that revenue. To encourage deep thinking on this critical aspect of revenue management, the worksheet lists three topics for consideration by the RMM Team:

> ***Subjects and Objects***. In considering this topic, the RMM Team must establish a reasonable estimate of the number of objects and/or subjects covered by the taxes, fees and service charges, then compare this estimate with current experience. If a "gap" is identified, the Team should formulate management plans to increase compliance, stating the estimated additional amount expected.
>
> ***Remittances***. In its study of potential, the Team must consider the possibility of "leakage," such as a business operator keeping a portion of the sales tax collection by submitting false reports, or, in the case of off-the-books cash transactions, no reports at all. (On the other hand, possessors of "dirty" money, also drawn from the underground economy, seek to "launder" it by making it subject to taxation. Although the receipts are welcome, this practice makes revenue collectors unwitting partners in illegal enterprises.) As every revenue collection system

confronts possibilities for the unlawful diversion of collections, or evasion, the RMM Team is well advised to review collection procedures in detail with experienced auditors, recommending action to tighten up procedures, where indicated.

Delinquency. In cases of persistent delinquency, the RMM Team should review the arrears, account by account, and, if the responsible officials are lax in pursuing delinquents, recommend vigorous action to collect amounts outstanding and to forestall new delinquencies.

3. ***Population Change.*** In general, changes in population size and composition influence revenue. But, the impact of population changes may not affect all revenues proportionately. Consequently the RMM Team should examine revenue sources for the applicability of the population factor, consulting expert opinion. To determine the revenue impact of population changes, the Team must quantify the relationship between population aggregates and particular revenues, establishing per person correlations, such as, movie tickets per person, restaurant meals per person, etc. These correlations can then be applied to population projections to derive object and subject data which can be used to calculate the amount to be attributed to impending population changes.

4. ***Change in Real Per Capita Income.*** Changes in real per capita income have an impact on many revenues. As incomes rise, people tend to increase their use of restaurants, and travel more, using hotels. This tendency increases hotel and restaurant sales tax revenue, if that tax is properly added to each bill and the proceeds faithfully remitted. As increases in real wealth work their way through an economy through "multipliers," the RMM Team should consult knowledgeable economists in assessing the impact of this factor on revenues clearly subject to its influence.

5. ***Change in Currency Value***. Changes in the value of currency, usually inflation, will automatically affect revenues with rates based on a percentage of the value of subject transactions, provided prices are not controlled. To apply an inflation/deflation factor to price-sensitive revenues requires that the RMM Team determine an estimate of inflation/deflation for the year of the projection. As with factor 4, consultation with knowledgeable economists is advised.

6. ***Rate Changes***. This factor includes the revenue impact of changes in rate policies, and, most importantly, changes in rates to reflect the impact of changes in the value of currency on those taxes, fees and service charges which are fixed amounts related to objects and subjects, rather than prices. Revenues that are not price-sensitive must be made so by deliberate and timely action changing rates. Failure to adjust rates to reflect inflation is a very common policy failure in many jurisdictions. Consequently, the RMM Team must give this factor strong attention, and reflect its resolve in its action proposals.

Certain revenues are price-sensitive. For example, a sales tax rate is defined as a percentage of sales. Consequently, sales tax revenues automatically increase if the prices of taxed commodities and services increase, and, of course, fall if prices drop. As the property tax is levied as a percentage of market value, it also qualifies as price-sensitive revenue, provided property is revalued frequently. Likewise, a percentage tax on movie viewers generates a price-sensitive revenue, provided the ticket prices are set in a free marketplace. In contrast, revenues, such as fees for tolls, public parking, water and sewer services, and many other service charges, which have their rates defined as fixed amounts, are not price-sensitive, that is, revenue does not automatically increase when prices increase. Consequently, the frequency of the indicated studies and the frequency of rate revisions should be related to the currency valuation experience, usually devaluation or, as it is popularly called, "inflation." Very early in the RMM process, the Team should consult with competent authorities to determine assumed rates of change in currency

VI. MANAGEMENT: Pursuit of Attainment

valuation to be applied to the years covered by revenue projections. If the prospective annual inflation rate is relatively low, say, under 2.5 %, biennial, even triennial, rate adjustments might be acceptable. But, if annual inflation is averaging more than 2.5%, waiting two or, perhaps, three years, to adjust rates will surely impinge on service and development programs.

7. *New Developments*. This factor encourages the RMM Team to consult with relevant officials to identify the character and timing of revenue-related developments over the projection period.

8. *New Revenue Sources*. This factor encourages the RMM Team to explore new revenue possibilities.

9. *Procedural Changes*. This factor encourages the RMM Team to explore the impact of rules, regulations and procedures other than those related to rates, which, if changed, could result in increased revenues and/or their more timely receipt.

Once institutionalized, the management environment of resource acquisition is fundamentally shaped by the requirements of the RMM process, especially its data demands and action timetables. Each year, the RMM process should produce the following key products:

1) Coverage studies and recommendations
2) Studies and recommendations concerning relationships between revenue and costs of service and collection
3) Rate revision proposals

The second procedures is undertaken to provide a solid basis for attaining the third, the most important of all RMM events: adjusting and updating the regulations governing taxes, fees and service charges.

Recognizing the critical importance of management, the RMM Team should also conduct an annual review of the efficacy of revenue collection. This review requires the RMM Team to assess the revenue-related activities throughout the jurisdiction. Management considerations include (1) the organizational complexities of the revenue collection process, (2) the special management requirements of revenue collection, and (3) the importance of time in collecting revenues.

Measuring collection effectiveness not only helps to attain additional revenue, but also helps to secure revenue equity by ensuring the coverage of all appropriate subjects and objects. Information on the potential subjects, objects and/or revenue must be deliberately sought by survey methods or by securing access to records and files maintained by relevant agencies. The coverage ratio is derived, as follows:

$$\frac{\text{Registered Subjects/Objects/Revenue}}{\text{Potential Subjects/Objects/Revenue}} \times 100\%$$

Keeping cost of collection ratios within the standard percentage set by the jurisdiction may require periodic organization and methods studies. Costs should include "direct" costs (salaries, supplies, etc.) and "indirect" cost allocations, including supervision, space costs, equipment depreciation, etc. The collection cost ratio is derived, as follows:

$$\frac{\text{Cost of Collection}}{\text{Revenue Collected}} \times 100\%$$

To be useful, costs and work time related to revenue collections should be recorded promptly, as incurred. If not a matter of accounting record, the RMM Team can apply cost finding procedures. (Interested readers can explore practical approaches to cost finding by consulting

VI. MANAGEMENT: Pursuit of Attainment

Joseph T. Kelley, *Costing Government Service: A Guide for Decision-making.* Chicago: Government Finance Officers Association, 1984.) With cost and revenue figures in hand it is then possible to derive the degree to which costs are "recovered" by payments by beneficiaries (users), or the reverse, derive the degree to which service is subsidized by other revenues. This experience provides benchmarks for projection and remedial action on rates when so indicated. Costs should include "direct" costs (salaries, supplies, etc.) and "indirect" cost allocations, (supervision, space costs, equipment depreciation, etc). Costs should also include the cost of collection. Amounts drawn from cost records for the most recently completed period(s) are divided by the amount collected for that period(s), as follows:

$$\frac{\text{Cost of Service}}{\text{Revenue Collected}} \times 100\%$$

Rate revisions are the most important research product. All recommended revisions should be based on the results of the indicated studies of collection cost and cost of service. The research foundation for rate revisions is also valid if the general price level is falling, rather than rising. The foregoing discussion has assumed the persistence of inflation. Although unlikely, periods of deflation may occur, requiring downward, instead of upward rate revisions. The practices advanced above to assist governments to cope with inflation will work equally well in periods of deflation.

Ideally, every tax and regulatory revenue should be subject to periodic studies, with managerial action and/or rate revisions recommended where indicated. Especially with regard to service charges, the cost of providing services should be determined each year, with rates promptly revised to meet the cost of service/revenue ratio standard. As a practical matter, however, governments may find it difficult to undertake a comprehensive set of studies and the consequent rate revisions each year, especially in the first years of RMM formulation, when governments will probably face significant gaps between the existing ratios and the standards here advanced.

It bears repeating that every revenue should be regarded as a "dependent" variable, that is, the revenue collected is a "resultant," traceable to the behavior of "controllable" and "uncontrollable" environmental, policy and managerial variables. Consequently, the RMM Team must examine the context of each revenue, then formulate projections which (1) reflect the influence of "uncontrollable" factors (population, currency valuation, economic activity, etc.) and (2) incorporate the revenue effects of recommended actions (coverage expansion, rate revisions, procedure modifications, etc.) having a probable impact on the timing and amount collected. At this point, I refer again to the revenue projection checklist of nine (9) factors which merit consideration by the assigned staff when projecting revenues. This recommended approach encourages the piece-by-piece construction of revenue projections, one year at a time, based on the revenue impact of proposed changes in revenue policy and management.

As previously noted, revenue sources are not equally important. Indeed, some are decisively more important than others, and, thus, deserve higher priority in assigning analytical work. As a general analytical process, assigned researchers should execute the following tasks:

1) Define issues, problems and opportunities
2) State goal(s), including multi-year targets
3) Identify collaborators and affected parties
4) Specify conditions required to secure goal attainment
5) Formulate work plans

Each task is briefly described, as follows:

VI. MANAGEMENT: Pursuit of Attainment

1) Achieving an adequate conception of the revenue in question is the first, and most important, step in revenue research. Revenues can (and should) be visualized as a dependent variables, defined in terms of issues, problems, and opportunities. This conception will influence the choice of goals(s), the identification of collaborators and affected parties, the specification of performance conditions, the composition of work plans and the subsequent performance reviews. Conceptually, the term, "problem," applies to a perceived gap between "what is," and "what should be." Problems arise when people perceive such discrepancies, and, then, define them as undesirable, that is, when reality is deemed unsatisfactory.

When this general problem concept is applied to typical revenue collection situations, two important performance gaps appear, one between the potential yield of any given revenue and the amount targeted, assessed and/or billed in any given period, the other between the amount targeted, assessed and/or billed in any given period, and the amount actually collected and deposited to the credit of the government. By definition, "potential" revenue exceeds that which is currently assessed or collected. To explore the coverage of any particular revenue, the RMM Team, and its assigned staff, will probably need data not readily available in the files, which will generally record only positive, rather than negative facts. In some cases, such as an advertising sign tax, the RMM will require field surveys to identify untaxed subjects and objects. In other cases, the RMM Team may make acceptable projections of potential revenue by using a combination of staff knowledge, existing data and reasonable assumptions, provided the action plan includes steps to test the projections. After all, potential revenue is only potential, if it can be collected.

2) Goal statements should include 1) action proposals reflecting identified performance gaps, and 2) projections of future revenue reflecting an analysis of conditioning factors. Using the factorial projection methodology, and starting with a base amount, RMM researchers should separately calculate the impact of each influencing factor, then add the amounts derived to arrive at a total estimate for the year. .

3) The implementation of an RMM is dependent on the effective cooperation of many officials and those subject to taxes, fees and service charges. The basic data files should provide a timely, accurate figure on the number of persons or organizations currently responsible for remitting payments, either as agents or principals. If the action plan for a specific revenue includes attempts to expand coverage, the RMM Team will necessarily formulate a new estimate of the number of subjects to support its estimate of potential revenue. In its consideration of affected parties, the RMM Team should review the collection experience, paying particular attention to complaints, delinquencies and evasions. This review of the behavior of affected parties may lead to recommended changes in procedure, and/or special training or publicity programs aimed at increasing voluntary compliance with the revenue

VI. MANAGEMENT: Pursuit of Attainment

laws. The Revenue Commentaries included in the RMM Report should disclose the extent of consultation with interested parties concerning proposed actions to be incorporated in the RMM, and indicate their degree of concurrence and commitment.

4) Meeting revenue collection targets requires coordinated, competently executed efforts. In formulating its proposals, the RMM Team must consider the practical aspects of implementation, the conditions which make performance possible. Performance conditions include institutional aspects (organization, staffing, staff capability, regulations, procedures, equipment) and the assumptions and standards which fundamentally influence the size, shape, direction, and feasibility of revenue proposals.

5) Work plans rest on theories of cause and effect. To properly formulate an RMM, the Team must evaluate the causal connection between the proposed action and the desired results. In cases of uncertain linkage between cause and effect, a common circumstance, the RMM Team may recommend an experimental action, aimed at building up better, more specific knowledge about performance conditions, revenue by revenue, for use in formulating future RMMs.

Given its historical impact on government purchasing power, and the likelihood of its impact in the future, inflation provides government officials with their most serious recurring revenue problem. Annual RMM recommendations for increasing rates on all non-price-sensitive revenues can certainly be justified. However, it is common sense, as well as sound managerial thinking, to address recurring problems with systemic, rather than a case-by-case, solutions. If the RMM Team expects rising prices to erode the purchasing power of non-price sensitive revenues for the foreseeable future, it should recommend adoption of a policy and supporting procedure for periodically adjusting fees and services charges. A systemic response to the inflation problem is considered the best option:

> *As a general rule, legislative bodies should avoid inserting fixed amounts when adopting its revenue-related legislation. Instead, they should adopt revenue-related legislation which incorporates a policy to protect the purchasing power of government revenues against the erosive impact of inflation by prescribing procedures requiring the timely adjustment of fee schedules and service charges by the jurisdiction's chief executive, setting standards for executive action, notice and reporting.*

The suggested legislation should 1) describe the problem addressed, 2) declare the policy of the jurisdiction with respect to the problem, and 3) set standards for policy implementation, including reporting requirements for legislative monitoring and timely notice to affected parties. The model presented below satisfies those specifications. It provides a vehicle for the exercise of legislative power to establish fees and service charges, and places the implementation of that policy under strict legislative controls, including a reporting requirement which provides a basis for legislative monitoring.

MODEL LEGISLATION: Effecting a Cost Recovery Policy

Whereas, the inhabitants of _____ [Jurisdiction's Name], and its visitors, will, in the course of

VI. MANAGEMENT: Pursuit of Attainment

their daily activities use its products, services and facilities, and

Whereas, the _____ [Name of Government] seeks to defray the net total annual cost of providing such products, services and facilities by imposing service charges, it is, therefore

Resolved, that the _____ [Title of Chief Executive] adopt a schedule of service charges for each fiscal year, effective on first day of each fiscal year, such charges calculated by the _____ [Title of Chief Financial Officer] to produce revenue equaling or exceeding ____% of the estimated net total annual cost for such products, services and facilities, excluding any estimated applicable grants from other governments, and it is further

Resolved, that, at least 30 days before the beginning of each fiscal year, the _____ [Title of Chief Executive] shall 1) report to the _____ (Name of Legislative Body) on estimated current year service charge revenue results, and 2) the charges to be imposed on the users of _____ [Name of Government] products, services and facilities during the next fiscal year, posting notice of a public hearing concerning the charges to be imposed and the justification thereof, and it is furthermore

Resolved, that the _____ [Title of Chief Financial Officer] reserve the revenue identified as depreciation allowances, such sums to be used for the timely acquisition of new or replacement assets, such acquisitions to be approved by the legislature, upon recommendation by the _____ [Title of Chief Executive].

This model provides 1) a timely, fair and effective method of preventing the erosion of purchasing power by inflation and 2) an explicit legislative declaration of its cost recovery policy (defined as a proportion of costs, e.g., 50%, 100%, 110%, etc.). Of course, the adoption of this recommended approach is dependent on an accurate calculation of costs. At minimum, the amounts collected should at least equal the cost of collection, such as expenditures for toll takers and parking lot attendants. Beyond that point, the amount of service cost recovered expresses the subsidy philosophy of the government concerned. Eliminating subsidies requires that service charges cover full costs, including indirect overhead costs and depreciation, plus provide a return for the employment of capital. The resistance to beneficiary payment policies is usually rooted in equity concerns, that is, the perception of economic hardship that prevents deserving potential users from accessing the subject services.

Obviously, the issues of cost recovery, principally "ability-to-pay," can be completely avoided by "privatizing" the provision of infrastructure and service. On economic grounds, "privatization" often offers an attractive alternative to the investment of public capital and subsequent expenditure for operation and maintenance by public forces. At the time of this writing, by all reports, governments across the world are actively pursuing the privatization option, especially those governments previously committed to the political philosophy of state capitalism. Realistically, however, the scope of true privatization (no public subsidies or service contracts) is limited by policy and/or technical considerations, and the fact that there is simply no profit in supplying many services provided by governments. In truth, governments provide many services less by willfulness than default. Consequently, across a broad spectrum of programs and projects, the government's problem lies less in shedding responsibility for service and infrastructure investments than in determining an appropriate degree of "cost recovery." Given this definition of reality, governments are well-advised to establish and maintain a resource mobilization process that can satisfy the demand

VI. MANAGEMENT: Pursuit of Attainment

for public capital by consistently probing the limits of cost recovery. A RMM Team, if established, can not evade confronting this issue, mandated, as it should be, to provide recommendations for improvements in the equity and sufficiency of revenues related to infrastructure emplacement and service programs.

RMM Report

In pursuing its work, the RMM Team accumulates valuable revenue-related information, potentially useful in shaping government policy. This information includes a) organized revenue-related data, b) studies of specific revenues, c) action proposals for improving revenue policy and collection performance, and d) revenue projections reflecting the implementation of the recommended action proposals. The usefulness of RMM information, however, depends on two interacting factors:

1) The willingness of policy and managerial leaders to use the results of the RMM research process to pursue the important public goals of revenue equity and revenue sufficiency.

2) The quality and timing of RMM Team reporting.

No one can guarantee the willingness of government officials to pursue important public values, but this much is certain: to discharge their responsibilities for revenue equity and sufficiency, government leaders require well-organized documentation concerning revenues within the general control of the jurisdiction. A timely RMM Report, prepared annually, is a significant step toward satisfying that requirement. Essentially, the Report should include: a) comments on the implementation of current year initiatives, especially those yielding unsatisfactory results; b) comments on the efficacy of revenue management; and c) concise reports on research results for specific revenues. These reports should use a standard format, as follows:

- Definition of issues, problems and opportunities
- Goals (including recommendations and projections)
- Collaborators and Affected Parties
- Conditions of Performance
- Work Plan

Also, the specific revenue reports should incorporate a table displaying collection history and forecasts, providing the reader with a perspective when reviewing the research findings and recommendations. Projection assumptions and methodology require careful and complete documentation. Finally, the RMM Report should provide a comprehensive table displaying the collection history and the multi-year projections for all revenues covered by the RMM.

Management Implications of RMM Implementation

The very nature of revenue collection has implications for management practice. Revenue collection officials must be ever attentive to "negatives," rather than "positives." As a general rule, what's not happening to revenues is more important than what is. Unless carefully designed to focus on delinquents, outstanding receivables, and unrealized revenue "potentials," the forms, procedures, records and reports related to revenue collection will inevitably center on collected, rather than uncollected funds. On balance, revenue officials should strive to limit the amount of staff time devoted to receipt and recording of revenues (positive data) in favor of increased staff attention to delinquents, overdue receivables and coverage deficiencies (negative data).

Revenue collection officials must also be ever attentive to the timing of receipts. As a general rule, time is not on the side of revenue

VI. MANAGEMENT: Pursuit of Attainment

collectors. The collectibility of revenue receivables tends to deteriorate, rather than improve with time, as the status of people, and their property and businesses, continually change with the changing circumstances of life. Delinquencies must be addressed promptly, before the first day of delinquency, if possible, to reduce the possibility of losses. Government liquidity, that is, its ability to meet its obligations, when due, depends on the timely receipt of revenues.

In sum, the RMM Team must be able to assess the reasons for significant "shortfalls" in performance, and encourage the formulation of recommendations for corrective action. (This process is of great interest to treasury officials, ever alert to revised estimates which alter cash flow projections) As stressed before and repeated here for emphasis, the failure to formulate work plans, and to conduct periodic performance reviews thereon, represents a very serious management deficiency. If performance data is not available to facilitate assessments of the efficacy of collection-related activity, the RMM Team should forcefully address this deficiency by recommending the formulation of the necessary work plans and the monitoring of planned activities and stated goals therein.

Even though, in certain cases, they may not approach potentials, the revenue targets incorporated in annual budgets must be treated as key management goals. Consequently, as an essential step in its periodic performance reviews, the RMM Team should examine the realization-to-target record for the last completed fiscal year, seeking (1) documented reasons for significant variations, positive as well as negative, and (2) documented management responses to perceived problems, especially lagging revenues. Assuming that its RMM process is initiated at the mid-point of the current fiscal year, the RMM Team should also examine the year-to-date realization of current year targets, provided the interim period target amounts have been thoughtfully, rather than arbitrarily, set, as in an arbitrary division of annual revenue targets by 12 or 4 to identify monthly or quarterly targets, respectively. Such arbitrarily set interim period targets are worthless and misleading.

Revenue-related officials should not only strive to collect the full potential of assigned revenues (effectiveness), but should stress economic and efficient collection procedures. Consequently, from year to year, the RMM Team should strive to reduce collection costs, increasing the net sum available for funding desirable programs and projects. Regarding fees for licenses and permits, collection costs should be less than the amounts collected. As indicated below, the relationship between the "cost" of collection and collected revenue may be also expressed in terms of work time, as follows:

UNIT MEASURE	DESIRED TENDENCY
Amount Spent per Amount Collected	Down
Amount Collected per Amount Spent	Up
Work Hours per Amount Collected	Down
Amount Collected per Work Hour	Up

Guided by period-to-period comparisons of collection ratios and unit measures, the RMM Team should formulate proposals to improve the relative efficiency of all collections. Ideally, every tax and regulatory revenue should be subject to coverage and cost of collection studies, with managerial action and/or rate revisions promptly adopted to meet the standards. Similarly, with regard to service charges, the cost of providing services should be determined each year, with rates promptly revised to meet the cost of service/revenue ratio standard.

Program Managers as Revenue Producers

Governments in the United States, and elsewhere, tend to concentrate major revenue collection responsibility in an official heading a specialized revenue collection unit, but, for reasons of cost and public convenience, delegate certain collection duties to program units. By organizational logic, the relationship between the chief collector and the officials

VI. MANAGEMENT: Pursuit of Attainment

of revenue-collecting program units is functional and collaborative, rather than authoritative. Given this common organizational arrangement, RMM formulation and implementation depend on 1) the skill of the jurisdiction's leading revenue collection official in securing cooperation from the revenue-collecting program managers, 2) the quality of the revenue management practices established, within the collection units, and 3) the active interest and support of the jurisdiction's chief executive.

The recommended formal resource mobilization process provides a jurisdiction-wide mechanism facilitating the constructive involvement of program managers in revenue production. Their active participation tends to increase consideration given to the application of the beneficiary payment principle in programs with cost recovery potential. Further, governments seeking to deeply embed the beneficiary payment principle in their system of budgetary finance may find that including funding data in programmatic cost center arrays is a good way to foster the revenue responsibility of program officials—a form of organizational behavior devoutly to be desired. (In this connection, the reader will recall that I opened my discussion of revenue mobilization with the observation that governments typically fail to require their program officials to pursue revenue potentials with the same intensity they devote to the formulation and advocacy of desired expenditures.)

At this point, consult Exhibit 6.8 A, *Model Performance Style Budget*. There the reader will note that the model budget includes a "Funding Plan" with its total exactly balanced to the total to be invested in programmatic activities. In concept, this format approach features a display which lists all revenues directly attributable to particular program of activities. This requires that all program-related revenues be identified with cost center classifications and codes. If the total of program-related revenues is less than the total programmatic investments, which is usually the case, other revenue sources must be tapped to effect a balance. In the model budget, the amount of program-related revenue is estimated to exceed the proposed investment. In this case, the balancing requirement is satisfied by showing the excess negatively, in effect, as a contribution to general revenue which can be assigned to support of other programs which do not generate sufficient revenue to meet costs. The Model Budget shows the Funding Plan adjacent to the cost center array it supports. The close association of funding plans with expenditures arrays in budget-related documents promotes staff identification with revenue production, and facilitates monitoring of revenue projections and collections during periodic performance reviews. This format approach is strongly recommended.

...

Cash Managers as Revenue Producers

Achieving goals related to liquidity and cash management requires coordinated actions involving every sector of a government. To play their role in the process of budget implementation, cash managers, usually treasurers, require 1) reliable information about prospective receipts and disbursements throughout the fiscal year and 2) effective influence with the key officials who can dynamically influence the flow of receipts and disbursements to maintain sufficient liquidity at all times.

In governments of general jurisdiction, cash flows toward the treasury from a complex of sources, including an ever-changing mix of taxes, regulatory fees, service charges, loans and grants. All these sources require unremitting management attention to ensure timely receipt, deposit and temporary investment, until needed to pay obligations. To ensure maximum investment earnings, every government should formalize its cash management process, frequently reviewing performance, especially the collection of outstanding receivables. Fundamentally, investment earnings depend on the interplay of 1) investment amount, 2) investment duration, and, 3) interest rates. Of these three variables, interest rates are the most problematic, being set by market forces and the decisions of monetary authorities.

In contrast to the capriciousness of interest rates, the size and duration of investments are much more controllable, and can be favorably

VI. MANAGEMENT: Pursuit of Attainment

influenced by coordinated, jurisdiction-wide management action, provided the finance establishment can transcend its own boundaries to supply government-wide leadership for a formal cash management program. Formal cash management programs foster the needed collaboration by fixing attention on the managerial factors affecting investment earnings.

If authorized to invest portions of its cash not immediately needed to pay pressing obligations, government cash managers, can be significant revenue producers, and, thus, should formulate and execute work plans aimed at the maximization of investment earnings. These work plans should focus on cash flow dynamics, best captured and controlled by means of a "Cash Flow Projection." These projections register the impact of receipts and disbursements on cash balances opening a specified period, which could be daily, weekly, monthly or quarterly, depending on circumstances. Benchmarked against recent history, cash flow projections provide cash managers with a basis for testing forecasts and assumptions about the flow of receipts and disbursements. Obviously, if the jurisdiction is using a formal revenue mobilization process, similar to that recommended, cash managers should have a good database for their planning.

If experience is any guide, cash managers frequently suffer serious information deficiencies, inhibiting their ability to make timely payments and invest maximum amounts not immediately needed. Information not only costs time and money, its assembly and communication requires the cooperation of responsible agency managers. These programmatic officials will forecast receipts and disbursements with various degrees of accuracy. To help register and evaluate such forecasts, cash managers are strongly advised to formulate work plans incorporating a cash flow projection, revising it regularly, based on accumulating experience. Benchmarked against recent history, cash flow projections provide treasurers with a basis for testing forecasts and assumptions about the flow of receipts and disbursements. In general form, for any given future period, cash flow projections include the following elements, an opening balance, plus expected revenues and receipts, minus expected disbursements, and the resulting ending balance.

As with all management activity, cash management programs require frequent review. Comparing year-to-date performance results with the targets set forth in the cash management work plan, this review should include a "stand-up" presentation by the cash manager, preferably given at a meeting of the senior officials of the jurisdiction. In these performance reviews, cash managers should discuss the efficacy of the key supporting practices identified in the cash management work plan, especially collection and timely deposit of receipts and disbursement forecasting by all accountable program officials. These presentations should include recommended procedural improvements needed to meet liquidity targets, and targets for investment amounts and duration.

The accuracy of cash flow projections depends on many factors, especially a) active pursuit of outstanding receivables, b) scheduling the payment of payables; c) prompt deposit of cash, and d) accurate disbursement forecasting by all service program leaders and cost center managers. Thus defined, cash managers confront a problem of considerable complexity. To think constructively about the management of cash, and to communicate their findings and recommendations to their collaborators, cash managers are advised to participate vigorously in the process of resource mobilization. Participation in a jurisdiction-wide RMM process not only provides data for the cash flow projections, but can foster needed jurisdiction-wide collaboration by focusing attention on the controllable factors affecting liquidity and investment earnings.

Fundamentally, investment earnings depend on the interplay of 1) investment amount, 2) investment duration, and, 3) interest rates. Of these three variables, interest rates are the most problematic, being set by market forces conditioned by the actions of central banks throughout the world. Because interest rates fluctuate, reflecting the mutability of market conditions, and, increasingly, the volatility of world capital markets, treasury officials can not be held strictly accountable for making good on their forecasts of investment earnings. They can, however,

VI. MANAGEMENT: Pursuit of Attainment

be held accountable for investment size and duration. In contrast to the capriciousness of interest rates, the size and duration of investments are much more controllable, and can be favorably influenced by coordinated management action, *provided* cash managers can transcend the boundaries of the treasury to exercise an acceptable degree of "functional supervision" with respect to all officials with revenue-collecting responsibility. .

The investment of cash should not to be considered a treasury sideline, based on ad-hoc decisions and guesswork. Despairing of accurate forecasts, many cash managers cope with uncertainty by using "rules of thumb." By their very nature, these arbitrary formulas usually err on the side of caution. Experience suggests that a regularly updated cash flow projection encourages treasury officials to develop and apply experienced-based decision rules which will help increase the ratio of funds invested over a period of time. Maximizing investment potential requires that cash flows be a prime subject of government-wide managerial thinking, planning and collaboration. Recognizing that important variables lie in hands outside the treasury, indeed, outside the finance establishment, governments are advised to ensure a strong role for treasury leadership in the total resource mobilization process. Treasurers (presumptive cash managers) must venture beyond the boundaries of their office to influence those operations which affect their ability to maximize investment yields. Governments may gain as much, or more, from this institutional leadership as they might from the exercise of pure investment savvy.

A cautionary note is in order: The introduction of procedures designed to increase investment earnings must cost less than the prospective gains. After all, investments to improve collection procedures (more frequent audits, pursuing delinquents, etc.) might cost more than can be gained in investment earnings at prevailing, or even higher interest rates. Then too, delaying vendor payments to permit and prolong investment periods, a frequent practice, may have an unfavorable impact on procurement prices and delivery, offsetting investment gains. Also, the investment of cash is by no means a costless activity. Consequently, treasury work plans should disclose the costs of earning investment income.

As in all sectors of well-managed finance establishments, efficacy should be an ever-present concern, in this case, concern directed to the costs of borrowing money. Obviously, it is best that governments do no borrowing at all, thereby eliminating interest payments. Indeed, using a "pay-as-you-go" approach, the funds reserved to pay for capital projects can be invested until needed, earning interest. With lead time to build up reserves, even large projects can be financed without incurring long-term debt. Next best, borrow for short periods, as the short-term market typically offers the lowest interest rates. If a government feels compelled to issue long-term debt instruments, the most costly financing alternative, the term should be a short as possible to limit interest costs. The alternatives in managing government indebtedness are explored at some length in Part 4, *Rationale: Aims of Attainment*.

The problem of uncooperative officials, and inaccurate or untimely forecasts, may be sidestepped by entering into investment contracts with banks or by participating in investment pools. "Interest from the day of deposit to the day of withdrawal," is certainly an attractive alternative to a treasurer tired of the unending battle with colleagues to determine cash flows. For a price, both methods shift a jurisdiction's investment decisions to competent institutions, bring a respectable return, and sharply reduce information and coordination requirements.

As investment returns are related to the size of investments, cash management programs encourage, indeed, demand the concentration of balances. When legally mandated, or politically dictated, bank account fragmentation is clearly a serious impediment to efficient management and investment of cash. Other issues may also arise in developing and executing formal cash management programs. Investment pools, for example, "ship money out of the jurisdiction," reducing local bank lending opportunities. At least that is the argument. Furthermore, socio-economic interests are sometimes associated with banks, which request

VI. MANAGEMENT: Pursuit of Attainment

deposits for the good of the cause, so to speak. Issues of a socio-economic character, such as bank account fragmentation, or attempts to coordinate cash management and socio-economic policies, must be given serious consideration within the framework of a formal cash management program. In fact, the overall success of a cash management program, measured by results, may hinge on how well the responsible cash manager and other finance officers handle politically sensitive socio-economic issues, if such issues surface in the jurisdiction.

As budget implementation proceeds, revenue and expenditure transactions intersect in the treasury bank accounts, where liquidity is the dominating concern. Governments maintain credibility by meeting their obligations, when due. As expressed in Part 1. *Core Agenda*, liquidity is the *sine qua non* of finance management, public and private. In precise terms, during budget implementation, receipts should equal or exceed authorized disbursements, lest cash balances ebb away. As pointed out above in the discussion of accounting support for budgeting, allotments and reservations provide proven mechanisms to establish a controlling linkage between program spending and the liquidity situation in the treasury. With regard to receipts, however, mechanisms linking collection processes with the treasury's liquidity situation are inherently less efficacious. Clearly, it is easier to modulate the flow of disbursements than to secure receipts which may be more dependent on the behavior of economic and social variables than policy and management actions. But, having given due weight to this basic limitation, it is still advisable to establish an institutional linkage between cash management concerns and the procedures for mobilizing revenues.

With few exceptions, government finance leaders find that maintaining desired levels of liquidity is an unending struggle to collect revenues and control expenditures. In the battle to maintain liquidity, rationalized banking practices can be an important asset.

In principle, given adequate accounting, government jurisdictions require only one bank account, and, perforce, one sequence of numbered drafts against that account. In practice, however, this principle is honored with "lip service," if at all. Governments maintaining hundreds, even thousands of accounts have been reported. In one noted case, during its flirtation with bankruptcy in 1974, the City of New York was reported to have thousands of bank accounts. One can only imagine the magnitude of the reconciliation problem this entailed, if even addressed at all.

As a widespread practice, fragmentation of banking practice must be a response to compelling realities. Indeed, government officials tend to maintain multiple bank accounts for a variety of political, administrative. geographical and legal reasons, including placating politically potent banks. Large scale jurisdictions have deconcentrated and decentralized programmatic units, many with revenue collection responsibility. Getting scattered collections promptly deposited requires convenient banking facilities.

Bank accounts are used to reserve funds for specific purposes. The impulse to maintain a bank account to sequester cash for a specific purpose is rooted in fear that the cash in question will be diverted to other purposes. Universally, benefactors tend to require dedicated bank accounts for their bequests, grants and loans. Undeniably, segregating cash in dedicated bank accounts provides a feeling of enhanced security for concerned interests. Unquestionably, inadequate accounting is the most compelling technical circumstance fostering fragmentation in banking practice. Given the availability of computerized accounting, however, the task of reserving assets for specific, particular purposes can be provided by an accounting system organized for the task. As governments across the world adopt and implement computer-based systems and generally accepted accounting standards, the availability of accounting procedures for reserving assets eliminates the principal technical reason for the proliferation of bank accounts. However, even this facility may not contain the impulse to establish bank accounts for fund protection. It must be remembered that, in the last analysis, financial security depends on the integrity and effectiveness of a jurisdiction's administrative and financial controls.

VI. MANAGEMENT: Pursuit of Attainment

Obviously, concentrating cash in as few bank accounts as possible facilitates cash management and the maximum investment of available balances at interest. Expert opinion tends to recommend one account for payrolls and another for vendor payments, with a minimum number maintained for special purposes. The availability of wire transfer technology supports this policy. This "minimalist" approach makes tracking and auditing bank account activity easier and at reduced expense.

3. Resource Utilization: Solution-Centered, Results-Oriented Budgeting

The Key Task: Budget Appraisal

As regrettably noted in Part 5, many chief financial officers are not responsible for budgeting. Thus, the depth of direct finance leadership involvement in the process of resource utilization varies with particular organizational arrangements. Unquestionably, the organizational location of the budget function is a telling indicator of relative emphasis. Indeed, one may safely assume that more stress will be placed on program, rather than finance values, in jurisdictions where budget formulation and implementation is not vested in the finance establishment. However, even if not directly responsible for budget formulation, finance leaders have a deep and abiding interest in the allocation process, because that process inevitably pits financial concerns against programmatic interests. Additionally, and significant for my purpose here, the ways and means of budgeting vary by jurisdiction, making generalizations about best practice problematic. Nevertheless, reflecting my experience, I dare say that governments can apply certain tested concepts and methods, which, if diligently implemented, can help their leaders "optimize" the deployment of public capital—the key ideal of public finance work.

The following commentary on resource utilization assumes that the recommended anticipatory process, organized and conducted under the leadership of the jurisdiction's chief financial officer, results in the issuance of the chief executive's call for the formulation of the upcoming year's budget. As the final document of the recommended anticipatory process, the Budget Call should be its most consequential document. (I am well aware that, in many jurisdictions, the Budget Call is a perfunctory document, short on directions and long on forms)   As befits the purpose of this essay on managerial thought in public finance work, my commentary dwells a formulation process shaped by a research-referenced Budget Call. As documents designed to facilitate coordinated efforts to attain the "best" allocation of scarce resources, Budget Calls are prime managerial instruments. In best practice the jurisdiction's chief financial officer should be responsible for the drafting and issuance of the Budget Call.

Ideally, budget formulation procedures should be designed to produce thoughtful, well-documented budget proposals, that is, proposals justified by the application of efficacy criteria, and thus can be deemed to have *intrinsic* merit. It is important to note at this point that the *relative* merit of budget proposals is a complex question, requiring the application of additional criteria. (My thinking about the task of budget appraisal, that is, evaluating the *intrinsic* and *relative* merit of budget proposals, is treated at length in a companion volume, *Budgetary Thought for Budget Officers,* Amazon, 2016).

Arguably, budgets and budget procedures now rival lawmaking as the most important instruments of governance. If so, this marks a signal development in the sweep of history because political thinkers have generally held that the making of laws by accountable legislators, and their faithful execution by accountable executives, was the essence of "good" government. However, even if we discount speculation about the relative importance of these two fundamental processes as public policy vehicles, the centrality of budgeting in contemporary governments is undeniable. Moreover, as the stakes grew with the growth of government, so did a perception that the forms and procedures of budgeting influence budgetary outcomes, that is, the process, itself, can not be regarded as an impartial instrument of policy. Giving this

VI. MANAGEMENT: Pursuit of Attainment

perception due weight, since the end of World War II, countless officials have tried various solution-centered, results-oriented alternatives to the traditional Line-Item form of budgeting (LIB). Their efforts to employ solution-centered, results-oriented budgeting have met with varying degrees of acceptance, enthusiasm and success in a variety of jurisdictions throughout the United States, including its Federal Government, and, increasingly, the world. In assessing this experience, one must admire the tenacity of numberless officials, who, despite manifest difficulties and disappointments, kept striving to bring the benefits of solution-centered, results-oriented budgeting to their jurisdictions. As evidence of this tenacity, pursuant to the adoption of the Government Performance and Results Act, 1993, officials of the United States Government made yet another attempt to employ the prototypical form of results-oriented budgeting, namely Performance Budgeting (PerB).

Concerning Budget Format and Procedure

By advancing a new way of channeling budgetary thought and action, the introduction of PerB, the earliest systematic alternative to LIB, stimulated thinking about the potential impact of formats and procedures on policy and management decisions. As is well known, this led to the development of three additional alternatives to Line-Item Budgeting, and to each other, namely, Program Budgeting (ProB), the Planning/Programming/Budgeting System (PPBS) and Zero-Base Budgeting (ZBB). Although they differ in procedural detail, all four alternatives to Line-Item Budgeting encourage officials to specify relationships between applied resources and results. Regrettably, however, the advocates of these alternatives to LIB directed attention to the novel resource allocation features of their favored approaches, slighting the necessities of budget execution, especially the requirements of appropriate administrative and accounting support. To this day, accountable officials have not satisfactorily addressed the implementation issues of solution-centered, results-oriented budgets, that is, budgets that support action resolving issues, solving problems and seizing opportunities—their true rationale.

The generally weak response to the implementation challenge of solution-centered, results-oriented budgeting is de facto recognition of manifest hazards and intrinsic difficulties. I will address the implementation challenge later on.

By directly associating agency appropriations with input summaries (personal services, contract services, etc.) or objects of expenditure (salaries, electrical charges, etc.), Line-Item Budgeting provides clear accountability for estimates, procurement, encumbrances and disbursements. Referencing commodity classifications and codes, assigned staff can accurately charge payments for personal services, commodities and contractual services to appropriate line-item budget allocations. Although acknowledging these virtues, critics rightly point out that Line-Item Budget formats and procedures do not explicitly focus attention on official accountability for performance. Now, obviously, even though they may be working with Line-Item Budgets, program leaders and cost center managers continuously think about performance. However, the format and procedures of the typical Line-Item Budget do not require them to systematically calculate, document and maintain specific relationships between applied resources, production techniques and results, variously defined as output/outcome/impact variables. Given the seemingly remorseless growth of public services throughout the world, this shortcoming is a serious deficiency. With the productivity of public capital defined as a core concern, it logically follows that public finance officers should express an abiding interest in forms of budgeting which relate allocated resources to well-defined issues, problems and opportunities, despite manifest hazards and intrinsic difficulties of implementation.

To date, the evidence paradoxically indicates that many jurisdictions have been willing to introduce forms of solution-centered, results-oriented budgeting, but have been slow or unwilling to support the introduction with appropriate administrative and accounting

VI. MANAGEMENT: Pursuit of Attainment

arrangements, condemning the enterprise to superficiality, if not outright failure. With specific reference to budgetary accounting, knowledgeable public officials, especially experienced budget officers, trace the failure to effectively practice solution-centered, results-oriented budgeting to accounting deficiencies. Experience strongly suggests that collateral changes in the supporting institutional arrangements must also complement the installation of the various alternatives to Line-Item Budgeting. Significantly, in the United States Government, the provisions of the 1996 Federal Financial Management Improvement Act support the latest attempt to install Performance Budgeting by requiring federal agencies to install management accounting. Although progress is reportedly lagging, the injunction to provide appropriate accounting support gives this newest effort a fighting chance to succeed, in contrast to previous attempts to install various forms of solution-centered, results-oriented budgeting without devoting sufficient attention to the administrative and accounting conditions of success.

The administrative elements of solution-centered, results-oriented budgeting embrace procedures related to a) data, b) documentation, and c) work planning. A discussion of these topics will be followed by a commentary on dynamic monitoring.

A) Performance Data Articulation and Use

Obviously, the first essential element needed for the successful conduct of solution-centered, results-oriented budgeting is the *articulation and active use of performance data*. Success absolutely requires 1) an appropriate array of performance indicators and 2) their effective use throughout the budget cycle. The second component of this two-component formula requires that performance indicators must prove effective instruments of budget allocation and implementation. This stress on effective use of performance indicators subjects the budget process, itself, to a performance test, that is, accountable officials must show that they are using performance indicators to allocate and implement budgets. This formulation directs attention to the critical role of official leadership in the successful employment of the tools and techniques of solution-centered, results-oriented budgeting. Putting it bluntly, given the essentially problematic nature of "performance" by public service agencies, it takes persistent, principled official leadership to make budgeting, itself, perform.

Truly a variable, "leadership" differs radically from administrative and accounting practices, which can be institutionalized with reasonable assurance that their prescriptions will influence behavior in desired ways. Leadership is a personal, rather than an organizational attribute, inherently idiosyncratic. However, the exercise of desired leadership action is not completely dependent on the vagaries of fortune. Leadership behavior can be taught and learned, as proven by the careers of military and business school graduates, and the cadre of "managers" providing non-partisan leadership in localities with the council-manager form of government. Ultimately, as human action of a desired kind rests on congruent belief, official action favoring performance articulation and use depends on internalized ideas and ideals. To express principled leadership, accountable officials must be inspired to champion performance articulation and use even when so doing can damage their position and deflate egos. It is this author's hope that this "what-to-think-about-it" essay will have this desired effect.

Sad to say, every jurisdiction of any size will have its quota of officials who, by inclination and vested interest, will resist any accountability system they cannot control. Identifying appropriate performance indicators, and overcoming resistance to their effective employment, requires accountable officials who relentlessly invest their time and attention in the definition, collection, validation and dynamic use of performance indicators. Given statistical probabilities, the desired leadership attributes will not be uniformly possessed by the members of any sizable cadre of accountable officials. Officials naturally rising to this desired standard of behavior do not occur in great numbers. Recognizing the problematic nature of performance in public programs,

VI. MANAGEMENT: Pursuit of Attainment

governments choosing to employ solution-centered, results-oriented budgeting, and succeed at it, have no choice but to support this choice by investing in administrative and accounting procedures that foster these leadership attributes, including systematic training and technical assistance programs provided to the entire cadre of accountable officials. (More on the subject of training later on.) Furthermore, accumulating experience indicates that officials who wish to use performance data in adopting and implementing budgets face a variety of impediments — a spectrum of endemic and endogenous difficulties found in legislative and administrative situations everywhere. The following commentary explores this critical problem, suggesting organizational and procedural solutions.

Essentially, an appropriation represents a legislative act of faith. In adopting budgets, appropriation authorities *assume* a rather linear relationship between their programmatic intentions and eventual results. Or else, why bother? For the mathematically minded, the production function of public budgets can be expressed algebraically by the equation, $y = f(x)$. In this equation, "y" equals the output/outcome/impact resulting from the application of "x" amount of resources, using various production techniques. However, it is well known that the production function assumed by an act of appropriation is frequently inadequately implemented, and its operational effects problematic. The experiments with various forms of solution-centered, results-oriented budgeting represent attempts to specify the relationship between the programmatic intentions assumed by an act of appropriation and eventual results. As indicated by the following list, the relationship of appropriations to results can be, and is, addressed in a variety of ways:

- Common practice: Responding to agency requests, program documentation and testimony, legislators appropriate in good faith, assuming that results, variously understood, will be forthcoming.

- Appropriations are authorized in increments, contingent on demonstrated performance.

- A substantial "base" appropriation is initially authorized, followed by incremental allocations, contingent on demonstrated performance.

- Independent objective/subjective ratings of agency performance influence legislative consideration of agency budget requests and subsequent appropriation allotments by administrative authority.

- Improvements in performance are rewarded with increased funding. (Assumes that public agencies normally perform sub-optimally, unless so stimulated.)

- Uncommon practice: Appropriation amounts, and the underlying program design, are influenced by the systematic application of formal allocation criteria, such as performance ratios, investment returns, marginal productivity calculations and mathematical models.

For all who are interested in the effective budgetary use of performance information, the last point in the list is the most desirable practice. Ideally, the relationship between appropriations and results should be reciprocal and dynamic, that is, appropriations should result in the anticipated results. In turn, results should influence the behavior of management and appropriation authorities. In reality, as noted by a legion of interested observers and practitioners, appropriation authorities (and, regrettably, many administrative officials) have not been noticeably

VI. MANAGEMENT: Pursuit of Attainment

impressed by presentations of operational results. Otherwise, how can one account for the frequency of instances where funds continue to be provided in the face of manifest performance disappointments and outright programmatic failures?

One likes to think that legislators (and administrative officials) place a premium on attaining anticipated results for funds expended. Often, they do not! Nevertheless, it would be rash to attribute legislative inattentiveness to sheer indifference. Generally, legislators do care about appropriation effectiveness. However, this concern is all too often superseded by more pressing legislative considerations, shaped by partisanship and the pressure of special pleas from socio-economic formations. And, as is well known, the agents of those formations interested in appropriations can be counted on to devalue and discredit performance data when indicated results may affect future budget allocations. Also, many legislators can be counted on to protect favored programs from performance-based criticism. Further, and even more disappointing, administrative agency leaders have been known to excuse, devalue and discredit negative operating results. Finally, as in all things legislative, the attitude of legislative leaders toward performance data and interpretations is a crucial factor. Legislatures lacking leaders who champion program efficacy (effectiveness, efficiency and economy) are not likely to develop and sustain a constituency interested in the budgetary use of performance data.

When and where it occurs, legislative disinterest in the budgetary use of performance data and interpretation is not only a serious procedural deficiency, but undoubtedly reduces administrative enthusiasm for the managerial use of performance data. Stating this thought positively, legislative attention to performance begets administrative attention to performance. Some observers and practitioners have also been concerned about administrative disinterest, attributing the lack-luster performance of administrative officials in the managerial use of performance data to foot-dragging and studied indifference. Indeed. It is a rare government that does not harbor officials, who, by inclination and vested interest, resist any accountability system that may report results potentially damaging to egos and future budgetary support.

Although program managers may actively resist performance evaluation, a policy of passive resistance is most likely. Obviously, only persistent executive leadership can ensure the faithful performance of key procedures throughout the jurisdiction. Experience suggests that this leadership commitment must be supported by special staff assignments, and vigorous follow-up, to authoritatively express the jurisdiction's commitment to solution-centered, results-oriented budgeting.

Budget officers and accountants continuously work with figures representing money. Data concerning results, however, is almost always non-monetary data. This data is unique to the program or project in question, and is almost always developed and recorded by the concerned program or project officials. This latter characteristic tends to render performance data suspect, especially to finance and budget officers because it is collected and presented by personnel who have a compelling interest in "looking good." In most governments, performance data is captured "catch-as-catch-can," stored in ad-hoc filing systems and occasionally related to expenditure and revenue reports by program leaders. Typically:

- Program and project personnel, who count, register and report events thought useful in evaluating performance, originally record performance data at work sites.

- Performance data is entered into records which make up fairly elaborate files, including original source documents, reporting forms and ledger-like records.

- Reporting and tabulation errors are rife in such "uncontrolled" recording systems (usually systems where money and auditors are not involved).

VI. MANAGEMENT: Pursuit of Attainment

The problems associated with performance data can be mitigated if officials are willing to take steps to guarantee data validity, such as, strictly enforced internal controls on the collection of data, independent surveys, sampling studies and field audits. Because performance data is so difficult and expensive to validate, few governments even try. Further, with reference to strict application of the above-cited criteria, one must not expect more precision than the subject matter allows, a wise observation of Aristotle. Certainly, it is fair to state that the expense of validating performance data is deemed a sufficient deterrent by most governments to inhibit the development and maintenance of credible performance data arrays.

Associating fees and/or service charges with performance indicators is an effective way to ensure the validity of performance data, because where money is involved, reporting procedures will fall under the scrutiny of accountants and auditors. With the fee schedule known, revenue reports can be organized to provide evidence of the volume of use, service or activity. Additionally, if performance data can be made subject to internal accounting controls, responsible program managers will be much more likely to foster the use of mechanical and electronic counting devices, and establish and enforce administrative controls, such as, double entry or cross-footed data recording, and tabulations and calculations which reduce the possibility of error.

To reinforce the key point, given the problematic nature of performance in public service programs, only persistent, principled official leadership, expressed through supporting institutions, can make solution-centered, results-oriented budgeting, itself, perform. Consequently, governments seeking to employ solution-centered, results-oriented budgeting are well advised to invest in, and enforce, administrative and accounting procedures specifically centered on the a) definition, b) collection, c) validation, and d) dynamic use of performance indicators. How best to attain firm institutionalization of these four inter-related activities?

Performance indicators range from descriptions of specific events and items to abstract concepts. They also vary in conclusiveness — ranging from indicators identified with "instrumental" program activities to indicators describing final programmatic "end-products." Instrumental performance indicators are very valuable because they provide the rationale for the formulation and execution of work plans, especially in complex programs where several interdependent units and/or processes are contributing to the attainment of a single end result. As they tend to identify specific countable events or items, instrumental performance indicators are not usually controversial. Given the problematic nature of performance in public service programs, however, one can frequently expect interested parties to challenge the representativeness, validity and measurability of indicators describing programmatic end-products, especially when indicated results may negatively affect budget allocations. Nevertheless, it is clearly better to identify "end product" indicators, and suffer controversy, than to have none at all. It is equally obvious that effective performance concepts and related data must be logically associated with programmatic activities. Therefore, *program and budget documentation* provides the best source of performance concepts which will command respectful attention from significant actors in the budgetary drama. Embedding performance information in budget documentation is a basic step in institutionalization.

In recent years, significant efforts to improve performance were underway in the United States, including an effort initiated by the Obama administration, to identify and remedy outstanding problems and invigorate the existing federal government performance system. Performance reporting by state and local governments attracted the concern of the Government Accounting Standards Board (GASB), which has developed "Suggested Guidelines for Voluntary Reporting of Service Efforts and Accomplishments," In a collateral (but independent) effort, a coalition of eleven public interest groups, working though a National Performance Management Commission staffed by the Government Finance Officers Association, published

VI. MANAGEMENT: Pursuit of Attainment

"A Performance Management Framework for State and Local Governments." These noteworthy efforts focus on the collection, use and dissemination of performance data, assuming, rather than addressing, the accounting requirements of solution-centered, results-oriented budgeting.

B) Program and Budget Formulation and Documentation

As noted, even if chief financial officers do not directly supervise budget officers, they have a vital interest in the quality of the budget formulation process. Exhibit 6.7, *Program and Budget Formulation and Documentation*, presents a suggested list of seven inter-laced topics to guide the formulation and documentation of solution-centered, results-oriented budgets. Requiring these seven related statements will tend to have predictable effects on the budget proposal process, all desirable, as follows:

1) Increase the probability that proposed allocations have a strong rationale, are well considered, and are anchored in specified relationships between intentions and results.

2) Provide a logical scheme guiding budgetary thinking, effectively 1) defining program rationale by defining issues, problems and opportunities, 2) setting goal(s), 3) identifying collaborators and affected parties, 4) specifying conditions of performance, 5) composing work plan(s), 6) formulating budget details, and 7) considering alternatives. The topical sequence is especially effective in centering thought on the ways and means of implementation.

3) Encourage an iterative thought process. The interrelatedness of the topics encourages budgetmakers to "go back and forth" among them, adding and amending as they develop the text of each topic. In this connection, the phrase, "the devil is in the details," points up the usefulness of shifting from the general to the particular, and then back again. By alternating levels of abstraction, this iterative process stirs the mind, sparking ideas, clues, cues, insights, and scenarios.

4) Provide a logical scheme for the composition and presentation of an appropriate interpretative text. As the text is open to choices concerning the level of abstraction, numeric displays can be inserted in text to provide selected levels of detail in support of general propositions. As a rule, no numeric display should be inserted in a text without interpretation.

5) Provide a base of evidence and logic to support dynamic implementation monitoring, facilitating the comparison of accumulating results against original intentions.

VI. MANAGEMENT: Pursuit of Attainment

EXHIBIT 6.7 Program and Budget Formulation and Documentation

	STATEMENT	SPECIFICATIONS
1	RATIONALE	A concise statement of the perplexities to be addressed, defined as issues, problems and opportunities justifying the budget. Identifies causal relationships (correlations) between key variables and desired results. .
2	GOAL(S)	As targets, performance indicators are defined in practical, measurable, time-bound terms.
3	COLLABORATORS AND AFFECTED PARTIES	In addition to parties (or units) providing (upstream) or receiving (downstream) assistance from the unit in question, identifies those to be served and/or regulated by the proposed activities, providing insight into the conferred benefits.
4	CONDITIONS OF PERFORMANCE	Description of factors required to produce goal attainment. These include institutional aspects (organization, procedures, staff capability, regulations, procedures, equipment, etc.), and most important, the assumptions and standards which influence the size, shape, direction and feasibility of proposed programmatic solution to the situation described in Statement #1.
5	WORK PLAN (Preferred Solution)	A two-part statement reflecting the preferred solution to the situation described in Statement 1. The first part provides a matrix, listing activities or tasks, assigned work hours allocated by time periods or milestones, and pertinent performance data, including ratios, such as output per work hour or unit costs. The second part provides a commentary relating the planned work to Statements 1, 2 and 3.
6	BUDGET	Supporting the preferred solution, a proposed budget (balanced by revenue) displays cost centers, performance data and interpretation.
7	ALTERNATIVES	A concise description of programmatic options considered, but rejected in favor of a preferred solution supported by a proposed work plan and allocation. Considerations include objectives, mix of resources and production techniques. These options should include at least one lower and one higher cost alternative to the recommended allocation, including the estimated impact on performance indicators.

Experience with this topical scheme attests to its salubrious effect on the quality of budget documentation, promoting the use of evidence and logic in the development of proposed budget allocations. To substantiate the premium placed on logical thinking and evidence, all cost center allocations should be documented according to the criteria cited above. Requiring such documentation provides a strong basis for performance data articulation and usage throughout the budget cycle. These seven statements deserve the extensive consideration to be provided momentarily.

In those jurisdictions where its chief executive submits a comprehensive budget document (in book and computerized form) for consideration and adoption by its appropriation authority, additional criteria apply. Because an adopted budget represents an understanding between legislators and program officials on what is to be done, bought or sought, the style and content of published documents should meet literary, rather than, let us say, public relations or accounting standards. An informative content, clarity and brevity are the prized virtues. Public budgets should be compact and readable, the acid test being the ability of policymakers and citizens to gain an unaided grasp of the program implications of expenditures and revenues. Budget narratives should integrate and explain all numerical displays. This means, of course, that a great deal of thought must go into the layout of budget pages. If in book form, pages should be printed on both sides. Summaries need to be carefully organized, as they control the number of program titles to be shown, hence the number of pages required. The literary quality of budget documents is a matter of topic selection and emphasis. The rules are 1) choose a level of abstraction which does justice to the issues involved in each program, and 2) avoid extensive detail (there is no space to waste) and generalities. In addition to accuracy in all computations and estimates, every budget document should reflect the underlying thought. This requirement means that budget preparation formats should correspond, as much as possible, to the format and content of the published budget.

VI. MANAGEMENT: Pursuit of Attainment

This also tends to ensure that the literary ideals of "good" budgeting are widely diffused among program officials.

At this point, consult Exhibit 6.8 (A & B), *A Model Performance Budget,* This two-page exhibit provides an indicative example of a budget book text displaying expenditures and revenues related to output/outcome/impact indicators. Funding a technical high school, the model incorporates a section allocating proposed investment (expenditures), presented in cost center order, a funding plan balanced to the proposed educational investment, an array listing estimated benefits accruing to the proposed investment, a performance data array presenting targets, a "cross classification" linking programmatic cost centers to education purposes, and unit cost calculations. These arrays are accompanied by an interpretive text.

EXHIBIT 6.8 (A)   A Model Performance Budget

SECONDARY EDUCATION
Technical High School

COST CENTER	BUDGET
Auto/Aero/Power	1,200,000
Business	420,000
Construction	480,000
Electrical/Electronic	720,000
Graphic Arts	1,020,000
Health Services	240,000
Mechanical Trades	1,300,000
Services	629,000
Total	6,000,000
FUNDING PLAN	
State Aid	2,000,000
Industry and Business Grants	4,500,000
Property Taxes	(500,000)
Total	6,000,000
ESTIMATED BENEFITS	
Personal Satisfaction	+ but ?
Diffusion of Knowledge	+ but ?
Broadened Options	+ but ?
P.V. Extra Income Per Student	85,140

Rationale. This budget funds 1500 students, 83% of total applicants, lowest ratio in Tech history. See the Five-Year Forecast for a discussion of this problem. Achievement ratios are expected to rise, but under expectations.

LAST YEAR	THIS YEAR	INDICATOR	BUDGET
80	85	% Above Reading Norm	90
75	80	% Above Math Norm	85
90	92	Attendance Ratio	95
85	87	Graduation Rate	90

As also noted, the graduation and attendance ratios, estimated to improve this year, are set higher next year. The marginal cost of attaining targets is estimated at $100,000 in computer expense and extra counseling. Curriculum design is based on annual surveys of skill demand in the community, and alumni "feedback." The distribution of resources to the School's dual objectives is displayed by the cross-classification.

VI. MANAGEMENT: Pursuit of Attainment

EXHIBIT 6.8 (B) A Model Peformance Budget

COST CENTER	ACADEMIC ATTAINMENT	VOCATIONAL ATTAINMENT
Auto/Aero/Power	480,000	720,000
Business	170,000	250,000
Construction	190,000	290,000
Electric/Electronic	290,000	430,000
Graphic Arts	410,000	610,000
Health Services	100,000	140,000
Mechanical Trades	520,000	780.000
Services	250,000	370,000
Total	2,410,000	3,590,000
Number of Students	1,500	1,500
Unit Cost	$1,607	$2,393

INTERPRETING ESTIMATED BENEFITS. Graduates are expected to add an estimated average of $10,000 to their annual income during the first 20 years after graduation. This incomes stream has a present value (PV) of $85,140, discounted at 10%. The public's investment in the average graduate is currently estimated at $16,000. After age 16, students contribute their time, measured by foregone earnings, estimated at an average of $10,000. Thus, the investment, private and public, in a technical education is estimated to total $26,000. Subtracting this investment from $85,140 yields a net present value (NPV) of $59,140 attributable to the Technical High program. Additional benefits are listed. The notation "+ but?" indicates that these benefits are deemed positive, but are of unknown value

MARGINAL PRODUCTIVITY. The academic attainment budget is up $100,000, balanced by a decrease in the budget for vocational attainment. In the opinion of the faculty, this shift will not reduce their ability to reach the indicated targets.

FIVE-YEAR FORECAST. Holding unit costs constant, the budget may be expected to rise by $400,000 each year to accommodate enrollment to 1,800 students, the design capacity of the school

	BUDGET	STUDENT ENROLLMENT
Budget Year	$6,000,000	1,500
Furure Year Two	6,400,000	1,600
Future Year Three	6,800,000	1,700
Future Year Four	7,200,000	1,800
Future Year Five	7,200,000	1,800

As befits the concept of solution-centered, results-oriented budgeting, to qualify as a cost center, a cost aggregation should be linked to a measure of performance. As emphasized, every cost center should be associated with a manager who shall have sufficient authority to be accountable for meeting, and exceeding, performance targets. To provide documentation for operating and maintenance budgets, and to stimulate thought and planning, every cost center manager should undertake the following tasks:

1) Describe program rationale by defining the issues, problems and opportunities to be attacked programmatically.
2) State goal(s) as measurable, time-bound, practical objectives.
3) Identify collaborators and affected parties.
4) Specify the conditions required to secure goal attainment.
5) Formulate the preferred solution(s) and a work plan(s).
6) Formulate a budget in a multi-year perspective
7) Identify alternatives considered, but rejected

Tasks 1 through 4 constitute the diagnostic phase of budget formulation. All seven tasks, taken together, provide the preferred approach to the formulation of solution-centered, results-oriented programs, and their supporting budgets and work plans. Constituting a set of guidelines for budget formulation documentation, these seven tasks are discussed in considerable detail below. For a snapshot version of these guidelines, revisit Exhibit 6.7, *Program and Budget Formulation and Documentation.* .

1) Rationale: Define Issues, Problems and Opportunities To Be Attacked Programmatically. Public programs are variously designed

VI. MANAGEMENT: Pursuit of Attainment

to a) resolve issues, b) solve problems or c) seize opportunities. However described, accountable officials formulating program and budget proposals tend to visualize programmatic situations in "problematic" terms, that is, as "problems" to be solved by programmatic activity. (Here a note about terminology is required as I am using the term, "problem" as a convenient abstraction also covering "issues" and "opportunities." After all, both issues and opportunities, although they refer to qualitatively different situations, must be converted into solvable problems to be addressed programmatically).

Theoretically, the term, "problem," defines a perceived gap between "what is," and "what should be." Problems arise when people perceive discrepancies between "what ought to be and what is," and, then, define them as undesirable. For example, consider a common problem in government-vendor relationships: vendors *ought* to be paid no later than 30 days after receipt of their invoice, but reportedly this rule is frequently violated. In this case, the accountable finance officer should address this perceived gap between ideals and reality by determining the cause(s) for laggard payments, then revise accounts payable procedures.

How should accountable finance officers go about framing specific goals related to the prime concerns listed in the core agenda? First, accountable officials should visualize each concern as "problematic," that is, open to diagnostic thinking by a questioning mind. Reaching this state of mind requires inquiring officials to resist the ever-present tendency of the human mind to jump to conclusions. *In terms of time and attention, diagnostic thinking in a problematic situation deserves the greatest weight in the goal-setting process.* In defining an issue, problem or opportunity, in the context of budgetary documentation, one should be specific, as scientific as possible, and brief. The following guidelines should be helpful:

- Explore the logistical and demographic characteristics of the situation. What, why, where, when, who and how questions are helpful in this regard. (Remember: implementation is the Achilles' heel of policy and programming!)

- Reference facts. Avoid unqualified comparative and relative terms, such as, "many," "most," "inadequate," etc.

- Identify causal relationships, noting correlations, critical factors, controlling variables, predicates, etc. *Identifying and defining "controlling variables" is the most important step in applying managerial thought to finance work, and, indeed, to any public program.* All programs rest on theories of cause and effect, notably expressed by the linear equation: $y = f(x)$. They provide the "raison d'etre," or rationale, for budgets, and the activities they finance. To be satisfactory, statements concerning program rationale should identify the variables, which, if programmatically attacked, can alter the problem situation in desired ways. Moreover, identifying gaps that are to be programmatically closed puts boundaries around proposed solutions. As noted below, budget proposers may amplify their theory of causation presented by their commentary on Performance Conditions.

- To keep rationale statements brief, incorporate material by reference, stick to the point, and use data arrays. Obviously the findings and recommendations of pertinent studies and audit reports will be helpful in this endeavor, and

VI. MANAGEMENT: Pursuit of Attainment

> such references should be noted in commentaries concerned with program rationale, that is, with issues, problems and opportunities.

Dwelling on this last point, references to the findings and recommendations of pertinent studies and audit reports can be brief, and sources footnoted. This tends to ensure that pertinent study recommendations and audit findings receive appropriate consideration during the problem formulation phase. If pertinent study and audit findings and recommendations do not influence the content of proposed work plans and budget, such omissions require explanation.

As both issues and opportunities must be transformed into solvable problems to merit budget consideration, the term, "problem" can be used generically. As noted above, a problem can be visualized as a gap between *what is* and *what should be*. Most assuredly, the diagnostic thinking called for by the third point, causal relationships, is a response to perplexity. Obviously, awareness of a problematic situation precedes a search for solutions.

It is best that budget officers adopt a skeptical cast of mind when reviewing statements of program rationale, lest they led to dwell on symptoms, or worse, erroneous questions. Moreover, it should be noted, budget review is not an academic exercise. Reflecting time constraints, the diagnostic process described by the third point must be oriented toward action (decisions), rather than knowledge for its own sake (an academic preoccupation). Such "decision-related" research must be of sufficient scope and depth to identify the "controlling variables," Because the identification of "controlling variables" justifies actions which might decisively alter problematic situations in desired ways, they logically influence the choice of goals, the identification of collaborators and affected parties, the specification of performance conditions and work plan(s).

It is always tempting to employ conventional wisdom in defining problem situations. Suppose a program leader or cost center manager has been assigned to formulate a work plan and budget for the collection of parking violation fines. A poor collection ratio could be blamed on judicial leniency toward offenders when they are brought to judgment, the residential mobility of violators, the "scoff-law" behavior of perennial violators, etc. Although such definitions may be "true," do they describe a situation which may not be efficaciously addressed programmatically, with intent to alter it in desired directions? The fact that the assigned staff may not directly attack certain variables, such as judicial leniency in settling cases, even though the negative impact on collections is significant, and can be specified, makes this type of controlling variable worthless in a problem statement. Indeed, serious consideration of such variables tends to excuse, rather than encourage, a search for those controlling variables which, if attacked programmatically, can enhance performance. Causal variables can also be deemed valid, but their impact may too weak to justify specific program and budgetary commitments. For example, *teacher accountability for student achievement* describes a valid, but inherently weak correlation. Vast sums of money, public and private, are annually allocated in reliance on this theory of educational efficacy. (To my mind, positing *student accountability for student achievement,* provides an alternative controlling variable centered on the ways and means of learning, rather than teaching.) The reader will find further comment on the influence of causal variables in educational programming and budgeting later on in my discussion of work plan formulation.

Blaming poor performance on inadequate staffing is also a causal variable frequently appearing in problem statements. Although such observations may be valid, they do not belong in problem statements because they do not address the cause of problems, but instead identify failures to respond appropriately to programmatic problems, properly defined. Finally, in passing, we should note that mission statements are often confused with problem statements. Because mission statements assume programmatic solutions, rather than define issues, problems and opportunities, such statements are best formulated and expressed in the context of work plans.

VI. MANAGEMENT: Pursuit of Attainment

Although brevity is prized, the problem diagnosis must be sufficiently broad and deep to identify the key variables which may be made subject to programmatic activity. At this point, consider the sample problem and goal statement which follows: It draws from a review of accounting procedures in an American city of 250,000 citizens:

"In the 1978-79, a total of 150,905 transactions were registered in our accounting system. As originally submitted, 142,712, or 94.6%, of these transactions were accepted, as initially entered. The remaining 8,193, or 5.4%, were rejected for the following deficiencies: 1) insufficient budgetary balance to permit recording of encumbrances, payment vouchers and payrolls, 2) incorrect coding, 3) lack of agreement between the total of items and amounts cited in batch controls, and 4) incorrect dates. By type of document, errors occurred most frequently in the processing of a) budget entries, especially transfers, b) payroll charges and c) encumbrances for purchase orders and contracts.

A sampling study of the correction process indicated that an average of 12.4 days pass before these deficient entries are corrected and successfully re-entered, consuming an average of 14 minutes of work time per item in the process. The direct cost of work time and other expenses to effect these corrections was estimated at $25,000. Additionally, in 76% of the cases, complaints concerning late payments to vendors were related to original entry deficiencies and the time lag in their correction. Errors were traced to poor design of forms, classification ambiguities, overly complex codes, and deficiencies in staff behavior, including, most notably, procrastination in recording needed budget modifications.

The fact that the rejected entries were eventually corrected and successfully re-entered, suggests that remedial administrative action directed at the causes of error can increase the rate of correct original entries. As some error is inevitable, a 99% acceptance rate is set as the performance target for original entries in the coming year."

In addition to identifying key variables, the sample statement directs attention to causal relationships between these variables and an undesired outcome (erroneous entries), even though the relationships, themselves, are not mathematically specified. This points the way to programmatic action which might decisively alter the "problem" situation in desired ways. *Indubitably, identification of critical controlling variables and causal relationships is the first and fundamental step in program and budget formulation.*

As most organizations maintain cost center continuity over the years, budget formulation documentation should also include interpretations of current year progress, measured against stated targets. This provides an indispensable platform for the development of proposed work plans for the upcoming year.

2) State Goal(s) As Measurable, Time-bound, Practical Objectives. Goal statement composition is best achieved when accountable officials engage in a structured diagnostic process embracing 1) rationale, 2) identification of collaborators and affected parties, and 3) performance criteria, that is, specification of the conditions needed to ensure goal attainment. If pursued vigorously, and with scholarly rigor, this diagnosis should produce goal statements which satisfy the criteria for such statements. Experienced managers avoid completely verbal goal statements in favor of statements embracing numerical terms. For example, concerning the obligation to pay obligations when due, the following statement provides sufficient precision about ways, means and ends to meet established criteria for goal statements:

VI. MANAGEMENT: Pursuit of Attainment

During the next fiscal year, the controller and treasurer, assuming the requisite degree of cooperation from program leaders and cost center managers, intend to pay 99% of vouchers no later than 30 days following receipt of vendor's invoice.

Providing another example, referring to the quality of accounting, the following statement provides sufficient precision about when, who and what to meet the criteria for goal statements:

During the upcoming fiscal year, the ABC Accounting Unit intends to increase the rate of accurate original entries from an estimated 94% in the current year to 99%.

Goal statements flow logically from the problem diagnosis. Goals provide a foundation for work plans and the subsequent periodic performance reviews. Goal statements should express measurable, time-bound and practical objectives. Goal statements with numbers are better than completely verbal statements. Numerical goals tend to ensure that chosen goals are practical and measurable. To be practical, a goal must be attainable by a specific time. Remember, success in budget implementation depends on choosing goals which are practical, that is, attainable. Obviously, work plan composition, featuring milestones (performance checkpoints), require numerical goal specifications. .

To re-emphasize, goals provide an indispensable, irreducible ingredient of managerial thought. Goals infuse work, and work plans, with meaning and direction. They provide a platform for the assessment of performance. Because managers are justified by aims sought and attained, the composition of goal statements requires the most careful consideration. In composing goal statements, consider using the following parts of speech:

> **Time:** Specify duration or deadline in an opening dependent clause.
> **Responsibility:** Identify agent of action as the subject of the sentence.
> **Commitment:** Use a verb to express the form of action.
> **Impact:** A verbal phrase, or indirect object, may be needed to express impact.
> **Goal:** Express as the complement or objective of the sentence.

Examples of appropriate language inserted into the recommended sentence structure:

> **Time:** *After_____, ,... During _____, ...By _____,... etc.*
> **Responsibility:** *the _____ team...the _____ unit...the _____ staff...etc.*
> **Commitment:** *will...plans...aims...intends...etc.*
> **Impact:** *to increase... to improve... to reduce.. to produce... to conduct...etc.*
> **Goal:** (Specify the goal in measurable terms) e.g:, *"from an estimated 94% in the current year to 99% next year."*

3) Identify Collaborators And Affected Parties. As experienced program officials know all to well, within a complex government organization, program units are usually dependent, to some degree, on the effective delivery of services by other units, notably centralized process agencies. In turn, program units may deliver services to other program units. Overall government efficacy is frequently dependent on recognizing and nurturing these "upstream" and "downstream" relationships.

The responsibility of budget officers for trans-organizational relationships (whether contemporary, upstream or downstream of any

VI. MANAGEMENT: Pursuit of Attainment

particular unit of government) has been previously noted, and is re-emphasized in my commentary about Statement 4, below. Further, every program has a clientele, willing or not. An accurate description of affected interests lends precision to the goal statement and makes it possible to evaluate impacts and benefits. Affected interests comprise those, organized or not, perhaps even unborn, who are to be affected by the expenditures outlined in the multi-year financial projection. Because the description of impacts and benefits depends on a good description of program clientele, it pays to be as accurate as possible in identifying affected parties.

4) Specify Conditions Required for Goal Attainment. To ensure that programs and budgets are based on sound operating concepts, proposers should prepare a commentary on performance conditions. This commentary should focus on the criteria, standards, and assumptions which infuse and support proposed work plans. Program officials should use this commentary to provide evidence of operational competence in attaining performance targets. As noted in the commentary on program rationale, every programmatic activity rests on a theory of cause and effect. In primary health care programs, for example, allocations are assigned to prenatal care on an assumption that significant health benefits will accrue to mothers and babies. In another example, the attainment of family planning goals is assumed to be partially dependent on certain postnatal events which are keyed to a timely post-partum examination of recently delivered mothers. There is no doubt about it: correlations, or causal relationships, provide the firmest foundation for program planning and implementation. Proposers should consider, and document, the connection between their proposed activities and the desired effects. When goals rest on specified causal factors, the relative effectiveness of these factors in goal attainment can be measured, and, if indicated, result in corrective action to close perceived performance gaps. Performance feedback, in general, is known to have positive effects on achievement. (Its an important causal variable in educational programming.) Work plans and budgets should, therefore, reflect commitments to take advantage of this powerful causal concept.

Reflecting the specialized nature of production, many programs are based on the application of professional or craft standards. These standards influence the size, shape, and direction of programmatic activity. Therefore, expenditure requirements reflect their influence. Failure to recognize, fund, and enforce performance standards is a major source of waste, inefficiency and ineffectiveness in government programs. Standards abound. As a case in point, public works organizations have established standards for road construction and maintenance. In hospitals, nursing teams seek to apply standards to patient care. Such conceptions are derived from experience and, thus, deserve serious considerations in the formulation of work plans and budgets. In yet another example, drawn form a primary health care budget proposal, noted the following performance conditions.

> "Currently, we do not conduct independent checks for quality of service in the clinics. In 1987-88, we plan to initiate a system of spot checks to assure quality care, including a systematic sample of patient experiences and opinions. Although clinic operators are not regulated by appointments, screening procedures ensure that needy/urgent cases receive priority treatment."

As previously noted, in complex organizations, all units are dependent, to some degree, on the effective delivery of services by other units within the total organization. Budget officials have a particular responsibility to ensure that the performance of program units is not hampered by the poor performance of accounting, engineering, maintenance, purchasing, printing, human resources, legal, and other centralized process agencies. For the benefit of their superiors and budget officers, program leaders and cost center managers should

VI. MANAGEMENT: Pursuit of Attainment

clearly point out these dependencies, and the effect of poor delivery on their performance.

To recapitulate, correlations, or causal relationships, provide the firmest foundations for program planning and implementation. The recommended diagnostic focus is designed to discourages premature adoption of programmatic answers, favoring instead, consideration of what, why, where, when, who and how questions. Thus, program leaders and cost center managers are encouraged to assess the program environment before settling on how-to-do-it, operational arrangements, and supporting budgets. Provided that the diagnosis provides sufficient grounds to justify further consideration, they may proceed to the development of program approaches. Formulation of a work plan(s) and budget follows the determination of a preferred program design. Together with related statements on Rationale, Goal(s) and Collaborators and Affected Parties, this required commentary on Performance Conditions completes the diagnostic phase of the budget formulation process.

5) Formulate the Preferred Solution(s) and Work Plan(s). Referencing the diagnosis, define and document the production program giving the most promise of attaining stated goal(s), efficaciously, and with least negative side-effects. Essentially a management proposal, this statement describes the coordinated deployment of resources, in time and space, applying specified tools and techniques to resolve the issues, solve the problems and/or seize the opportunities identified in Statement 1.

This proposed production program will necessarily specify presumed linkages between input and output variables. Drawing an example from educational practice, teaching "causes" learning. The presumed linkage between systematic instruction (measured by work time, costs, or curricula specifications) and student performance is undoubtedly the most important presumption in the educational practice, now, and in the past. But, there are others. In fact, educational programs are based on a number of presumptions about the cultivation of learning, such as age grouping, ability grouping, pupil/teacher ratios, educational attainments of teachers, teacher experience, etc. Each of these conceptions is granted a certain degree of conventional validity and, as a consequence, is treated as an important causal variable within school environments. The programmatic and budgetary implications are obvious. The responsibility of program and budget reviewers is also obvious: Presumed, but unproven, linkages should not be accepted at conventional value. Each should be assessed, seeking to specify its impact as an independent variable on student performance.

Specification of linkages is exacting, and I might add, exasperating work. Referring again to teaching-learning relationships, linkages believed to be productive resist specification, leaving their contribution to student achievement undocumented, but still conventionally appreciated. Yet, even if presumed causal relationships are vexing, no program leader, cost center manager or budget officer should turn away from this work. If production functions are unspecified, alternatives cannot be properly assessed and benefits ascribed.

What to do? In cases of uncertain linkages, budget officers are advised to recommend an action-research, or experimental, approach to allocations, aimed at building up better, more specific knowledge of production functions for use in future budgets. Indeed, treating all program allocations as experiments is the best way to combat the ever-present inertial tendency of the appropriation process. An experimental approach is aided-and-abetted by referencing both linear and multi-variate correlation equations, where the relative strength of independent variables "influencing" the distribution of resources can be illuminated.

Unquestionably, computer technology has made it far easier for officials to employ mathematical modeling. No jurisdiction can go far wrong by expecting its program leaders and cost center managers to employ mathematical modeling as a technique of programming and budgeting. The practice of mathematical modeling has many valuable side-effects, including, most importantly, inescapable inducements for critical thinking. With the advance of computer technology, it is easier

VI. MANAGEMENT: Pursuit of Attainment

to add multiple identifiers to a jurisdiction's chart of accounts, exploit the utilities of management accounting and model expenditure patterns.

It is axiomatic that those who cannot maintain an adequate conception of overall mission and effectiveness are forced to specialize in trivia, suffering impaired judgment and reduced relevance in the bargain. Modeling procedures enable accountable public officials to rise above the flood of minutia. In order to model, they must 1) slice through facts and values to isolate key programmatic variables presumed to make significant differences in performance, and 2) allocate resources accordingly for the attainment of desired goals. If they can specify the relationship of key variables to one another, and to desired goals, they will be able to construct and use models in programming and budget formulation and implementation. Although one must be cautious of logical pitfalls in interpreting correlations, thus recommend only their experimental use, I freely predict an expanding role for correlation studies in the future of public budgeting.

As hypothetical statements, models involve an ordered set of assumptions about causes, effects, and objectives. Models can be very elaborate, but not so necessarily. Variables abound! The search for variables can put a variety of viewpoints to work. Indeed, modeling exercises offer opportunities for constructive participation by collaborators and affected parties identified in Statement Three of the suggested budget formulation and documentation topology (See Exhibit 6.7). Allocation proposals developed according to the specifications listed in Exhibit 6.7 help to identify likely independent and dependent variables that can be used to build models. The search for variables should also include reviews of technical and critical literature related to the subject matter in question.

By exploiting existing data sources, or by organizing special data arrays, officials can employ correlation studies to assess the relative weight of independent variables. If a selected independent variable is found to be sufficiently influential in practice, the budgetary implications are obvious. On the other hand, should any independent variable prove to have little or no impact on the dependent variable (the objective), other variables may be substituted in the equation, and tested for significance,

It is one of the great advantages of modeling that, once equations have been established, a model builder can test likely variables, searching for that combination of variables which reduces the amount of "unexplained" variation to a minimum. While not minimizing the computational problems involved in modeling, it is fair to say that problems of data availability and validity will prove the most vexing. Measurement problems should not cause us to turn away from significant variables. After all, if we give up because of measurement difficulties, we will not be able to model at all, as many of the most significant variables in public services resist measurement.

Summing up, the abstract nature of models centers attention on important and effective variables, to the exclusion of all else. Their use especially benefits budget officers, who are frequently distracted by peripheral issues and administrative trivia. Additionally, modeling practices treat budgets as rather continuous experiments, undermining the inertial power of customary practice. Models belong in every jurisdiction's budget toolbox. Definitely, program leaders, cost center manager and budget officers should cause them to be built and used.

With a preferred solution in hand, the program proposer can proceed to develop the required work plan(s) for the deployment or the requested resources.

6) Formulate a Budget, Plus a Two-Year Projection, Including a Funding Plan. This statement should include a multi-year projection of program costs and a financing plan (taxes, grants, service charges, etc.). By bringing the future into the present, this projection helps to alert budget reviewers to the implications of the alternatives preferred by budget proposers. Be sure that each year's funding estimates equal or exceed the proposed expenditures. For an indicative example, again turn to Exhibit 6.8 (A & B), *A Performance Budget.* Funding a technical

VI. MANAGEMENT: Pursuit of Attainment

high school, this two-page budget document displays expenditures and revenues related to output/outcome/impact indicators. Repeated here for the reader's convenience, it is there noted that the model incorporates a section allocating proposed investment (expenditures), presented in cost center order, a funding plan balanced to the proposed educational investment, an array listing estimated benefits accruing to the proposed investment, a performance data array presenting targets, a "cross classification" linking programmatic cost centers to education purposes, and unit cost calculations. These arrays are accompanied by an interpretive text.

7) Identify Alternatives And Reasons For Rejection. Budget proposal documentation should conclude with a brief discussion of alternatives considered, but rejected. This requirement presumes that program proposers are truly "managers" who explore programmatic options; that is, different ways to achieve outputs and goals, including serious consideration of production techniques which reduce unit costs and/or improve output per work hour. A commentary on alternatives provides reviewers with an opportunity to evaluate the recommended preferred approach, and its supporting work plan, within a context of approaches and alternative production techniques. Required consideration of alternatives puts a premium on consistency in the evaluation of options, including, most crucially, the one recommended as the preferred solution, It also provides assurance that alternatives were, indeed, seriously considered, thus inspires confidence in the proposed budget and work plan(s) as thoughtful responses to issues, problems and/or opportunities identified by Statement 1.

C) Work Plans

To provide a solid foundation for the implementation of solution-centered, results-oriented budgets, government leaders are well advised to require the formulation of work plans by *every* supervisor, these being absolutely necessary for the conduct of periodic formal performance reviews. Proper work plans incorporate performance indicators as targets. Thus, the requirement for the formulation of work plans by every supervisor encourages the identification and dynamic use of performance information—managerial behavior devoutly desired. In my judgment, work plans formulated by all supervisors is the *best* way to validate performance indicators proving useful in budget formulation, adoption and implementation Work plans are illustrated in Exhibits 6.10 through 6.12, amplified by details concerning their formulation and use. The following list provides a set of general procedures for work plan formulation::

1) Identify work activities/tasks assigned to each cost center.

2) Identify and quantify desired output(s) units associated with activities/tasks

3) Determine, list and estimate prices of input units (work hours, kilowatt hours, square meters/feet, mileage, etc.) and other resources (e.g,: contracts) needed to attain the estimated output units.

4) Determine the total cost center allocation by adding all cost components.

5) Where applicable, calculate unit cost or cost per unit of output.

6) Where applicable, calculate output units per work hour or work hours per output unit, and any other pertinent performance ratios. The *desired tendency* of selected ratios:

VI. MANAGEMENT: Pursuit of Attainment

    Cost per unit of output should go   DOWN.
    Output units per cost should go   UP.
    Staff time per unit of output should go   DOWN.
    Units of output per staff time should go   UP.

7) Compare all ratios to past and current experience. If comparisons do not show movement in the desired direction, review production techniques and associated inputs, seeking improvements in productivity and/or lower input cost or work hours.

As indicated, work plans are the essential foundation for the conduct of periodic formal reviews. Distinguished from the passive practice of after-the-fact reporting, the dynamic use of performance data serves to illuminate the conceptual problems and issues which bedevil the process of performance articulation and usage under the best of circumstances. To qualify as "dynamic," the reviews should be conducted "before-the-fact," that is, 2/3rds of the way through the current reporting period. So scheduled, the reviewing officials have time to authorize "corrective action" in cases of impending failure of work supervisors to meet targets. Consequently, in addition to providing the entire performance articulation process with a compelling rationale, the active use of performance data during budget implementation encourages and supports desired managerial behavior.

Also, consider the advice of Pressman and Wildavsky, cited previously, that the means of implementation should be built up in the course of program formulation. Courses of action which look good analytically may not look practical to implementers. Involving potential implementers in the analysis of alternatives is a good way to avoid wasting time and resources on the study of unrealistic approaches.

Considered as subsidiary ledgers, established and maintained by supervisors, work plans are fundamental management instruments.

Managerial Thought for Public Finance Officers

The formulation and execution of formal work plans, periodically reviewed and updated, no later than quarterly, is a prime means of securing performance accountability. Although they have proven merit at all levels of government organization, the preparation and execution of work plans are especially useful at basic levels of organization and supervision, the points of service and product delivery. As they list activities and tasks, every official immediately accountable for the work of others should formulate and execute work plans. At minimum, work plans embrace the following elements: a) Activities/Tasks; b) Effort, expressed in work hours, and, if available, costs; c) Targets, expressed in terms of outputs/outcome/impact indicators; d) Checkpoints/Milestones; and e) Performance Ratios. Schematically, these elements can be arranged as shown in Exhibit 6.9, *A Work Plan Model*.

EXHIBIT 6.9 A Work Plan Model

	PERFORMANCE ELEMENT	PERIODS				TOTAL
		1	2	3	4	
1	Activity/Task – Work Hours					
	Cost					
	Output					
	Performance Ratio					
	/__ /					
N	Activity/Task – Work Hours					
	Etc.					
	Total Work Hours					
	Authorized Absences - Hours					
	Total Paid Hours					

Work plans may display data discretely, period by period, providing totals in the last column at the right. As an alternative, one may display data cumulatively, with each period's data added to the prior

VI. MANAGEMENT: Pursuit of Attainment

period. Consequently, each period provides a year-to-date total, with the last period's figures also serving as the year-end total. If desired, both formats, the discrete periodic totals and the cumulative year-to-date approaches, can be used simultaneously to provide maximum insight during the review process. The sample Work Plan, Exhibit 6.10, identifies reading proficiency as an activity/task in a primary school. As noted, work plans usually embrace multiple activities and or tasks. Covering multiple activities/tasks, the sample work plan marks Grade Four as a comprehensive center of performance responsibility in the Alpha Primary School.

EXHIBIT 6.10 Alpha Primary School, Grade Four Work Plan

	ACTIVITIES/TASKS	Q1	Q2	Q3	Q4	Total
1	READING PROFICIENCY					
	Cost (direct $)	4,000	12,000	12,000	12,000	40,000
	Teaching Time (hours)	144	432	432	432	1,440
	Pupil Time on Task (hours)	3,600	10,800	11,800	12,800	39,000
	TOT/TT (hours)	25.0	25.0	27.3	29.6	27.1
	Cost/TT ($/hour)	27.78	27.78	27.78	27.78	27.78
	Above Reading Norm (%)	70.0	75.0	79.0	82.0	
N	OTHER ACTIVITIES, etc *					
	Total Work Hours	144	432	432	432	1,440
	Add Authorized Leave (Hours)	36	36	36	36	144
	Total Paid Hours	180	468	468	468	1,584

* List additional activities/tasks, including related supporting services charged to the cost center but not easily or accurately assignable to the programmatic activities and/or tasks.

As demonstrated by the examples, work plans should incorporate performance ratios, or standards, whenever possible. Indeed, unit measures, such as, unit cost, cost per unit, output per work hour or work hours per unit of output provide a strong foundation for work plans. As previously noted, work plans can be organized by periods other than quarters, monthly, for example. Also please note that work time forms the basis of work plans. At this point, consult Exhibit 6.11, *Work Plan: Finance Director's Office* Based on work hours, this plan displays data discreetly, quarter by quarter. This plan is based on work hours. Work time can be calculated by hour, week, month or year. As it reflects time-on-task, work time embraces all forms of effort, regardless of payment concept, including that of staff, whether permanent, part-time or temporary, overtime payments, and time of contractors, if used. In contrast, paid time forms the basis of budgets. Thus, at the bottom of the sample work plan, these two different concepts are reconciled with the addition of a calculation of "authorized absences." This usually includes vacation leave, sick leave, holiday pay, etc.

Inevitably, work plans require adjustment as the work proceeds. As dynamic documents, work plans should always register the best current estimates of work time commitments and output delivery dates. Therefore, performance reviews provide an opportunity to assess progress, and, if necessary, adjust future work time allocations, expected performance, and performance delivery dates. These reviews will provide the government with sequential opportunities to ensure goal attainment by encouraging, and authorizing timely corrective action in those cases where results are falling short of expectations. Frequently, the accountable officials will find it necessary to assign additional assistance to lagging activities, drawing on the unallocated work hours provided for contingencies. (Exhibit 6.11 includes contingent provision for unanticipated tasks.) Where lagging results reflect deficient inter-agency collaboration, also a common occurrence, corrective action will probably require the active intervention and assistance of accountable officials. Additionally, performance reviews tend to pinpoint recurring productivity problems — problems which can only be solved by systemic changes in assignments and/or operating procedures.

VI. MANAGEMENT: Pursuit of Attainment

EXHIBIT 6.11 Work Plan: Finance Director's Office

	ACTIVITIES/TASKS	Indicator	Q1	Q2	Q3	Q4	Total
1	**Fiscal Policy Formulation**	Work Hours	410	320	320	365	1415
	Annual Financial Report	Document	+30				
	Annual Strategic Plan	Draft			+240		
	Budget Call	Draft			+240		
	Multi-year Capital Program	Advice					
	Annual Budget	Advice					
2	**Systems Development**	Work Hours	140	90	45	45	320
	Improve Accunting Accuracy	Tests	+30				
	Reduce Processing Lags	Tests		+60			
	Improve Collection Ratios	Tests	+30				
	Organization Development	Sessions	TBD	TBD	TBD	TBD	
3	**General Administration**	Work Hours	280	325	375	325	1305
4	**Miscellaneous Tasks**	Work Hours	90	185	180	185	640
5	**Performance Reviews**	Work Hours	20	20	20	20	80
	Quarterly Presentations	Corrections	+60	+150	+240	+330	
	Total Work Hours		940	940	940	940	3760
	Add Authorized Leave (Hours)		100	100	100	100	400
	Total Paid Hours		1,040	1,040	1,040	1,040	4160

NOTES:
Including the Finance Director and a Secretary, this two-position work plan is based on a work year of 260 paid days, eight hours per day, or 2,080 paid hours. Authorized absences are estimated at 25 days per position, or 200 hours (Vacation Leave, 15 days, or 120 hours and Sick Leave, 10 days, or 80 hours).

Manpower planning is an integral part of the budget formulation process, especially in problem-centered, results-oriented budgeting which requires the composition of work plans based on work hours. The composition of work plans based on work time effectively determines manpower requirements prior to the start of the fiscal year. It is work plans which justify proposed personal service allocations and, eventually, periodic allotments.

In sum, if one might say that diagnostic documentation, particularly the specification of program rationale and goal(s), endows a budget allocation with its soul, a work plan(s) certainly supplies its heart. Deemed as the most feasible response to the problem situation, as diagnosed, a work plan represents the action requirements of the preferred solution. Ideally all officials, regardless of rank, who supervise the work of others should formulate and execute work plans. Certainly, because they conduct primary activities and tasks, officials at the basic level of organization and supervision should formulate and execute work plans.

During budget implementation, following periodic performance reviews, allotments are awarded to supervisors based on acceptance of their work plan for the ensuing period. Of course, the financial position of the government may require budget adjustments during the fiscal year. In that case, performance targets and the associated work plans should be adjusted prior to adjusting allotments. This same sequence of action should govern the work of budget officials when adjusting budget requests during the budget formulation process. Solution-centered, results-oriented budgets are based on targets and associated work plans. Consequently, expenditure modifications must be preceded by modification of performance targets and associated work plans, including manpower.

Concluding Thoughts about Budget Appraisal

Chief financial officers entrusted with budgetary responsibility are well-advised to recruit talented budget officers who can assist them in the challenging task of assessing the *intrinsic* and *relative* merits of existing and proposed budget allocations. Charged with maintaining the integrity of the budget system, as well as its productivity, they must ensure that budget officers maintain a service, rather than control, orientation toward officials. Consequently, the work time of budget officers is a key resource, to be allocated with great care. As a general rule, the work time of budget

VI. MANAGEMENT: Pursuit of Attainment

officers should be distributed in three approximate ways, 1/3 reserved for program-related research, 1/3 devoted to program performance reviews (including site visits), and 1/3 for desk-bound duties, including budget formulation. Further, programmatic assignments should be rotated among budget officers to build up knowledge about linkages between programs. To maintain their productivity and relevance, chief financial officers are advised to conduct frequent performance reviews of budget officer activity.

A proposed budget allocation may be said to have intrinsic merit if its estimated programmatic effects and affects satisfy objective criteria, principally, the desired tendencies of the performance ratios listed in Exhibit 4.2, *Allocation Criteria*. A proposed allocation may be said to have relative merit if its estimated effects and affects are deemed more valuable, on objective grounds, than those attributed to potential competitive allocations. Selecting proposed allocations to be made subject to such comparisons is a key decision, which should, if possible, reflect the application of consistent, objective criteria. Obviously, all proposed capital investments, considered as a group, should be subjected to comparative analysis. Grouping criteria might also include all proposed allocations involving requests for a) added staffing, b) expenditure increases exceeding a set amount or percent, or c) "overtime" payroll payments. Once a comparative grouping has been determined, various formal techniques of appraisal can be applied to assess the relative merit of proposed allocations, such as those displayed by Exhibit 4.2, *Allocation Criteria*. An extended commentary about applying the concepts of budget appraisal listed in Exhibit 4.2 appears in my companion volume, *Budgetary Thought for Budget Officers* (Amazon, 2016).

4. Controls: Dynamic Monitoring

Dynamic Use of Control Procedures

In the context of this essay, the term, "dynamic," refers to control procedures which provide a basis for action "before-the-fact." Obviously, the most effective control procedures alert accountable officials to emerging situations in time for remedial action.

Sad to say, accountable finance officers must emplace and maintain "controls" designed to thwart those bent on looting the public treasury. Conventionally, finance-related work concerns money, but only a small number of public employees, notably cashiers, actually work with cash. These employees must be closely supervised and subject to frequent audit. Those authorizing contracts, purchase orders, payrolls and payment vouchers must also be vigilantly supervised and audited. These employees work with documents incorporating numbers representing money. These numbers, and their various meanings (interpretations) are the "raw material" of finance work. To properly address the policy and administrative aspects of their work, finance officials must develop and maintain process controls which guarantee the integrity, accuracy, relevance and timeliness of finance numbers, whether destined for files or transfer to others for their active use. Numbers must be handled with appropriate speed, yes, but above all, correctly and accurately. Additionally, because they so deeply influence government policy, accountable finance officials must interpret numbers thoughtfully, with due regard for the reader's interest and understanding. This latter point has very substantial implications for the format, content and accuracy of budgets and financial reports. Controls on reported numbers are required as errors (and lies) are common, one is tempted to say endemic, in too many governments.

Although higher math and statistical techniques are sometimes required, especially in the work of budgeting and financial planning, finance employees routinely use standard arithmetic processes (addition, subtraction, multiplication and division) to relate finance numbers to one another. The possibility of error is ever-present, particularly in single entry data aggregations, not subject to double entry discipline. As single entry aggregations, (e.g., number of paid vouchers per month, number of requisitions processed per month, etc.), performance report accuracy can never be taken at face value. Computer-based spreadsheet

VI. MANAGEMENT: Pursuit of Attainment

technology is helpful in this regard, provided that controls on data entry and output are strictly regulated and enforced.

The incidence of misappropriation of assets and procurement corruption among government officials is continuously worrisome. The potential for wrong-doing is ever-present, and often difficult to detect and prevent. Universally, public and private organizations rely on "internal controls" to maintain the integrity of their operations. Well known to accountants and auditors across the globe, these control techniques include requirements for formal delegation of approval authority, segregation of duties to compel multi-party reviews, counter signature requirements, timely, effective reconciliation procedures, and sealed competitive tenders for contract awards. Nevertheless, experience indicates that, even when such controls are in place, opportunistic officials, contractors, assorted vendors and self-seeking citizens never cease trying to evade them in illegitimate attempts to get something of value from governments. Of course, employees enjoying "inside knowledge" can spot and then exploit system weaknesses.

Many consider internal auditing as the "front-line" against wrong-doing and inefficacious procedures. Reflecting my experience, I have found that internal auditors, left to their own devices, tend to define their mission as pure investigation and reporting. Fearful of compromising their objectivity while pursuing their fault-finding missions, they tend to limit interactions with the subject management. During the course of their investigations, they are reluctant to engage with the subject management as their discovery proceeds and their findings develop, preferring to finish their work with a report on findings and recommendations—an example of "after-the-fact" reporting. Applying a philosophy of "dynamic" controls, the role of internal auditors could be broadened to include technical assistance, that is, helping the subject management correct faults as they are discovered and validated. In addition to their findings and recommendations, auditors would then also report remedial actions initiated and/or completed during the course of an engagement. Furthermore, the fault-finding methodology usually leaves the response to audit findings and recommendation in the hands of those found at fault, a problematical situation, to say the least. Adding technical assistance to the job specification of internal auditors promotes a timely and effective response to documented operational deficiencies.

Significantly, the application of computer technology to administrative work tends to empower subordinates, in addition to supervisors. Knowledgeable observers report that computers increase the complexity of operations, and, thus, the opportunity for misappropriation of assets and procurement corruption. Using computers for access to unauthorized internet sites is reportedly very prevalent, resulting in misappropriation of work time and equipment.

Effective implementation of controls simply can not be taken for granted. Collusion is always a possibility. The very monotony of implementation breeds carelessness and perfunctory performance in the enforcement of administrative and financial controls. Facing the ever-present danger of control lapses, accountable finance supervisors, especially chief financial officers, must continuously display a "nose" for scandal and lax management, reinforcing this leadership disposition by subjecting the system to periodic formal reviews.

As noted in Part 2, *Instrumentalities,* administrative and financial controls add costs, measured in work-time and other expenses. As financial controls serve to prevent loss, their efficacy in discouraging misappropriation of public assets and procurement corruption can only be assumed, never proven. The benefits conferred by administrative process controls are also not measurable, but they are justified by their contribution to efficient, economical goal attainment. (One hopes that the benefits of administrative controls exceed the cost of implementation.) If systematically embedded in operating standards and progress reports, administrative process controls provide managers with timely information about the status of production. *After all, goal attainment failure is a prime source of waste in government, greater, by far, than losses by misappropriation and procurement corruption.*

VI. MANAGEMENT: Pursuit of Attainment

With respect to budget monitoring, reviewing an "after-the-fact" expenditure report may be equated to "examining an unlocked barn door after the horse has been stolen." Only by the vigorous and continuous use of dynamic process controls can accountable officials learn of impending production shortfalls in time to effect corrective action to ensure goal attainment.

At several points, I identified work plans as the first of a quartet of recommended instruments of implementation. The following discussion explores the contribution of the other three instruments.

Allotments.

Allotments are important instruments of budget control. Annual appropriations represent terminal controls. They do not provide checkpoints as a basis for performance feedback. Appropriation allotments can play a positive—perhaps dynamic—role in program execution because they can be made discretionary in amount and timing. It is timing that makes the allotment process so valuable. By allotting portions of an appropriation for expenditure at specific times, it is possible to set up a spectrum of intermediate control points which make it more likely that significant variations from work plans will be discovered early enough for corrective action. For best results, allotments must be tied to specific performance objectives. Otherwise (and this is a common observation about allotments), the apportionment process becomes merely an accounting ritual to authorize further spending. If, on the other hand, allotment decisions are preceded by consultation with program managers about specific targets, apportionment can be an effective implementation instrument.

In best practice, appropriations are allotted periodically, based on expenditure plans provided by the responsible program agencies. Although, fundamentally, allotments depend on estimates of cash availability, appropriations are supposed to fund government policies and programs over a certain time period, usually one year, secured by revenue estimates. Therefore, in theory, budgets should be emancipated from constant association with the short-term cash management problems. Unless financial officials predict a total shortfall of total estimated revenue in relation to the total of appropriations, budget officials should be free to recommend work plan allotments for periods of at least three months — such work plans to reflect the results of periodic, before-the-fact, performance reviews.

Many governments allot appropriations during the fiscal year, by quarter or by month, with quarters preferred. Allotment procedures require close collaboration between agency program managers, budget officers, accounting staff and treasury officials. Experience indicates that allotment procedures can degenerate into a rather arbitrary accounting ritual (annual appropriation divided by 4 quarters or 12 months, for example) unless allotments are related to performance review procedures, and other operating requirements, listed as follows:

- A "realistic' budget, that is, a comprehensive statement of estimated expenditures and year-end obligations, balanced to a conservative revenue estimate.

- A "Cash Flow Projection," prepared and updated monthly, such statements showing available balances as well as the projected inflows of revenue (including loan proceeds) for the remaining portion of the financial year. This provides the key vehicle for the maintenance of liquidity and a stable allotment process.

- Quarterly allotment requests accompanied by expenditure projections for the remaining quarters. Provided that program expenditures to date, plus allotment requests and projections

VI. MANAGEMENT: Pursuit of Attainment

are within the budget, and provided that the latest estimate of the government's year-end fund balance is positive, allotment requests by agency officials should be approved, this predictability encouraging program planning and performance.

- An Allotment Reservation Plan, executed in orderly fashion, conditioned by reference to the "Cash Flow Projection". This Plan identifies expenditures which can be deferred to specific times later in the fiscal year, such as, equipment acquisitions, new program initiatives and inventory replenishments.

Dynamic Use of Performance Reviews.

Unless strong performance review procedures are established, budgeting degenerates into an annual estimating and accounting ritual. More than any other part of the budgeting repertoire, it is the institutionalization of periodic performance reviews which invests the budget system with "managerial muscle." When conducted as formal affairs, periodic performance reviews tend to stimulate desirable organizational behavior, as follows:

- Anticipation of periodic formal performance reviews strongly influences behavior in the intervals between reviews.

- Conduct of the review, itself, influences behavior as the participants reach understandings and agreements concerning actions to be taken by particular parties.

- Reviews promote collaboration among units which have the resources or responsibility to assist the subject supervisor solve problems defined during review proceedings.

- The reviews stimulate accountable officials to initiate corrective action

Effective organizations attain stated goals. Efficient organizations attain stated goals at "minimum or lowest" cost. Assessing the effectiveness and efficiency of any activity requires the development and maintenance of data, and data arrays, as follows:

- Effort devoted to stated intentions, expressed in terms of money and/or work-time.

- Results related to stated intentions, expressed in terms of output/outcome/impact indicators.

- Calculations dividing effort by results, or results by effort. (performance ratios)

- Additional measure(s) or ratio(s) drawn from a comparable situation, facilitating evaluation of a subject ratio.

To be readily available for work plan formulation and the subsequent performance reviews, the required performance data must be identified, recorded and reported. As incurred, costs and work time must be associated with appropriate activities and/or tasks identified in work plans, then summarized at pertinent milestones. Similarly, performance data must be recorded and summarized. Over time, using performance as a guide, responsible officials will be in a position to encourage

VI. MANAGEMENT: Pursuit of Attainment

the formulation of plans to improve the relative effectiveness, efficiency and economy of program operations, that is, *reduce* unit costs and unit times of results, or, putting the case positively, *increase* results per work hour and per amount expended.

The institutionalization of periodic formal performance reviews provides the budget system with "managerial muscle." Performance requires comparison to give it significance, or meaning. In the following abstract calculation, significance is given to a stated performance by deriving a variance by subtracting an ideal, standard or target from it, both stated, of course, in similar terms:

Performance
<u>(Ideal/Standard/Target)</u>
Variance

These terms can be absolute numbers, or unit measures or other performance ratios. In addition to revealing the magnitude of variance, the subtraction will provide an indication of the direction of the variance in that the stated performance will equal (=), exceed (+) or fall short (-) of the stated ideal, standard or target.

Performance reviews provide formal opportunities for supervisors to address the officials and units that affect their ability to attain their goals, presenting a) results compared to intentions for the completed prior period, b) revised estimates of results related to intentions for the current period and c) projected intentions for the upcoming period. The projections also form a solid basis for allotment requests and for cash management planning.

By design, the reviews should be conducted by strategically constituted Performance Review Committees 2/3rds of the way through the selected milestone period, toward the end of the second month of each quarter, for example, if work plans are organized by quarters. So timed, with 2/3rds of the period completed, responsible officials have sufficient experience to calculate revised estimates for the current period, conditioned on proposed action plans for the remaining 1/3 portion of the period.

These timely reviews provide the government with sequential opportunities to ensure goal attainment by encouraging, and/or authorizing timely corrective action in those cases where results are falling short of targets. At the 2/3rds point, if the projected unfavorable variances are deemed significant, the accountable officials still have time remaining in the period to authorize corrective action (adjusted staff deployments, changed procedures, etc.) to put the performance for the period "back on track."

The seven elements of data involved in the typical Performance Review are displayed in the simplified model shown below:

PAST PERIOD	**PRESENT PERIOD**	**FUTURE PERIOD**
Performance	Estimate	
(Target)	(Target)	Target
Variance	Variance	

As recommended, formal performance reviews provide supervisors periodic opportunities to address their colleagues and superiors concerning the performance of their units, no later than every quarter. Ideally, supervisors should provide a "stand up" presentation, supported by visual aids, where appropriate. All presentations should reference the commitments registered in current work plans, with significant variances indicated and explained. In general, experience indicates that the subject supervisors will trace variances between intentions and results to one, or more, of the following factors:

A. Unanticipated changes in input prices.
B. Unanticipated changes in volume and type of applied resources, including staffing.

VI. MANAGEMENT: Pursuit of Attainment

C. Unanticipated performance from assigned physical assets.
D. Unanticipated and uncontrollable changes in the production situation which invalidate original production assumptions.
E. Environmental contingencies.

Variances in unit measures are most frequently traced to factors "A" and "B." In an economy subject to significant inflation, unanticipated cost variances are to be expected, as prices cannot be accurately predicted, even for the near future. Factor "C" is often cited to explain variances from period to period, especially if new technology has been introduced. Equipment failure, and/or delays in equipment repair also frequently cause negative variances. Significantly, factor "D" considerations often include shortfalls in services and/or goods due from other units of the government. Factor "E" refers to accidents, including natural and man-made disasters, which interfere with the conduct of work.

As indicated by the first requirement in the following set of suggested specifications for the establishment and maintenance of a performance review system, the procedures should be established by authoritative regulation:

- Performance review procedures to be formally adopted.

- Cost center managers (all who supervise the work of others) to be provided with a forum for oral, written and visual presentations.

- To provide supervisors with a supportive audience, reviews to be conducted by a committee whose members are selected for their capacity to assist the concerned supervisors attain stated targets.

- To provide opportunities for corrective action in pursuit of targets, review sessions to be conducted periodically, 2/3rds through the current reporting period,.

- Reviews to cover the prior reporting period (results related to intentions), current reporting period (estimated results related to intentions), and next recording period (projection of intentions).

- The committee secretariat (assigned budget officers) to document proceedings, reporting formally to accountable officials regarding recommended corrective actions to forestall failure to meet stated targets. .

Representatives of significant staff agencies, especially budget, human resources and other relevant centralized process units, are expected to participate in these periodic reviews to help cost center managers solve production problems. This procedure encourages the attainment of performance targets during the year, via timely corrective action. Most important, frequent reviews pinpoint recurring productivity problems — problems which require systemic changes in operating procedures, cost center by cost center.

Work plans require adjustment as the work proceeds. As dynamic documents, work plans should always register the latest current estimates of work-time commitments and target dates. Therefore, performance reviews provide an opportunity to assess progress, and, if necessary, adjust future work-time allocations, and, perhaps, output delivery dates.

VI. MANAGEMENT: Pursuit of Attainment

In recommended practice, budget officers should be assigned the responsibility for organizing and coordinating the performance review process. The following steps will be required:

1) Appointment of Performance Review Committees
2) Designation of Committee chairperson and secretariat
3) Arrangements for time and place
4) Timely notification to all participants
5) Provision of projection equipment
6) Provision for seating an audience
7) Conduct of the review
8) Preparation of the Review Committee Report

As indicated by the suggested performance review specifications, listed above, these reviews should be treated as formal occasions, with the staff assigned to each activity/task granted appropriate time for presentations. Performance reviews expose the fallibility of plans, for whenever intentions are compared to results, variances are the rule. Consequently, work time overruns and missed deadlines are to be expected. Considering the inherent fallibility of plans, the Performance Review Committee should strive to maintain a positive, rather than punitive, review atmosphere—avoiding fault-finding and criticism in favor of problem solving and corrective action. To be a continuously effective instrument of budget implementation, a formal system of performance review requires the establishment and maintenance of a positive, rather than punitive, managerial atmosphere. *The importance of this ethical principle cannot be overstated.* The critical test of a review system lies not in how it reacts to successful attainment of targets, but the reverse. As things usually go, program leaders and cost center managers will fail to meet targets. With reference to the subjects and objects of review, superiors and colleagues, alike, should shun fault-finding and criticism in favor of understanding, problem solving and corrective action.

All cost center teams are dependent, to some degree, on the effective delivery of services by other units (upstream) within the government and in turn, may have units (downstream) dependent on them. As an example, primary care services in health centers may be abjectly dependent on timely responses to requisitions for goods and/or services from centralized medical stores and laboratories. Performance Review Committees and, especially, the budget officers servicing them have a special responsibility to ensure that the performance of cost center teams is not hampered by the poor performance of staff agencies, such as, maintenance, purchasing, personnel, legal and other centralized process agencies. Furthermore, many important goals of government require continuous collaboration between its major program agencies. Responsibility for trans-organizational relationships (whether contemporary, upstream or downstream of any particular unit of government) is the particular responsibility of budget officers, as they are in the best position to identify and solve relationship problems.

By textbook definition, managers are assumed to pursue productivity and productivity improvements. So stated, this axiom locates the "cause" of productivity in managers, per se, giving no weight to the influence of managerial environments. In business organizations, the objective reality of economic survival tends to permeate the entire work environment. Everybody "gets the message," so to speak. However, in public service units where work is not subject to the spurs of profit and competitive pressure, productivity improvements do not seem to effervesce unless consciously (on principle) cultivated by leadership and design. Typically, government work environments provide managers with little incentive (or authority) to seek systemic productivity improvements. Experience indicates that, standing alone, solution-centered, results-oriented budgeting will not automatically enhance operational efficacy. Additional administrative mechanisms specifically targeted on productivity are required, especially a systematic program of agency manager training and technical assistance, working within a periodic performance review system.

VI. MANAGEMENT: Pursuit of Attainment

As noted above, periodic formal performance reviews not only enhance the likelihood that performance targets will be attained during the year, via timely corrective action, but also spotlight recurring productivity problems — problems which require systemic changes in operating procedures, cost center by cost center. To address these problems, many governments have established specialized management research teams, which may be found incorporated in budget units, associated closely with them, or standing alone. These units can not enjoy a solid institutional basis for securing the implementation of their recommendations if they rely on an ineffective "study-and-report" methodology. Reflecting experience, management research units are well-advised to abandon diagnostic-prescriptive approaches in favor of cost center manager education and technical assistance, working within a periodic performance review system. By working closely with cost center managers within a reporting cycle, management research units can work on an agenda established by cost center managers, giving the management research staff a strong institutional base for the implementation of productivity improvements.

In sum, performance reviews expose the fallibility of plans, for whenever intentions are compared to results, variances are the rule. Consequently, cost variances. work time overruns and missed deadlines are to be expected. Considering the inherent fallibility of plans, all participants in performance reviews should strive to maintain a positive, rather than punitive, atmosphere— avoiding fault-finding and criticism in favor of problem-solving and corrective action.

As stressed before and repeated here for emphasis, the failure to formulate work plans, and to conduct periodic performance reviews thereon, represents a very serious management deficiency

Corrective Action

Immediately following the conduct of a performance review, the committee secretariat should prepare a draft report for the committee's consideration. Addressing significant performance "shortfalls," this report should recommend corrective actions to be taken by the accountable agency program leader and the accountable officials of the units identified during the review as sources of assistance. In general form, performance reports should outline 1) performance to-date, 2) problems encountered, 3) recommended corrective actions. 4) performance targets for the period to be covered by allotment requests, and 5) recommended allotment(s).

The identification of the recommended corrective action is not always easy. The term itself is an abstraction covering a variety of types of action which might be appropriate in given situations. Not all production problems are immediately solvable. Moreover, experience indicates that productivity improvements are far easier to identify than to implement. In many cases, the action to be recommended is rather like a "band-aid" rather than a genuine problem resolution. Frequently, reviews pinpoint recurring productivity problems — problems which require systemic changes in operating procedures, cost center by cost center. As emphasized, representatives of key staff units and centralized process agencies are expected to participate in these periodic reviews to help agency managers remove the causes of recurring production problems.

Closing Thoughts about Implementation

Embracing a set of management tools, I have advanced the concept of dynamic monitoring as an efficacious way to enhance goal attainment. But, before turning to the vital subject of management motivation, a few general thoughts about the implementation of public programs and projects, and, by implication, the appropriations which fund and finance them..

Essentially, adopted budgets represent an act of faith by appropriating authorities—an attempt to shape the socio-economic future in desired ways. As such, appropriations simultaneously authorize, direct and limit the behavior of implementing authorities. As universal experience

VI. MANAGEMENT: Pursuit of Attainment

unequivocally testifies, results often fall short of legislative expectations, if these be known via the form and documentation of appropriation acts. As public budgets have expanded in recent decades, this regrettable situation has attracted critical attention from many knowledgeable observers and practitioners. (The reader will recall my earlier observations about the performance gap between legislative expectations about output/outcome/impact and eventual results.) The history of budget reform can be interpreted as a struggle to achieve stronger causal connections between legislative intentions, if made transparent, and results, if also rendered transparent. In this endeavor, the spotlight inevitably falls on the institutional foundations of budget implementation. Accumulating experience indicates that public officials who wish to use performance data in budget adoption and implementation face a variety of impediments — a spectrum of endogenous and exogenous difficulties found in legislative and administrative situations everywhere. The generally weak response of public officials to the implementation challenge is de facto recognition of manifest hazards and intrinsic difficulties.

As more and more of the world's financial resources are subject to budgeting by governments and an increasing number of non-profit organizations, the scope of the implementation problem is enlarging. Overcoming impediments to more effective budget implementation is especially important for democratic governments, which are inherently subject to more implementation impediments than authoritarian regimes. Authoritarian regimes have a survival stake in their effectiveness, and can use means not available to democracies to "make good" their decisions. Consequently, in the continuing competitive struggle with authoritarian governments, democracies have a significant stake in finding ways to overcome budget implementation impediments.

As suggested, the implementation problem can be addressed by inspired officials using procedural tools, readily at hand, but not usually found "working hand-in-hand." In administrative terms, these tools comprise inter-related practices which require firm institutionalization. Toward that end, I identified and explored a quartet of institutional determinants needed for successful implementation of solution centered, results-oriented budgets Repeated here for emphasis, these four determinants are 1) effective articulation and use of performance information; 2) an elaborate, flexible classification and coding scheme; 3) accounting procedures which facilitate the aggregation of non-monetary performance data, formally correlated with measures of effort and monetary data; and 4) continuous management utilization of four inter-related instruments of implementation. These four instruments include a) work plans, b) allotments, c) "before-the-fact" periodic formal performance reviews and d) timely corrective action. Effective budgeting is best assured by using an institutional framework integrating these determinants and instruments, with accounting procedures providing the glue. Here a cautionary note is appropriate: As these four determinants are mutually reinforcing, the absence or limp implementation of one reduces the effectiveness of the others.

Obviously, the effective employment of the implementation determinants and instruments noted above depends on managerial energy and direction. Through precept and example, leading officials must actively express and cultivate the *will-to-achieve* — a most important, but problematical, leadership quality. This quality varies naturally from official to official. Consequently, government leaders desiring to formulate and implement solution-centered, results-oriented budgets must take concrete steps to encourage and reward expressions of the will-to-achieve by their managerial cadres, especially those directly accountable for production.

5. Management Motivation: The will-to-achieve

At this point, I hope that the reader has given serious consideration to the overall thrust of this essay, comparing my observations, examples and recommendations with familiar situations. The reader may also have noticed that, thus far, I have drawn my inspiration, and my examples, from the bloodless realm of technique and procedure, unaccompanied

VI. MANAGEMENT: Pursuit of Attainment

by systematic references to managerial motivation which inevitably conditions all forms of programmatic implementation.

Regrettably, mere pedagogical works (including this one) recommending an ensemble of techniques, cannot kindle the will-to-achieve in the mind of a finance manager who lacks vision and courage. It is easy to cite specific factors which inhibit finance managers and reduce their will-to-achieve, such as, 1) rules restricting management rights to discipline or remove less productive workers, 2) inadequate budgetary support for so-called "overhead" operations, management accounting, analytical staff, etc., 3) fragmented organizational structures, facilitating buck passing and risk avoidance, and 4) little or no relationship between pay and output. Further, given the intrusive political atmosphere surrounding many finance establishments, it is not surprising to encounter supervisors who disavow their motivational responsibility. They avoid accountability, seek approval from their superiors unnecessarily, and obey orders without question, regardless of qualifying conditions. They exude negative attitudes about productivity issues. They talk of inhibitions, emphasize barriers, stress missing ingredients, excuse low productivity, and thus shun accountability for productivity improvements. True enough, finance officials often face a number of formidable barriers, such as, organizational fragmentation (often justified by the time-worn concept of "checks and balances"), inadequate budgeting and accounting procedures, low capital/labor ratios, and a "control" rather than "service" orientation of finance personnel.

As the barriers are inter-related, mono-dimensional approaches to the productivity problem (such as, professionalization of employees, or increasing the capital/labor ratio.) often are only marginally effective. Nevertheless, here and there. one finds examples of determined and inspired finance managers who have built-up efficacious operations in spite of the inhibitions characteristic of public service everywhere in the world. Reflecting training and experience, they confidently pursue the craft of finance management with knowledge and dexterity. If some can achieve, all can aspire!

Although they report the usage of various repertoires (evidence that there is, perhaps, no magic in any technique or even in any given ensemble of techniques), students of productivity tend to agree on the crucial role of leadership in achieving productivity. In this regard, I was impressed by Myron E. Weiner's exploration of this subject in *"Management Repertoires"* published in *Connecticut Government*. (Institute of Public Service, University of Connecticut, Winter, 1977.)

In simple social settings, leadership is expressed by persons persuading others to do what they want done, without recourse to authority, or coercion. In the complex environment of bureaucracies, the concept of leadership includes issuing orders, as well as attempts to persuade, making bureaucratic leadership very potent, indeed. In settings suffused with authority, supervisors are expected to issue orders, and subordinates expect to receive and obey orders. In such settings, pure expressions of persuasive "leadership" are not usual, but exceptional. Subordinates are usually disposed to accept orders, even when offered as suggestions. Given this predisposition, sufficiently motivated chief financial officers/finance directors should be able to 1) ensure staff competence via training, and 2) lead staff across the bridge from knowing about the instruments of efficacious management to their vigorous application. The following traits are commonly attributed to productive managers:

- Crave a deserved reputation for productivity.

- Pursue goals based on consultation, research, planning, and dynamic monitoring.

- Demand accountability by results (from oneself, colleagues and subordinates).

- Stress innovation, training and organization development.

VI. MANAGEMENT: Pursuit of Attainment

Unquestionably, these traits of productive managers can be taught, learned and, then expressed in executive action and procedures, especially the provision of in-service training programs taught by respected, knowledgeable trainers. Proven in practice, in-service training is an effective way to attain and maintain the requisite institutionalization of efficacious management. Formal in-service training programs not only can produce desired increments of staff knowledge and skill, but also can have desirable sociological effects by establishing expectations of achievement by all participants. Although the sources and springs of human motivation are multiform, and at least partly instinctual, we know for sure that individual human behavior is heavily influenced by the words and deeds of others, especially if individuals want to be esteemed by their fellows. From time immemorial, the concept of leading by precept and example has been extolled. In modern times, training specialists acknowledge the sociological principle by designing training programs which apply the concept of the "training diamond," graphically shown below:

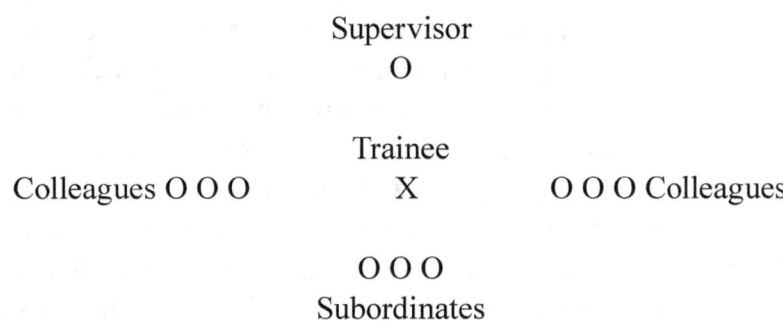

Persons working in hierarchical settings typically have a supervisor, colleagues laterally and may have subordinates. Increasing the knowledge and skill of any hierarchically-situated individual is most effective if significant others (located at the four points of the diamond) surrounding the trainee (located at the center of the diamond) are taught to expect the application of the newly acquired knowledge and skills by the trainee.

Successful program and budget implementation depends on persistent, principled official leadership — a personal, rather than an organizational attribute, inherently idiosyncratic. As the critical variable, leadership presents a pedagogic challenge. As behavior depends on internalized ideas and ideals, desired leadership behavior can be taught and learned — proven by the careers of military and business school graduates, and the cadre of city managers providing non-partisan leadership in numerous localities.

All members of a finance establishment who are accountable for the work of others, the supervisory cadre, should be taught managerial thinking, that is, they should be taught to view their work though the lenses of efficacious management. (The implications of this requirement for academic curriculum design will be discussed shortly.) And, as emphasized above, to develop rank and file expectations of leadership behavior, it is equally important to expose all members of the finance establishment to the efficacious management philosophy. Consequently, an in-service training program, featuring on-the-job examples and applications, is the best way to entrench the recommended techniques and procedures. A thorough in-service training program can develop and maintain a competent cadre of finance supervisors, and, if the practice of efficacious finance management is institutionalized and rewarded, the cadre may be expected to express the essential will-to-achieve.

By their very nature, in-service training programs vary significantly in content and quality from place to place. Ideally, in-service training should extend beyond instruction in office practice to provide systematic continuing technical education. Anything less represents an unsatisfactory state of affairs from a pedagogical point of view. In this perspective, the training and certification programs currently offered by the Government Finance Officers Association (GFOA) and the American Government Accountants (AGA) are significant. They not only testify to the demand for on-the-job training, but stimulate it. Also,

VI. MANAGEMENT: Pursuit of Attainment

representing a form of "post graduate" education for public finance officers, these programs cast light on their academic preparation.

The GFOA's 2015 web site, provides a profile of its 18,310 members. In addition to indicating that 93% of its members work for local governments, 55% are certified public accountants and 42% hold prime management positions as chief financial officers/finance directors. Moreover, the GFOA web site lists 604 members who have been designated as *Certified Public Finance Officers* (CPFO). As an indicator of demand, the web site also states that 390 GFOA members took the certification exams in 2014. The AGA's web site states that more than 14,000 members have been designated as *Certified Government Finance Managers* (CGFM). (However, an unknown, but substantial number of these CGFMs were "grandfathered" in when the certification process was initiated.) Reportedly, about 400 AGA members take the CGFM exam each year. Significantly, the large number of members of the AGA designated as CGFMs also attests to the importance of undergraduate and graduate accountancy studies, albeit the coursework focus is enterprise, not governmental accounting.

Reportedly, those who take the exams, and win certification, feel an enhanced sense of competence and employability, more "professional," so to speak. However, from a systemic point of view, these certificate and training programs suggest that the academic preparation of public finance officers lacks technical breadth and depth — the essential foundation of a "professional" identity. This same lack of concentrated coursework dedicated to a specific civil service occupation can be noted in the academic preparation of budget officers, many of whom work within finance establishments.

Emphasizing the value of in-service training is not to slight the importance of the academic preparation of public finance officers. Indeed, The GFOA membership data points up the importance of academic studies focused on accounting and management skill. Significantly, many public finance officers, especially those with accounting backgrounds, think of themselves as "professionals" participating in public financial management. A professional orientation toward one's work is usually acquired by attending a graduate school. In general, graduate schools, in various fields of knowledge and skill specialization, seek to produce competent, employable professionals. This is no less true for the graduate education of public administrators, including public finance officers. Thus, the intellectual and job-related behavioral aspects of a "professional" identity are an enduring curriculum concern. .Essentially, professionals are expected to 1) acquire valued specialized knowledge, 2) apply acquired knowledge in accordance with acknowledged technical and ethical standards of practice, and 3) express affective neutrality (impartiality) in all cases requiring "professional" judgment. Additionally, for those thousands of finance officers who become supervisors of finance-related units (especially chief financial officers/finance directors), we must add the crucial "managerial" skill, that is, the capability to think and act "strategically." As managers, as well as professionals, public finance officers in supervisory positions are expected to know how to efficaciously attain desired objectives by deploying human and material resources in time and space, giving due weight to resistance and opportunities — the strategic conception. .

Typically, with a single occupation and skill-set in view, professional school faculties can easily link the attributes of "professional" identity to specific job requirements. In sharp contrast, graduates of public administration schools work in various capacities, e.g., municipal manager, budget officer, public finance officer, program administrator, etc., occupations with different knowledge and skill requirements. This circumstance has led (compelled may be a better term) the schools of Public Administration/Affairs (PA/A) to offer a core curriculum, supplemented by a limited number of specialized knowledge and skill-based electives. As noted previously, the GFOA and AGA training and certification programs provide evidence that the PA/A schools are not strong centers of skill development and professional identities, nor can they be. As the amount of available faculty and student time is limited,

VI. MANAGEMENT: Pursuit of Attainment

the typical PA/A curriculum simply cannot offer concentrated studies in the knowledge and techniques of specific civil service occupations.

As indicated by the GFOA membership profile, a substantial number of public finance officers have studied accounting. The number of public finance officers with graduate degrees from schools accredited by the National Association of Schools of Public Affairs and Administration (NASPAA) is probably substantial, Clearly, students of public administration and accountancy have the best chance of arriving on-the-job with some appreciation for the ways and means of public finance, although the pertinent coursework varies in breadth and depth from school to school. Also, students of business, enterprise finance and economics, come to public finance (and budgeting) work with pertinent analytical skills. Additionally, with reference to budget officers, the general requirement of critical thinking and clear expression favors undergraduate liberal arts studies.

A few decades ago, the typical curriculum of PA/A schools rested on a relatively sharp image of the public administrator as a non-partisan "manager," working within political environments to advance the values of effectiveness, efficiency and economy — the efficacy triad. The blurring of this image tracks to the influential 1968 Minnowbrook Conference. The conferees questioned its relevance as the key ground for PA/A curriculum. In the years since, as the image of the non-partisan manager faded, PA/A faculties offered more generalized courses, justified by multi-dimensional images of public administrators. Knowledgeable observers have characterized this drift in curriculum design as displacing public administration in favor of political science. More critical observers, taking a strictly "professional" development point of view, point out that learning the ins-and-outs of public policies, the ephemeral result of political negotiation, bargaining and compromise, is no substitute for time spent acquiring perennial technical skills forming a professional identity. .

Striking a balance between teaching policy perspectives and technical skills has been a long-standing concern of PA/A school faculties.

Managerial Thought for Public Finance Officers

Evidence of this perennial pedagogic challenge surfaced in 1984 when the American Society for Public Administration (ASPA) assembled a 30-member task force on budgeting and financial management curriculum reform. The deliberations of this task force were summarized by James R. Alexander in an article in Public Budgeting and Finance. Autumn, 1984. In addition to observations about curriculum diversity among PA/A schools, he noted that "MPA programs are not generally designed as explicit training programs for specific agencies or specific levels of financial management, and the technical skills included as required elements in the core graduate program constitute more of a general exposure than a sophisticated training." A sampling of the current offerings of PA/A schools indicates that curriculum diversity among PA/A schools, and a balance between required general courses and professionally-oriented electives are still the rule. It is fair to conclude that courses centered on finance management and budgeting, considered as technical, professional subjects, remain an important, but not dominant curriculum consideration.

VII. CONCLUDING NOTES

...draws the stands of this essay together with some final thoughts about public finance work.

At the beginning of this essay, I advised readers that I was to dwell on the intellectual requirements of efficacious finance work. In so doing, I gave official behavior focused on government effectiveness, efficiency and economy an absolute positive value, that is, behavior that is always praiseworthy, regardless of circumstances. Of course, "circumstances" do matter, notably those stemming from the political environment surrounding, and in many cases, penetrating the work of public finance officers. Readers, especially those with experience, probably noticed that I avoided delving into the conditioning power of politics and political influence on the behavior of public finance officials, and may fault me for that omission.

It is not lack of experience that caused me to slight the subject, as I have served various governments as chief executive, finance director, budget director, treasurer and revenue collector. During this service, I experienced "pressures" to favor this or that action, such as, grant revenue-related relief to favored parties, hire politically connected individuals, relax work discipline for politically connected employees, maintain cash balances in politically potent banks, and award non-competitive contracts as requested. That I was subject to these and many other special pleas was not surprising because I had early learned that politics pervades the environment of public finance officials, and, perforce, may significantly influence their thinking and behavior in ways not recommended by this essay..

My vulnerability to the pressure of special pleas varied significantly, depending on laws and customs in different jurisdictions. In my experience, pleas for special consideration tended to rest on unique circumstances. Unlike administrative situations, which are usually defined by settled regularities, political situations rarely recur in the same way. Logically, valid conclusions concerning appropriate behavior must rest on demonstrated regularities. It is the very singularity of these pressures which dissuaded me from offering advice and instruction on appropriate lines of thinking and action for finance officers suffering the pressure of special pleas.

In exploring the role of politics in public finance work, one must distinguish between special pleas and policy-related pleas. Power relationships are not all one way. Public finance officials can and do have considerable influence in many jurisdictions throughout the world. Chief financial officers are properly involved in the development and implementation of programmatic, financial, and, in sovereign jurisdictions, monetary policies. In my own career, for example, I recommended many policies to political leaders with varying degrees of success, such as, "pay-as-you-go" project funding, direct issuance of citizen-subscription bonds, multi-dimensional budgeting, and cash reservations to fund asset depreciation. In every government, sovereign or otherwise, its chief financial officer counts as an important official. Indeed, in sovereign jurisdictions, the chief financial officer is likely to be a key member of the ruling party, and, as such, is expected to advance partisan policies as well as respond to general and special pleas from partisan sources.

Viewed in broad perspective, every day, in thousands of jurisdictions, thousands of political leaders demonstrate that they favor "sugar" rather than "medicine," efficacy aside. Regrettably, from my point of view, pragmatism is the working principle of most politicians most of the time in most jurisdictions. In my official and consulting career, I encountered few political officials who consistently supported the values

VII. CONCLUDING NOTES

advocated by this essay, and who would appreciate its content. Most supported efficacious finance practices only when it was expedient, i.e., when their constituencies, or the circumstances of the time allowed, or demanded it. As participants in the great game of hopes and promises, politicians can not be faulted for being more interested in programmatic values and their re-election, rather than the rather abstract values of efficacious financial practice.

In sum, in this essay, I avoided dwelling on the political aspects of public finance work because the pressures of special pleas stemming from political environments are usually unique, and lacking regularity, are essentially beyond the reach of educators and essayists who would offer advice and instruction. Certainly, it is not the business of an essayist who has invited the reader to join him in exploring ideas and ideals transcending circumstances. (In passing, I should note that some authors have found enough regularity in political environments to offer advice. In this regard, I found the following authors and their works to be illuminating: Niccolo Machiavelli, *The Prince*; Max Weber, "*Politics as a Vocation;*" and Charles E. Merriam, *Political Power.*)

Throughout this essay, I assigned responsibility for managerial thinking to "accountable" finance officials, ignoring the obvious fact that supervisory officials vary widely in the scope of their authority, their competence, and in the number supervised. However, by any measure, the key accountable finance official is a jurisdiction's chief financial officer. Under various titles, in various jurisdictions, chief financial officers supervise the most important unit in the hierarchy of government organizations. In essence, this essay provides support and encouragement for chief financial officers who wish to express and incorporate the values of effectiveness, efficiency and economy in finance work proper, and throughout government operations. Obviously, the line of thought and action advanced by this essay will not be of much benefit to self-interested, compliant finance officials who do not have the vision, self-respect and enough steel in their spine to strongly represent the managerial values of efficacy to the political order. I look askance at chief financial officers who merely preside, buddha-like, over finance establishments. Chief financial officers of this cast provide a poor leadership model for the governments they serve, and, most important, are likely to neglect their fiduciary responsibility as custodians of the public's money.

What of the future? As previously pointed out in Part 5, and repeated here to provide context, in differentiated modern societies, the values of responsibility and accountability are at war with one another. In this context, "accountability" refers to authoritative action exercising the discretionary powers of an office in accordance with law and/or a code of official conduct. "Responsibility" refers to authoritative action subject to correction by those in control, or those affected. If one is totally responsible, one has no authority. (On the contemporary scene, the distinction between accountability and responsibility can be clearly seen in controversies over the formal review of official action and performance by citizens.) As the complexity of modern society advances, administrative organizations differentiate in an effort to respond, that is, satisfy the conflicting demands of a steadily growing array of sub-groups, sub-cultures, and differentiated environments. Under the impact of differentiated interests, governments expand, and official response to stimulus tends to replace the reasoned exercise of authority.

Organizations and "management" are justified by goals sought and attained. Despite respect for this truism, it must be acknowledged that goal attainment tends to be elusive, no less in finance work than in other fields of government action. Indeed, the same environmental pressures which compel contemporary governments to do "more," paradoxically work to make goal attainment increasingly problematical. Further, goals are particularly hard to define and communicate in governments of general jurisdiction, which face a multitude of claims for service and privilege. Yet, despite the ambiguities which beset public policies and service, the prime concerns of government finance work can be defined, as I have attempted in this essay. This is the indispensable, irreducible ingredient of managerial thought applied to finance work.

VII. CONCLUDING NOTES

It is also abundantly clear that the pursuit of coordination and control no longer provides an adequate philosophy for the organization of finance work in the governments of North America, and, perhaps, the world. Governments also need finance establishments with planning and analytical talent capable of assessing the financial consequences of the interplay of social and economic tendencies, and help citizens and officials understand the impact of worldwide, national, regional and local trends. As the manifold influences of a world-wide economic system increasingly impinge on national, regional and local economies, government finance establishments must be governed and energized by analytical and planning values, without slighting their indispensable coordination and control contributions. Nothing short of a comprehensive, well-led finance establishment can attract and retain the talent necessary to balance, and forcefully express the complementary values of coordination, control, analysis and planning.

Ever facing the vicissitudes of the marketplace, finance officials, public and private, practice a craft which places a premium on knowledge and forethought. Inherently, the goals of finance work in government can never have the focused clarity that the "bottom line" confers on finance work in profit-seeking organizations. Yet, despite this lack of clarity, accountable finance officials (and all those concerned with public policy and programs) must never cease championing the ends and means of efficacious public finance. Based on experience and reflection, it is clear to me that the ever-present political aspects of government make the practice of finance management, with a requisite degree of competence, intrinsically more difficult in government than in private, profit-oriented enterprises.

As the constraints are greater, so is the challenge!

www.ingramcontent.com/pod-product-compliance
Lightning Source LLC
Chambersburg PA
CBHW070226190526
45169CB00001B/93